"Yale Magrass and Charles Derber have done it again. Following their excellent books on the nature of American capitalism, domestic and imperial violence, and resistance: *Morality Wars, Capitalism: Should You Buy It? Bully Nation*, and *Moving Beyond Fear*, they now extend and deepen their critical analysis of our past and the crisis-ridden present with *Glorious Causes*. It is a powerful call to study, understand, and confront the deep-seated ills that are tearing this nation apart. In an age of profound existential crises led by climate change and the growing threat of nuclear war, we must heed their sage advice that 'there is no more glory in glorious causes.'"

— **John Marciano**, Professor Emeritus, *SUNY* and Author, *The American War in Vietnam: Crime or Commemoration?*

"Yale Magrass and Charles Derber's study of 'glorious causes' is an in-depth discussion of why people act against their interests. They provide readers with a comprehensive, multidisciplinary analysis of a subject which has been frequently overlooked. Their chapters on the rise of the right, with popular support, and the failure of the left to come to terms with it, is particularly relevant to politics today. It is a book to be read and debated in classrooms and public meetings throughout the US and abroad."

— **James Petras**, Professor Emeritus of Sociology, Binghamton University.

"In an era of upheaval and political confusion, how can we understand the emerging world and still have hope for the future? *Glorious Causes* provides insightful answers. It not only explains the roots of America's deep trouble, but points to ways that we can re-imagine our country and make it once again a beacon for humanity."

— **Stephen Kinzer**, Author of *Overthrow, All the Shah's Men* and *Poisoner in Chief*

"Another way of looking at history — provocative, original, progressive."

— **Oliver Stone**, Hollywood director of *Platoon, JFK*, and *Born on the Fourth of July*.

"Fascinating, provocative and very timely! I found it very hard to stop reading, and when I had to momentarily, I was eager to get back to it. On every page, there's something startling to be learned about the past that is crucial to understanding our vertigo-inducing present. Highly recommended!"

— *Daniel Ellsberg*, the *Pentagon Papers* whistleblower and author of *The Doomsday Machine*

Glorious Causes

Drawing on historical cases of the American South before and after the Civil War, Europe – especially Germany – between the world wars, and the United States in Vietnam and its aftermath, this book takes a historical approach to explain the problems of capitalism in western democracies today.

Capitalist democracies proclaim equality, material prosperity and comfort but produce extreme differences in wealth and power. They promise security and peace, but deliver frequent wars. The promises broken, elites often turn to other visions – partially borrowed from feudalism – to win public support. Nations turn to honor, nobility and war as a way of winning over workers and legitimating the capitalist system itself.

Capitalism's contradictions often have produced a cultural divide. One side, "cosmopolitans" – urban – see themselves as citizens of the world, not one region or country, identify as secular, preach multi-culturalism, entertain state welfare systems, and are cautious about going to war. Their opponents, "traditionalists," breed among people who feel left behind, anxious and insecure, often embracing community, tradition, God and family.

The devastation of the world wars and the Third Reich led Europe to forgo visions of empire, militarism and glory and focus upon improving the quality of life for their own citizens. Although the United States does not need to experience comparable trauma, they should follow Europe's example: forget glory and instead build a better life for the American people. The last chapter will consider how such a change could emerge in the US and who might help fight for it.

Yale R. Magrass is Chancellor Professor of Sociology/Anthropology at the University of Massachusetts, Dartmouth. He is the author of eight books and over 60 articles, and frequently makes public appearances and presentations.

Charles Derber is Professor of Sociology at Boston College. An internationally renowned scholar and public intellectual, he has written 21 books, translated into eight languages, and more than 100 articles, including op-eds for the *New York Times*, *Boston Globe*, *Newsday*, *Truthout*, and others. He is internationally recognized, and has spoken on hundreds of television and radio shows.

Universalizing Resistance Series
Edited by Charles Derber and Suren Moodliar

Welcome to the Revolution
Universalizing Resistance for Social Democracy
in Perilous Times (2017)
Charles Derber

Moving Beyond Fear
Upending the Security Tales in Capitalism, Fascism,
and Democracy (2019)
Charles Derber and Yale R. Magrass

Forthcoming:

Disrupting Narratives of Deservedness
Changing the Stories that Hold Economic and
Racial and Inequality in Place (2020)
Chuck Collins

¡Viva Latinx!
How a New Generation of Organized Power Can
Win Elections and Transform Culture (2020)
Elisa Batista and Matt Nelson

For more information about this series, please visit:
https://www.routledge.com/Universalizing-Resistance/book-series/
RESIST

Glorious Causes

The Irrationality of Capitalism,
War and Politics

Yale R. Magrass and Charles Derber

NEW YORK AND LONDON

First published 2020
by Routledge
52 Vanderbilt Avenue, New York, NY 10017

and by Routledge
2 Park Square, Milton Park, Abingdon, Oxon, OX14 4RN

Routledge is an imprint of the Taylor & Francis Group, an informa business

© 2020 Taylor & Francis

The right of Yale R. Magrass and Charles Derber to be identified as authors of this work has been asserted by them in accordance with sections 77 and 78 of the Copyright, Designs and Patents Act 1988.

All rights reserved. No part of this book may be reprinted or reproduced or utilized in any form or by any electronic, mechanical, or other means, now known or hereafter invented, including photocopying and recording, or in any information storage or retrieval system, without permission in writing from the publishers.

Trademark notice: Product or corporate names may be trademarks or registered trademarks, and are used only for identification and explanation without intent to infringe.

Library of Congress Cataloging-in-Publication Data
A catalog record for this book has been requested

ISBN: 978-0-367-26319-5 (hbk)
ISBN: 978-0-367-26320-1 (pbk)
ISBN: 978-0-429-29257-6 (ebk)

Typeset in Adobe Caslon Pro
by Apex CoVantage, LLC

 Printed in the United Kingdom
by Henry Ling Limited

From Magrass:
To Joel, who gave his all for nothing

From Derber:
To my students: our best hope to heal the world

CONTENTS

INTRODUCTION: NOT SUCH A WONDERFUL LIFE   xi

Chapter 1	An Irrational Cultural Divide: Cosmopolitans vs. Traditionalists	1
Chapter 2	The South Shall Rise Again: Finding Glory in Defeat	37
Chapter 3	Stabbed in the Back: The Master Race Shall Be the Master	81
Chapter 4	America Becomes Exceptional But Europe Prospers	127
Chapter 5	Weimar America: Vietnam, The Left, The Right & Reagan	153
Chapter 6	Making America Great Again: The Reagan in Trump and the Failures of Anti-Trumpism	195
Chapter 7	We Can't Afford Glory: Turning Toward Equality and Human Survival	232

NOTES   253
INDEX   270

INTRODUCTION

Not Such a Wonderful Life

In the 1985 movie *Back to the Future*, Marty McFly [Michael J. Fox] travels in a time machine from the 1980s to the 1950s. When he tells people of the 50s he is from the 80s, he is met with skepticism.

1950s person: Then tell me, future boy, who's President of the United States in 1985?
Marty McFly: Ronald Reagan.
1950s person: Ronald Reagan? The actor? [chuckles in disbelief] Then who's vice president? Jerry Lewis [comedian]?[1]

In the 1950s, Reagan was head of the Screen Actors Guild and led the purges of Hollywood actors, writers and directors who were suspected of having Left political sympathies, but the idea that he might, one day, become president must have sounded absurd.

In the waning months of the Reagan administration [December 1988, nearly 30 years before Donald Trump became president], *Mad Magazine* presented a parody of Trump, imagining him telling the story of the 1946 Christmas movie *It's a Wonderful Life*.

> George Baily [Jimmy Stewart] inherited a small building-and-loan business from his father. He lent money for mortgages. When people couldn't make their payments he told them not to

worry about it. What a schmuck! He should have foreclosed and kicked them out! He could have gotten a tax abatement and build condos, a high-rise office complex, and a gambling casino. He just didn't understand the art of the deal.

One day while checking George's books, the bank examiners found an $8,000 discrepancy. George's drunken uncle had lost the money on the way to the bank. Unless it was replaced, George faced criminal charges. I can't believe the guy didn't have eight grand to his name! I gave more than that to Ed Koch's [Mayor of New York] reelection fund – and I hate Ed Koch!

George panicked and decided to kill himself. But he was stopped by an old guy claiming to be an angel. George said he wished he'd never been born. So the angel took George to the past to prove his life had been meaningful. Ha! In my opinion, George was a total loser! He never made a million-dollar deal, he never had his picture on a magazine cover, and he never shook hands with Mike Tyson [champion boxer] or Don King [boxing promoter].

Anyway, George realized his life was okay and he returned to his family. His friends took up a collection to replace the money. George resumed his job at the building and loan company, barely scraping out an existence. This is a wonderful life? Come on![2]

During the Vietnam War, Jimmy Stewart was a reserve Brigadier General in the Air Force. When his step-son was killed in Vietnam, he reacted: "He wanted to serve his country . . . I don't think it's a tragedy."[3] On the other hand, Donna Reed, his co-star in *It's a Wonderful Life*, was the co-chair of *Another Mother for Peace*. We can wonder what Reagan would have done to her if she had been more politically active in the 1950s.

In the 1980s, Trump was already famous as a billionaire who articulated the philosophy look out for your own profit and don't care how much you hurt anyone else in the process. However, no one would imagine he would eventually become president. Long before he entered politics, Trump called anyone who challenged him a loser.[4] With that vocabulary, he perpetuated the idea that victims are weak and lazy and don't have the stuff to prevail. They deserve their fate and must submit to the triumphant. As a landlord, Trump brutally intimidated his tenants – cutting heat and hot water, refusing to maintain and repair his buildings which sometimes became rat infested – in the hope of driving them out of rent-controlled apartments that he planned to convert into condominiums.[5]

Trump's presidency has been treated as a fluke, but it actually represented a very old ideology of capitalism. When Trump became president, the media and liberals became nostalgic for Reagan, saying that Reagan would never do what Trump was doing. In reality, Trump was Reagan's heir. Reagan appointed Alan Greenspan as Chairman of the Federal Reserve. Greenspan's five terms as Chairman included two reappointments by Bill Clinton, which suggests his paradigm was accepted by some Democrats.

Greenspan regularly published with Ayn Rand, the self-proclaimed philosopher and novelist of capitalism. Her economics inspired Reaganism and Trumpism and had a long lineage, going back at least to the British workhouses of the early 1800s and the American gilded age of the late 1800s and early 1900s. She divided the world into two distinct orders of being: creatives and moochers. To defend her when her book *Atlas Shrugged* was badly reviewed, Greenspan wrote in a letter to the *New York Times*:

> *Atlas Shrugged* is a celebration of life and happiness. Justice is unrelenting. Creative individuals and undeviating purpose and rationality achieve joy and fulfillment. Parasites who persistently avoid either purpose or reason perish as they should.[6]

Similar to Trump's winners, Ayn Rand's creatives are chosen to rule by some higher, perhaps biological, force and, if unrestricted, will bring progress and prosperity to everyone. They must be motivated with the promise of greater wealth in order to fulfill their productive potential. She was convinced if they are unrestrained in their pursuit of fortune, their riches would "trickle down" and bring affluence for everyone, although, of course, ordinary people will never be as rich as they are. Unfortunately, creatives are often held back by the moochers – similar to Trump's losers. At various times, especially during the New Deal from 1932 to 1980, the moochers controlled the state, with disastrous results. The ruling moochers were the liberal professional–managerial class (PMC), bleeding hearts who were so selfish they could not bear to look at other moochers – poor parasites who might be homeless and destitute. To soothe the PMC's guilt, they used the state to give the extremely poor welfare and other government benefits. They may have improved the lives of the victims in the short run, but in the long run, they denied the poor the incentive to uplift themselves by their bootstraps and allowed them to wallow in their misery. The programs were presented as benefiting the poor, but they really served the PMC who have to be thrown out of power for the good of everyone else. The creatives are overwhelmingly businessmen. They must be free to do as they think right. Otherwise PMC government moochers will transform American capitalist democracy into a collectivist dictatorship. Ayn Rand warned:

> Businessmen are the one group that distinguishes capitalism and the American way of life from the totalitarian statism that is swallowing the rest of the world. All the other social groups – workers, farmers, professional men, scientists, soldiers – exist under dictatorships, even though they exist in chains, in terror, in misery, and in progressive self-destruction. But there is no such group as businessmen under a dictatorship. Their place is taken by armed thugs: by bureaucrats and commissars. Businessmen are the symbol of a free society – the symbol of America.[7]

The Capitalist class itself is divided over the cut-throat ideology of Rand-Reagan-Trumpism (also called neoclassicism and neo-liberalism), with some embracing it as a license to do whatever they want, but others fearing it is too blatant in telling the 99% they are on their own and the elite owes them nothing. Under neoclassicism, wealth did not trickle down; rather, from 1980 to 2016, the ratio of pay for the average

INTRODUCTION: NOT SUCH A WONDERFUL LIFE   XV

Standard & Poor's 500 American corporate CEO to the average worker grew from 42 to 1 to 347 to 1 as the percentage of national income held by the richest 1% doubled.[8] Capitalism strives to win the support of the 99% through a utilitarian pledge of a higher standard of living for everyone willing to work hard. It will be shared, but not equally. The gap between the 1% and the 99% shows this is not a promise kept. Accordingly, if capitalism is going to win the acquiesce of the vast majority, it must find another way of legitimating itself – a kind of glorious cause that is the subject of our book. This becomes urgent when inequality zooms up and workers are forgotten. In the first year of Trump's presidency, the stock market as measured by the Dow Jones Industrial average grew 27%,[9] but the wages of working people were stagnant, growing at 0%.[10] Wages, in fact, had been stagnant since the beginning of the Reagan presidency, creating a "Rodney Dangerfield" working class who just "can't get no respect."

Western Capitalist democracies proclaim equality, material prosperity and security but produce extreme differences in wealth and power. The promises broken, elites often turn to other visions – partially borrowed from feudalism – to win public support. Nations turn to glory, honor, nobility and war as an effective way of winning over workers and legitimating the capitalist system itself.

Drawing on glorious causes in the American South before and after the Civil War, Europe – especially Germany – between the world wars, and the United States in Vietnam and during the Reagan counterrevolution, this book takes a historical approach to explore the pursuit of war and power. We suggest that glorious causes are anything but glorious. Elites exploit them to galvanize support among a population to whom they bring mostly misery.

Capitalism's contradictions have produced a cultural divide. Borrowing terms from German sociologist Wolfgang Streeck[11], we call one side, "cosmopolitans" – mainly urban people, who see themselves as citizens of the world, not one region or country, identify as secular, preach multi-culturalism, champion racial diversity, entertain state welfare systems, and are cautious about going to war. Their opponents, called by both Streeck and us, "traditionalists," are primarily people who live in rural areas, reject welfare, tend to be racist, are super-patriotic, are often living paycheck to paycheck, feeling left behind and economically insecure, and culturally deplored. They typically champion community, tradition, God and family, and their race and nation.[12]

Materially, feudal peasants lived in a misery hardly anyone in the modern West could imagine. However, feudal ideology, resting heavily on Christian religion, offered a sense of ultimate meaning and purpose which capitalism cannot match, for capitalism envisions nothing higher to strive for than economic wealth. Under capitalist secular ideology, if life here on earth is bad, there is no compensation. Feudal Christianity gave hope of a better life in the next world, even if it can only be reached after death. While capitalist ideology teaches "you're on your own," psychologist Eric Fromm pointed out that even the lowest medieval peasants gained a sense of security from the knowledge that they had been assigned a place within the "Great Chain of Being":

> The Middle Ages have been idealized, for the most part by reactionary philosophers but sometimes by progressive critics of modern capitalism. They have pointed to the sense of solidarity, the subordination of economic to human needs, the directness and concreteness of human relations, the supranational principle of the Catholic Church, the sense of security which was characteristic of man in the Middle Ages[13] ... A person was identical with his role in society; he was a peasant, an artisan, a knight, and not an individual who happened to have this or that occupation. The social order was conceived as a natural order, and being a definite part of it gave man a feeling of security and of belonging.[14]

Feudal ideology does not obligate the ruling aristocrats to deliver anything concrete, observable and measurable. On the other hand, capitalism promises a prosperity that can clearly be seen. Hence, it is obvious when capitalists fail to deliver. Largely because capitalism was never able to eliminate economic and social insecurity, feudal values never completely died. To prevent discontent from going rampant in times of anxiety, capitalism might borrow a vision of ultimate purpose from feudalism. Feudalism teaches sacrificing yourself for some higher cause, which capitalism does not. Feudal values like honor and valor are more likely to galvanize soldiers to kill and die in war than the capitalist pursuit of profit. They might willingly forfeit their lives for their king or country, but not for Shell Oil. General Robert Baden-Powell, the founder of the international Boy Scouts, a British aristocrat who lived after capitalism reached maturity, offered feudal knights as models for modern boys to emulate.

> In days of old, when knights were bold, it must have been a fine sight to see one of these steel-clad horsemen, come riding through the dark green woods in his shining armour, with shield and lance and waving plumes, bestriding his gallant war-horse, strong to bear its load and full of fire to charge upon an enemy . . . Behind him (the knight) rode his group, or patrol of men – at arms – stout, hearty warriors, ready to follow their knight to the gate of death, if need be.[15]

The feudal crusades, with their devastation, plunder and massacre of tens of thousands of Moslems, Jews and Christians, were Divinely sanctioned missions to restore the Holy Lands from the heathens for Christ. While capitalism offers individual profit as a reward, feudalism promises God's grace, a place in the world to come, community and national identity, honor, valor, glory – all bringing a sense that you are part of some greater cause beyond yourself. Feudalism promoted the idea that if my God, my king, my community, my nation is great, I am great – an attitude that persists today and capitalism finds useful. It does not matter if I am a starving peasant or an underpaid worker; I am great! Since my side, whether tribe, nation or civilization, is sanctioned by some higher force – be it God, nature or whatever – it is good; its foe is evil.

The feudal ideology – now used and abused by capitalists and nationalists – is that you need not say "my country – right or wrong" because it can never be wrong. Germany is good! The Holocaust either never happened or else it was deserved and necessary, or both.

One side's war hero is the other side's war criminal. The Israelis may put the Palestinians behind walls in Gaza resembling the camps the Nazis put the Jews in (although there are no gas chambers) but that is OK because Palestinians are terrorists. Israelis fight with tanks, machine guns and planes; Palestinians fight with rocks, but Palestinians are terrorists. With the most powerful military the world has ever seen, the United States bombs villages, rounds up civilians and massacres those who resist, but again, that is OK because anyone – no matter how weak – who resists America's generous offer of civilization and democracy is a terrorist. John McCain, who later became a US Senator and Republican presidential nominee, bombed villages and killed civilians. The Vietnamese locked him up as a war criminal, but liberals maligned President Trump when he suggested he was not a hero. Actually, Trump's criticism of McCain was not that he committed atrocities but that he was insufficiently heroic because he was shot down. In a sense, Trump was right. The only real war crime is losing. The Americans, British and Soviets were able to put the Nazis on trial in Nuremburg because they won. Had Hitler won, he might now be lying stuffed in state in a mausoleum in the middle of Berlin.

When the 99% faces a declining standard of living, appealing to feudal values might help breed stability. Reagan successfully did this when Europe and Japan began to challenge American economic domination and America lost a war in Vietnam. In an extreme crisis, when capitalism is in danger of collapse, the capitalist elite has turned to fascism which melds capitalism with feudal thinking – and might again.

A compete merging of feudalism and capitalism would be difficult to achieve for they are logically incompatible. The Medieval Catholic Church labeled usury, avarice, pride and gluttony as deadly sins. The New Testament teaches: "The love of money is the root of all evil."[16] Ayn Rand openly called selfishness a virtue. She was a Russian-born Jewish atheist who considered religion a tool of moochers. Capitalists saw feudal aristocrats as lazy, parasitical and incompetent, while aristocrats considered capitalists upstarts, who grubbingly worked for money, and lacked grace, refinement and manners. The aristocracy saw themselves as endowed with a superior essence that biologically separated them from the common lot. With a grace given to them by God, they were "blue blooded" guardians within a "great chain of being," grounded in tradition, in which everyone was interconnected but had an assigned place. The goal was to maintain harmony, order and stability. As such, progress, trying to uplift yourself or seeking a profit was shunned. Living off of trade or industry was a sign of inferiority. The truly worthy glowed in their essence and their inherited status and need not work. Despite these differences, aristocrats and capitalists often intermarried, especially as the aristocracy lost the power to challenge capitalism.

Both supporters and critics of capitalism see it as undermining the sacred. Even Karl Marx, probably its greatest opponent of all, praised it for this. While Marx wanted to see capitalism overthrown, Max Weber, another social theorist almost as acclaimed as Marx, begrudgingly accepted it. However, he feared capitalism would lock people into "iron cages" where they would lack a feeling of meaning, purpose and direction, and he worried who or what would fill that void.

> To-day the spirit . . . has escaped from the cage. But victorious capitalism, since it rests on mechanical foundations, needs its support no longer. . . . like the ghost of dead religious beliefs. Where the fulfillment of the calling cannot directly be related to the highest spiritual and cultural values . . . No one knows who will live in this cage in the future, or whether at the end of this tremendous development entirely new prophets will arise, or there will be a great rebirth of old ideas and ideals, or, if neither, mechanized petrification, embellished with a sort of convulsive self-importance. For of the last stage of this cultural development, it might well be truly said: 'Specialists without spirit, sensualists without heart; this nullity imagines that it has attained a level of civilization never before achieved.'[17]

Weber feared capitalism, along with science and bureaucracy, would produce "disenchantment" without a mystical sense binding people together. Consequently, capitalism would be unstable.

> As intellectualism suppresses belief in magic, the world's processes become disenchanted, lose the magical significance, and henceforth simply 'are' and 'happen' but no longer signify

anything.[18] . . . Bureaucracy develops the more perfectly, the more it is 'dehumanized', the more completely it succeeds in eliminating from business love, hatred, and all purely personal, irrational, and emotional elements which escape calculation.[19]

Marx's critique of capitalism was much more brutal than Weber's. To rally the 99% against it, Marx and his followers on the Left addressed the rational interests of people they considered its victims. On the other hand, rightwing movements, including fascism, the American Christian right and the Ku Klux Klan, effectively won followers by offering an alternative to "disenchantment," and appealing to the "irrational", an alleged reality – not knowable through science, reason or empiricism. The Nazis openly attacked Marxists for believing promises of individual economic well-being offer sufficient motive. Hitler's inner circle thought people would feel inspired when individually promised nothing, but could sense they were part of some greater cause.

> The health of our people's soul is the basic question with which National Socialism is concerned. Adolph Hitler did not start with purely economic considerations . . . He did not promise his first followers and later the whole German people 'more earnings and less work,' as has been done earlier by Marxist demagogues. He promised us nothing. He achieved something psychologically unprecedented, in that he made demands rather than promises . . . He demanded of each individual the utmost in participation and a disposition prepared for action . . . Since the advent of Adolph Hitler, Volkdom and homeland, discipline, fidelity, and honor are again words of biological value in Germany![20]

Fascism may carry these ideals to extreme, but even in more democratic forms of capitalism, the rulers need a population that will be compliant employees and fight their wars. The Marines would have little trouble fitting into fascism. They recruit by proclaiming themselves "The Few, The Proud, The Brave" and expect subordinates to show they have the "right stuff" through blind obedience. The private is supposed to submit to the sergeant, who in turn must submit to the lieutenant, all the way up the hierarchy to general. This is little different from the feudal "great chain of being," which it may be modeled after, with the peasant expected to submit to the lord who also carries deference up the chain all the way up to king.

Feudal peasants seldom ventured more than a few miles from where they were born and felt strong affinity to their manor or village. In contrast, the largest capitalist corporations are cosmopolitan, transcending national boundaries, and as they become global, willingly sacrifice local communities to profit. Throughout much of American history, there was antagonism between large monopoly capitalists and people whom we shall call "traditionalists." Although there were traditionalists throughout the country, they were more likely to be found in the South and the interior than the Northeast and the West Coast and in rural communities rather than big cities. Traditionalists tend to be more patriotic and have stronger ties to community, family and religion. Some literally believe the universe was created in six days, as Genesis says. This is a belief that many cosmopolitans consider hilarious and many capitalists in biotech corporations in Boston and Silicon Valley consider actually dangerous.

Reagan did something that, at one time, would be considered unimaginable. He built an alliance between traditionalists and the corporate cosmopolitan elite. As of this writing, this alliance continues. It is referred to as conservativism and it is the core of the Republican Party. It brought us Trump. Around the time Reagan became president, there emerged a new movement which called itself the "New Right." With a bizarre merging of fundamentalist Christianity and Ayn Randian neo-classicism, it had close ties to Reagan. One of its leaders, Jerry Falwall, founder of the "Moral Majority," insisted despite two thousand years of evidence to contrary:

> The free-enterprise system is clearly outlined in the Book of Proverbs in the Bible. Jesus Christ made it clear that the work ethic was part of his plan for man. Ownership of property is biblical. Ambitious and successful business management is clearly outlined as part of God's plan for his people.[21]

Thirty years later, we still hear from Republican former senator and presidential candidate Rick Santorum:

> I believe in capitalism[22] . . . Capitalism actually encourages morality[23] . . . You can't ignore the reality that faith and family, those two things are integral parts of having limited government, lower taxes, and free societies[24] . . . Defend the church. Defend the family.[25]

The Moral Majority explicitly believed that America must rest upon fundamentalist Christian principles and that anything which violates these principles has no place within the American polity. They supported Israel more fervently than many Jews, but wanted to transform the United States into a Christian Commonwealth, where Jews might not feel welcome. Although in feudal Christianity, society supposedly assumed responsibility for the material well-being of the individual, in the Moral Majority's theocracy, individuals will have to fend for themselves in striving to fulfill God's will.

Since Reagan's presidency, the neoliberal aspects of the New Right's agenda have been largely implemented under both Democratic and Republican administrations. There have been drastic cuts to social services, tax cuts for the rich and escalating military spending. On the other hand, the moral-religious side has hardly been imposed. The United States is not a Christian commonwealth. Abortion is still legal. Evolution is still taught in most public schools. Nevertheless, hearing politicians deferring to their values, at least in rhetoric, may make traditionalists feel respected and therefore willing to accept the neoliberal program, even though it is against their material interests. It appears traditionalist will follow politicians who preach their values and affirm their great American status, even if their personal lives are full of sin. While in Hollywood, Reagan allegedly had affairs with Lana Turner, Ava Gardner, Doris Day, Betty Grable and Marilyn Monroe[26] and Trump cavorted with prostitutes.

Beginning with the Reagan era, the New Right has failed to improve the standard of living for most Americans, but it has successfully held political power. The Left has tried to appeal to the objective material conditions of the 99%, but the Right has assuaged their psychological anxiety. Why people hurt by neoliberalism would gravitate to its conservative agenda is a paradox we have been trying to understand by writing two volumes. In the first volume, *Moving Beyond Fear*, we focused on the "security story," how a sense that there are evil forces –both real and imagined – has created a yearning for strong authority and how liberals and the Left, as well as the Right, have responded. In this book, we consider how capitalism relies upon the seemingly non-capitalist idea that people seek meaning in their lives by looking beyond their individual identity to some greater cause – perhaps community, nation, king, God. War brings profit, but also a higher calling that brings honor but requires sacrifice of self and autonomy. As in *Moving Beyond Fear*, we suggest external threats – real or not – build solidarity. Among the demons whom people can be rallied against are cosmopolitans who reject tradition. These can be found among Leftist, countercultural bohemians, PMCs and some capitalists. In both volumes, we looked at how crises within capitalism produced polarization, intensify the need for hierarchical and unchallengeable authority but also can empower the Left. In extreme crises, fascism becomes plausible, although there may also be hope for increased humanitarianism.

The devastation of the world wars and the Third Reich led Europe to forgo visions of empire, militarism and glory, and focus upon improving the quality of life for their own citizens. Although the United States does not need to experience comparable trauma, they should follow Europe's example – forget glory and instead build a better life for the American people. The last chapter will consider how such a change could emerge in the US and who might help fight for it.

In this volume, we look at how capitalism claims rationality, but may actually be irrational. We suggest rationality does not always meet people's needs and this is something the Right understands better than the Left. We then look at three historical junctures: 1) the American South before and after the Civil War; 2) Europe, especially Germany, in between the World Wars; and 3) the United States during the Vietnam War and its aftermath, which intensified a cultural conflict that persists into the present. It can move us toward neo-fascism or social democracy. For democracy to prevail, the Left must understand irrationality and appeal to people's emotional as well as material needs.

1

AN IRRATIONAL CULTURAL DIVIDE

COSMOPOLITANS VS. TRADITIONALISTS

Chariots of Fire[1] won the Oscar as Best Picture in 1981. It is the story of Harold Abrahams, the son of a financier – a capitalist who may be rich, but as a Jewish Polish immigrant to England, lacked pure aristocratic blue blood. Harold entered Cambridge University immediately after World War I, when it was still largely a finishing school for aristocrats. At that time, Cambridge University provided upper class students with servants who had aristocratic airs and manners. When Harold was out of hearing range, the servants gossiped to each other that with a name like Abrahams, he wouldn't be joining the choir.[2]

At Cambridge, Abrahams became a champion runner but to improve his skill so he would have a serious chance at winning in the Olympics, he hired Sam Mussabini, a Turkish professional trainer. The Dean of Cambridge summoned Abrahams to his office to advise Harold that hiring a coach is not something a gentleman does; he is to rely on his innate ability, implying it must be in his blood. When Abrahams refused to obey, the Dean remarked that as a Jew, Harold must worship "a different God."

At the Olympics, the Prince of Wales met with most of the British running team. This is the same prince who later would become Edward VIII, the king who was forced to abdicate, ostensively for marrying

Wallis Simpson, an American capitalist without blue blood, but more likely, because he supported Hitler. Even though Abrahams was a British citizen and the Prince supposedly represented all of the British people, Harold was not invited to meet him. While Abrahams' victory would be Britain's victory, the prince invited the rest of the British team to dinner. However, he remarked that if you win, I will pay, but if Abrahams wins, you will pay.

Economic Winners: Cultural Losers

Under capitalist values, hiring a trainer to help you win the race is admirable. Under feudal values, it is a different story. Few people would want to return to the material conditions of feudalism. The richest feudal king or queen could not imagine the cell phones, the computers, the cars, the televisions that even the relatively poor have under capitalism. Electricity and indoor plumbing were unknown. For a feudal peasant, 35 was a long life. Any food other than bread and porridge was a luxury. In their huts, peasants would sleep on straw covering the dirt floor. Even Karl Marx, perhaps the greatest opponent of capitalism who ever lived, believed capitalism had to mature in order to create the wealth and technology which would make possible the humanistic socialism he hoped would replace it.

There is no question that capitalist economics, science and technology triumphed over feudal approaches, but the dominance of capitalist values is less clear. The feudal community, at least the way it is romantically remembered, offered a sense of belonging, order and meaning which capitalism undermined. Capitalist ideology promises material prosperity and the opportunity to compete to achieve it. There is no concept of ultimate purpose. Indeed, some capitalist theorists dismiss the search for ultimate meaning as an irrational fantasy. Like science, capitalism offers external objectively observable criteria to measure success and failure – mainly how much wealth you possess. How well you do is apparent here on earth. Western Feudalism is grounded in Christian religion. Jesus comforted: "Blessed are the poor in spirit, for theirs is the kingdom of heaven . . . Blessed are the meek, for they shall inherit the earth."[3] The ultimate reward is in the world to come. It has been mocked as "pie in the sky when you die." No matter how miserable you are in this life, there is always hope for better in the next. For a feudal peasant, faith was the highest virtue. The righteous feudal peasant accepted his place within the "great chain of being," obeyed and did not challenge authority or hierarchy. These are the same traits a capitalist employer would want in his lower ranked employees including janitors, maintenance workers, assembly line crew and cashiers, but he would need independence and creativity among his professionals and managers.

Under capitalism, failure is failure. Your fate is yours as an individual. If you didn't make it, there is something wrong with you and that's it. The capitalist promise of equality is contradictory. Everyone has an equal chance to compete but competition produces winner and losers. So, it is an equality which produces inequality. As Chuck Collins[4] pointed out, some people begin the race much closer to the finish line than others.

The feudal promise is vague enough that you can never be sure if it has been fulfilled or not. Whatever you can see in this world, you can never know what will happen in the next – especially since that world is inherently inaccessible to empirical observation. Even if all the empirical evidence suggests all you can look forward to is poverty, misery, disease and death, you can be vindicated as part of some greater cause. Your reward need not be individual; it can come through the victory of your community, nation or lord. To someone for whom capitalism did not deliver prosperity, an idealized memory of feudalism might be an attractive alternative. In the modern world, children are raised with feudal fairy tales, told by the Grimm brothers and Hans Christian Andersen, who wrote them in the 1800s, after the emergence of capitalism. Most children see them animated by Disney, one of the largest capitalist corporations, as little girls dress as Disney princesses. Although capitalism may have destroyed feudalism, it may find that feudal values helped maintain stability and would thus have a motive to restore them, at least in mutated form.

For much of the population, who never achieved the capitalist dream, the feudal sense that they do not have to rely upon themselves as individuals, that they can be part of some greater cause can offer vindication and a path to self-respect. This discomfort with capitalism and nostalgic yearning for the feudal past may have always existed, but it becomes more acute during crisis, when there is all the less reason to have faith in the capitalist dream. Capitalists can promise to share the wealth with the 99% in times of prosperity when the pie is expanding. In the immediate years after World War II, American economic dominance was so assured, that a large part of the white 99% could be offered a prosperity their parents could hardly dream of. In the 1970s when America showed signs of decline, capitalists protected their wealth by sacrificing the security and prosperity of the rest of the population. They closed factories or moved them abroad. In response, Ronald Reagan came to power, not by restoring the standard of living but by referring to feudal values of honor, valor, tradition and national greatness. In the 1930s as Weimar Germany collapsed, the corporate elite allowed Hitler to come to power. The Nazis offered a more extreme feudal-like vision of racial greatness and glory, which required exterminating Jews.

Early capitalists were merchants – often Jews and Gypsies – who were shunned in an aristocratic Christian society which looked down upon usury and working for a living. Their main interest was making money, not glory or valor through combat. Compared to aristocrats, they had a practical utilitarian mentality and could hardly understand dying for honor. In pre-capitalist societies, war for war's sake was often seen as an intrinsic good, a way to achieve honor and prove gallantry. As Christian aristocrats and knights led armies of peasants, they certainly sought plunder and booty, but they saw victory in battle as proof they held a special essence and were above the common lot. Courage and willingness to die showed worthiness. They sometimes claimed their higher status was sanctioned by God.

However as the capitalists shifted from peripheral outcastes to a class powerful enough to challenge the aristocracy for domination, they came to see the great fortunes that could be amassed by building vast empires through conquest. They learned that using armies to control other countries can lead to cheap raw materials, labor and markets. They saw that building weapons could be one of the most successful ways of achieving opulence. Although they may have not been particularly interested in militaristic glory, they embraced the money that could be made from war. They now needed a population who would be willing to fight and "support the troops." However, few would be willing to kill and die to find oil for Exxon. Feudal promises of heroism and national greatness would be much more likely to bring people to cheerfully march to the frontline.

Irrational Rationality

Capitalists rejected feudal irrationality and substituted science and progress to win workers to their side. But this was a fatal strategy. Their rationality not only lacked the feudal appeal to emotion but also brought an "irrational rationality" that left workers behind and forgotten. It offered neither the appeal of feudal irrationality nor fulfillment of capitalist promises.

Unlike aristocrats, capitalists put profit first. In peace or in war, capitalist profit depends upon forever introducing new products and procedures. Innovation is essential, so it regards progress, science and technology as virtues. Market exchange requires treating virtually everything as a commodity, something with measureable quantifiable monetary worth. Even humans are commodities, whose labor can be bought and sold, either voluntarily or through slavery. Accordingly, capitalism also needs mathematics, rationality and logic, as it shuns the sacred – the idea that things and people have intrinsic worth, valuable in themselves and not reducible to something else. Ayn Rand treated capitalism as the fulfillment of rationality: "The moral justification of capitalism lies in the fact that it is the only system consistent with man's rational nature."[5]

Capitalism also promises equality – equality of opportunity – where everyone has an equal chance, regardless of where they were born, to rise or fall according to their ability and ambition. Capitalism may value rationality, but it carries its own irrationalities. You can ask how logical it is to claim equality when the average corporate CEO is paid over three hundred times the average worker.

Capitalism and science are actually twins, both born in the enlightenment of the 1600s and 1700s or the "age of reason," when tradition was supposed be abandoned and science was supposed to replace faith as the path to knowledge and truth. Science elevates rationality to among the highest virtues. Although it treats faith as a dirty word, it rests on faith in the fundamentally unprovable assumption that all truth is ultimately learnable through human logic – largely mathematical – and observation. Enlightenment science prided itself as challenging feudal religious authority, but it created a new class of experts whose special wisdom was beyond question by anyone lacking their exceptional training and talent.[6] Anyone who doubted them is dismissed as ignorant and biased, an unforgivable sin. Whatever they prescribe is not a personal opinion, but objective truth. Claiming such enlightened understanding can either breed awe or resentment. It can produce a sense in much of the population that either 1) they are so brilliant that we cannot understand them and must simply accept their judgment on faith, or 2) they are arrogant elitist snobs who hold us in contempt and we need not listen to them.

The enlightenment was a reaction against feudalism and led to the industrial revolution, along with political revolutions in Britain, America and France. Perhaps more than the rest, the French Revolution viewed itself as the logical outcome of the enlightenment. It illustrates the irrationality of rationality. In its attempt to overcome the alleged superstition of the Catholic Church, it created a new religion, a Cult of Reason, where reason became literally an object of worship. Churches, including Notre Dame, were converted into Temples of Reason, with festivals and ceremonies venerating enlightenment ideals. In the Feast of Reason, everyone would revere a woman, acting as the Goddess of Liberty and dressed in red, white and blue – treated as sacred colors.[7] Statues of philosophers replaced statues of Jesus and saints. In their attempt to rationalize everything, they tried to measure almost everything as a power of ten. They introduced a new calendar which replaced the week with ten-day periods. That meant that peasants and workers would not get every seventh day off, but every tenth. This provoked anti-revolutionary feelings among peasants and workers who sensed that rather than being liberated from the aristocracy and the Church, their exploitation was being intensified.[8] Some of the effort to use decimals to impose rational measurements was successful. The revolutionaries created the metric system, which is still in use in almost all non-Anglo-American countries.

By the early nineteenth century British industrial revolution, capitalism and science melded, again accompanied by the irrationality of rationality. Calling themselves utilitarians, English philosopher Jeremy Bentham and his disciple Edwin Chadwick developed a calculus weighing pleasure against pain and convinced Parliament that codling the poor did them a disservice by undermining their incentive to uplift themselves. Bentham was certain that

> truths that form the basis of political and moral science are not to be discovered but by investigations as severe as mathematical ones[9] . . . Nature has placed mankind under the governance of two sovereign masters, pain and pleasure.[10]

Intentionally increasing the misery of the poor, they forced them to go into workhouses – virtual slave labor camps – or face starvation. Lacking ventilation and heat, the workhouses were frigid cold in winter and stifling hot in the summer. Diseases like tuberculosis, cholera and typhoid were rampant. Not only to save money, but also fearful that too rich a diet, including meat, would make the inmates feel overly entitled and spark their rebellious spirit, the workhouse guardians deliberately underfed them. In Charles Dickens' novel *Oliver Twist*, Mr. Bumble, the director of the workhouse, warns a cook: "Meat, ma'am, meat . . . You overfed ma'am. You raised an artificial soul and spirit in him, ma'am, unbecoming to a person of his condition."[11] The same policies that immiserated the poor made the emerging British capitalist class, also called Bourgeoisie, the richest elite the world had yet seen. In contemporary America, the same calculus weighing pleasure against pain has been used to justify minimizing welfare and other social services. Neoclassical economists present this ideology as objective science.

In twentieth-century America, the merging of science and capitalism produced "scientific management," another illustration of the irrationality of rationality.[12] Founded by Frederick Taylor, the goal was to consciously remove "all possible brain"[13] work from the laborer, making him essentially act as a machine, allowed no decision-making autonomy, whose every motion was under the control of management. As tedious and monotonous as assembly line work had been before, Taylorism made it more so. Taylor adopted a quantified maximization calculus similar to utilitarians and neoclassicists: "The principal object of management should be to secure the maximum prosperity for the employer, coupled with the maximum prosperity of each employee."[14] For their common benefit, the ignorant worker must submit to the judgment of the expert scientific manager. Although Taylor insisted the interests of employer and employee converged, he certainly expected the profits of the employer to vastly outweigh the wages of the employee. One union officer assessed Taylorist science as "[n]o tyrant or slave driver in the ecstasy of his most delirious dream ever sought to place upon abject slaves a condition more repugnant."[15] It is difficult to see what long-term benefit workers could get from scientific management for Taylor's goal was to ultimately remove the human element from the shop floor: "In the past, the man has been first; in the future the machine must be first."[16] No one can better act as a machine than a machine. From a capitalist point of view, replacing humans with machines may be rational for short-term profit, but in the long run, it is irrational for it may undermine the stability of capitalism. Displaced workers cannot consume, so corporations may be unable to sell their products and hence lose their profits. Even more precarious, displaced surplus people may be compliant but they could also, as Karl Marx predicted, attempt to overthrow the capitalist system as the source of their misery.[17]

Science aids corporate profit, which is more easily quantified than environmental impact. Energy and mining companies hire geologists to find petroleum and other minerals. They use sophisticated mathematical models to predict where such resources would be, but as rational objective experts, they are not supposed to allow subjective values, like concern for environmental impact, to impede their investigations. Global warming and related catastrophes are to be dismissed as "externalities." To fear destruction of the biosphere is irrational. As professionals, they are to act in the interests of their employers even if they personally worry they may be creating a worse world. As private citizens or employees of a university, government agency or environmental non-profit organization, they can investigate the potential for calamity. In fact, lay citizens owe almost all their knowledge of pending ecological devastation to warnings from independent scientists who project from mathematical models at least as sophisticated as those adopted by petroleum companies.[18]

Perhaps nothing better embodies the irrationality of capitalist rationality than military research. Physicist J. Robert Oppenheimer, generally considered the father of the atomic bomb, dreaded the possible cataclysm his own research might yield, but he followed the professional ethic of serving the interests of his sponsor and not letting his personal values interfere.

> I did my job, which was the job I was supposed to do. I was not in a position of policy making at Los Alamos. I would have done anything I was asked to do including making the bombs a different shape if I thought it was technically feasible.[19]

The Pentagon quantifies success using "kill ratios," the amount of death and destruction it endures measured against what the alleged adversary suffers. In assessing a new plane, the Air Force was pleased that it "Looks like the F-35 achieved an impressive 20:1 kill ratio at Nellis Air Force Base."[20] To create the appearance of objective neutrality, killing or maiming civilians and destroying their homes and other possessions is referred to by the sterile phrase "collateral damage." While it is estimated that the American invasion of Iraq resulted in over 180,000 violent civilian deaths,[21] Obama's Pentagon Press Secretary Rear Admiral John Kirby proclaimed: "No other military on Earth takes the concerns over collateral damage and civilian casualties more seriously than we do."[22] Pentagon analysts have calculated that 20 to 30 million deaths in a nuclear war are "acceptable losses."[23]

Capitalism: Ending Feudal Idyllic Relations

Both capitalism and feudalism foster militarism, but while capitalists care more for profit, feudal aristocrats fight more for glory. Capitalism is a class society with vast differences in wealth between the bourgeoisie and the ordinary citizens, but there is a claim that you can rise or fall according to your ambition and ability. On the other hand, feudalism was a caste society, ruled by aristocrats, where everyone was born with an essence, fixed in their blood, and assigned at birth, a place – lord, peasant etc. – for life. Everyone must accept their place as a link in "the great chain of being" and not seek personal advancement. Opposing the enlightenment and hoping to restore feudalism, Joseph de Maistre observed in the early 1800s, "We are all attached to the throne of the Supreme Being by a supple chain that restrains us without enslaving us."[24]

In feudalism, the goal was to maintain harmony, order and tradition, so progress was shunned. Whatever their individual achievement or station in life, everyone could feel they were a piece in some greater cause ordained by God. Aristocrats had an essence, intrinsic in their blue blood which separates them from the common lot and makes them inherently superior. People should be judged by what they *are*, not by what they *do*. Capitalists are impertinent upstarts, who do not deserve their wealth and power because they earned it by working rather than being born to it. They have little appreciation of higher purpose and lack refinement, grace and honor. The bourgeoisie would destroy order and tradition for the sake of money and profit and would not care whom they hurt in the process. American Southern plantation owners, who modeled themselves after European aristocrats, asserted their superiority over Northerners, whether capitalist, farmer or worker.

> Free society! We sicken at the name. What is but a conglomeration of greasy mechanics, filthy operative, small-fisted farmers, and moon-struck theorists? All the northern, and especially the New England states, are devoid of society fitted for well-bred gentlemen ... small farmers who do their own drudgery, and yet are hardly fit for association with a southern gentleman's body servant.[25]

Social climbers are not to be tolerated. They defy the natural order. With his aristocratic background, General Robert Baden-Powell advised his Boy Scouts in 1908:

> Don't be too anxious to push yourself on. You will get disappointments without end if you start that way . . . We are very much

like bricks in a wall, we each have our place, though it may seem a small one in so big a wall. But if one brick crumbles or slips out of place, it begins to throw undue strain on others, cracks appear and the wall totters.[26]

By Baden-Powell's time, the wall had tottered several times. From an aristocratic point of view, the capitalist and industrial revolutions turned the world upside down. Order was replaced by chaos. Estimated deaths during the French Revolution's Reign of Terror, instituted after the Cult of Reason fell, range as high as 250,000, including about 17,000 beheaded in the guillotine for the crime of having aristocratic blood.[27] While life expectancy for a feudal peasant had been about 35, by the 1850s it fell to about 25 for the poor in Liverpool and Manchester, largely as a result of the work houses.[28]

Although capitalist democracy promised freedom from caste bounds, it hardly ended inequality or alienation. Karl Marx praised it for ending a false sense of meaning, tradition, religion, purpose, direction, valor and community.

> The bourgeoisie, wherever it has got the upper hand, has put an end to all feudal, patriarchal, idyllic relations. It has pitilessly torn asunder the motley feudal ties that bound man to his "natural superiors", and has remaining no other nexus between man and man than naked self-interest, than callous "cash payment". It has drowned the most heavenly ecstasies of religious fervour, of chivalrous enthusiasm, of philistine sentimentalism, in the icy water of egotistical calculation. It has resolved personal worth into exchange value.[29]

The Irrational

In the wake of the devastation brought by the industrial and French revolutions, especially the Reign of Terror, romanticism emerged in Europe. It was a nostalgia for a view of feudalism, which had little to do with historical fact. It embraced the irrational, a reality which could not be understood through science, logic or empiricism. To romantics, the word irrational implied deeper understanding; it was not pejorative. As a romantic, Joseph de Maistre sought to defend the French monarchy against the revolution and he asserted: "True legislators . . . act on instinct and impulse more than reasoning."[30] Stephen Kinzer, hardly a romantic, laments that throughout most of human history, there was a sense that "reason offers little basis for morality, rejects spiritual power, and negates the importance of emotion, art and creativity."[31] Feudalism offered a sense of authority, where everyone knew and accepted their place and worked together for the common whole. Modern conservatism, including fascism and the American Christian right, descends from this vision.[32] Ironically, some people, impoverished or oppressed by capitalist competition, could gravitate to this hierarchical image as an escape from insecurity and anxiety. Most religions and spirituality are grounded in the irrational. It offers a sense that despite whatever misery you may experience in this life, there is ultimate goodness and purpose, perhaps ordained by God or some other divine force – built into the universe.

The irrational is to be understood through feeling, faith and tradition. It defies logical explanation. If you require empirical or analytical proof, that shows you do not understand it. Willingness to accept pronouncements that are logically contradictory is a sign of grace and faith. The Christian Trinity asserts there is one God who assumes three forms. There is an omniscient God who knows the future. So the future is predetermined, but we have free will. Irrational truth is knowledge that stems from your inner being, not observation or reason. Ordinary and chosen people can see the same phenomenon or read the same text, but the select will learn something from it that most can never understand.

De Maistre revealed:

> [W]riting? Was it not formed with a pen and a little black fluid? Does it understand what to tell one man and what to hide from another? Did not Leibnitz [a famous philosopher] and his maidservant read the same words there? . . .[33] God revealed nothing in writing . . . Christ left not a single writ to His apostles. He commended them not to books but to the Holy Spirit.[34]

If you are higher on the great chain of being, you are right because of who you are, not what you have studied. In traditional families, the father knows best because he is the father; the Pope is infallible because he is Pope; the king is right because he is king. This applies outside the West perhaps even more than in the West. In the musical *The King and I*, which is based on a real event, the King of Siam mockingly asks his children's English tutor: "Can woman be right and king wrong?"[35]

This is very different than scientific truth which is independent of who discovered it and does not rest on authority. As a 26 year-old underemployed clerk in the Swiss pattern office, Albert Einstein could make one of the most important discoveries in the history of physics. However when he was acclaimed as the greatest living scientist in the world, his asserting "God does not play dice with the universe" did not make it true. Art is closer to romantic reality. A Jackson Pollack painting may resemble the scribble of a three-year-old, but it is a masterpiece because Jackson Pollack painted it. Unlike scientific truth, irrational truth is understood instantly in its entirety or not at all. It cannot be explained by breaking it down into components. You either get it or you don't. As De Maistre reads the New Testament: "The Evangelists, describing the Last Supper . . . Indeed, we read, *Go, teach!* in their admirable history, but never teach *this* or *that*.[36]

The apostles did not have to be told what to teach; they had grace; they knew! Religious believers usually consider it futile to try to demonstrate the existence of God to infidels. If you try to analyze a joke for someone who did not laugh, it ceases to be funny. The aristocracy prided themselves on "good taste," unlike the plebian bourgeoisie, and anyone who has to have good taste demonstrated to them does not have good taste.

The Country: Getting In Touch With Irrational Reality

There is an assumption that contact with the ultimate irrational reality is extremely difficult in the modern city. Capitalism, in bringing industrialism and urbanization in its wake, uprooted peasants from the land and undermined the authority of landed gentry. Removal from nature, from the outdoors, was never seen as an unmixed blessing. Even adamant nineteenth-century defenders of the new capitalist-industrial order, like Horatio Alger, view the city as the seat of vice, sin and corruption. In *Ragged Dick*,[37] Alger depicts a New York which reeks with homeless children, near starvation, sleeping in the streets, beaten, forced to beg and steal. The children's condition does not alarm Alger. This is the burden they must bear until they prove themselves worthy of rising above their station. What disturbs Alger is that the children make an unpleasant sight, possibly even pose a physical danger, to the refined who must retreat to the country to find beauty, security and serenity.

Despite the brutality which Alger finds within the city, others worry that urban-industrial culture makes people, especially men, soft, unable to withstand challenge, lacking a sense of purpose and direction, out of touch with irrational truth, unwilling to sacrifice for the community, too ready to give into immediate personal whim. There was a belief that rural communities of the past provided a sense of being tied to higher powers. In the pre-capitalist world view, land was considered an intrinsic force, not reducible to a quantifiable commoditized form, with almost magical power. In *Gone With The Wind*, Gerald O'Hara, who tries to run his plantation like a feudal manor, tells his daughter Scarlet:

> Do you mean to tell me, Katie Scarlett O'Hara, that Tara, that land, doesn't mean anything to you? Why, land is the only thing in the world worth workin' for, worth fightin' for, worth dyin' for, because it's the only thing that lasts."[38]

Among Baden-Powell's motives for founding the Boy Scouts was a conviction that urban industrial culture provided material comfort and removed responsibility for physical survival from the individual. As a result, people, especially men, lacked the stamina and will of their predecessors.

> Very few fellows learn these things when they are living in civilized places, because they have comfortable houses, and soft beds to sleep in. Their food is prepared for them, and when they want to know their way they just ask a policeman.[39] . . . The truth is that

men brought up in a civilized country have no training whatever in looking out on the velt or the plains or in the backwoods. The consequence is that when they go into wild country they are for a long time perfectly helpless.[40]

There is a conviction that rural and perhaps pre-civilized life brought contact with some ultimate reality closer to way the people are supposed to live. Convinced that peasants lived a purer simpler life, French Queen Marie Antoinette built a peasant village on the grounds of the Palace of Versailles, which bore little resemblance to the poverty and misery in which real peasants lived.[41] Although hardly an aristocrat, French post-impressionist painter Paul Gauguin tried to escape the hustle and bustle of Paris by moving to Tahiti, where he believed he could find an idyllic paradise and explained:

> Civilization is what makes you sick[42] . . . I have come to an unalterable decision – to go and live forever in Polynesia. Then I can end my days in peace and freedom, without thoughts of tomorrow and this eternal struggle against idiots.[43]

Cosmopolitans and Traditionalists

Despite his desire to escape to the tropical South Seas, Gauguin was someone whom Wolfgang Streeck, emeritus director of the Max Planck Institute for the Study of Societies in Cologne, Germany, would call an "urban cosmopolitan." According to Streeck, a cultural conflict, which has been brewing for centuries, has intensified in recent years. On one side are prosperous, progressive cosmopolitans who takes capitalism's reliance upon innovation and science a bit too literally. Many – liberals, Leftists and bohemians – turn science's call to challenge tradition and authority to question the capitalist system, the bourgeoisie and the militaristic state, themselves. Often, they are freelance artists and intellectuals, or work in the sciences, entertainment, journalism, education and social services. Feeling secure enough to challenge dominant values and institutions is a privilege that comes with relative prosperity. Ironically, many within the bourgeoisie itself – especially globally oriented capitalists or capitalist particularly dependent upon science and innovation, such as entrepreneurs in high tech, biotechnology and media – can be called cosmopolitans. Cosmopolitans tend to live in cities, see themselves as citizens of the world, not necessarily any one region or even one country, identify as secular, sometimes adopt experimental bohemian lifestyles, preach multi-culturalism, critical thinking, denounce racism, entertain state welfare systems, and are cautious about going to war, but try to keep the poor away from their buildings. The other side can breed among people who feel left behind, anxious and insecure. They often feel they are not getting the rewards, recognition and deference their national or racial identity should make them automatically entitled to. They tend to live in smaller cities or rural communities, and can be small businessmen or workers barely getting by. Many of them are the very people who Karl Marx expected to be revolutionaries. We call them "traditionalists." They feel tied to their communities and embrace tradition, God and family, their nation and race. They sense disdain from urban cosmopolitans who regard them as provincial yahoos. Many see the cosmopolitans as deliberately trying to seed discord and discontent, virtual traitors willing to sacrifice the community, maybe even the nation, to their personal profit and their political and cultural agenda.

> Seen from the perspective of the provinces, of course, elite cosmopolitanism serves the material interests of a new class of global winners. Mutual contempt is reinforced by self-imposed isolation, both sides speaking only to and within their camps.[44]

Not all religious people are traditionalists. With a Ph.D. in chemistry and deep concern about global warming, Pope Francis should probably be considered a cosmopolitan.

Streeck should have pointed out the cosmopolitans can be divided into a least two subgroups that tend to be enemies. Wealthy capitalists against bohemians, tied to the Left, who are often socialists or pacifists with professionals on both sides. Capitalists, like Reagan and Trump, have rallied traditionalists to undermine the bohemians.

According to Nancy Isenberg, people struggling to get by in the American rural interior are

> regularly convinced to vote against its collective self-interest. These people are told that East Coast college professors brainwash the young and have nothing in common with them and hate America and wish to impose an abhorrent, godless lifestyle.[45]

Streeck suggests the gap between the cosmopolitan centers – in America, located mainly on the coasts – and the hinterland exceeds cultural differences between nations.

> Urban elites can easily imagine themselves moving from one global city to another; moving from New York to Ames, Iowa is another matter. National borders are less salient to urban elites than the informal borders between urban and rural communities.[46]

The conflict exists on both sides of the Atlantic Pond. In the movie *Did You Hear About the Morgans*,[47] a Londoner, played by Hugh Grant, adjusts to life in Manhattan instantaneously. However, he and his New York wife, played by Sarah Jessica Parker, feel they have entered another planet when they are forced to move to Wyoming, even though it is part of the same nation as New York.

There are contemporary urban cosmopolitans who, like Gauguin, seek to escape to the country for peace and serenity, although they often create their own enclaves rather than interact with the rural traditionalists. An influx of urban cosmopolitans from Boston and New York, including Bernie Sanders, transformed Vermont from one of the most conservative states to one of the most liberal.

Nevertheless, urban cosmopolitans often hold the country in contempt. As an early urban cosmopolitan, Karl Marx harangued about the "idiocy of rural life."[48] According to New York comedian Fran Lebowitz, "the outdoors is what you must pass through in order to get from your apartment into a taxicab."[49] Woody Allen has no romantic illusions about nature: "To me nature is . . . spiders and bugs, and big fish eating little fish, and plants eating plants, and animals eating . . . It's like an enormous restaurant."[50]

Traditionalist can be motivated more by symbolic cultural affinity than rational economic interests. Rightwing movements, including fascism and the contemporary American Republican party, are more in touch with the irrational and appeal to it more effectively than movements of the Left, which primarily breed among urban cosmopolitans. Among these are socialism, New Deal liberalism or the contemporary American Democratic party. American Republican politicians castigate cosmopolitans as foes of "family values." Trying to appeal to traditionalists, Republicans often oppose paid parental leave and government subsidized child care, largely because these permit mothers to work outside the house rather than be full-time housewives. Government involvement in the family, even if ostensibly intended to support the family and is in the family's rational economic interest, undermines it.

> God gave children to parents for a reason and it is their responsibility, not the state, to raise them[51] . . . Defend the church. Defend the family . . . Defend them against a government that wants to weaken them.[52]

Among the strongest evidence of cosmopolitan hostility toward the family is their tolerance of gay marriage, even though it has zero objective impact on any heterosexual family.

> Legalization of same-sex marriage compromises the institution of marriage and thus undermines the family built on the foundation of marriage . . . change the concept of matrimony, and the traditional family will cease to exist. And once the family is gone, society will fall apart.[53]

Politicians who galvanize support among traditionalists can come from the urban coastal elite. Trump presents himself as the embodiment of hinterland morality, but he is a three times married New York real estate mogul, who owns casinos in Las Vegas. Reagan was a divorcee from Hollywood, but he rose to power by allying two groups which had been historical enemies: the corporate rich, and those who felt disaffiliated but clung to traditional values. He pointed out they had a common enemy: coastal cultural elitists. He became president by denying Jimmy Carter reelection in a landslide. Although relatively liberal and tied to Wall Street, Carter was a born-again Christian, who taught Sunday School and owned a peanut plantation in Georgia. He was convinced the American people wanted to see him live like them as he wore cardigan sweaters and turned down the heat in the White House, during an oil shortage when motorists had to wait in hour-long lines for gasoline. He thought that if the people must face austerity, a president who also sacrifices would be popular. Reagan believed the American people wanted to see him live like royalty. If their lifestyle deteriorated, they would be reassured by a president who basked in luxury. Reagan was right and Carter was wrong.

> In 1980, Carter lost to Ronald Reagan, a man who understood precious little about southern culture, but knew all he needed to know about image making. His White House took on the trappings of a glamorous Hollywood set . . . He came to office rejecting everything Carter stood for: the rural south, the common man, the image of the down-home American in bare feet and jeans. Reagan looked fantastic in a tuxedo. A rumor made the rounds in 1980 that Nancy Reagan was telling her friends that the Carters had turned the White House into a "pigsty". In her eyes, they were white trash and every trace of them had to be erased.[54]

Living Like Kings
Under feudalism, the lavish lifestyle of royalty and aristocrats proved they were superior beings. They established their legitimacy through separating themselves from the common lot. The more superior, the more distant, the more powerful and capable of protecting they appeared. At least unconsciously absorbing an inferiority complex from feudalism, many within the bourgeoisie were not completely confident they were worthy of their dominant position and felt the need to prove they were a

select breed, with a superior biological essence and the dignity, manners, airs and aura of the aristocracy.

Merely having money is not enough to prove you are among the select. The bourgeoisie felt a need to show they were at least as deserving as the aristocracy, whom at one level they denounced, but on another level they envied. Capitalists had to prove they were worthy and the aristocracy provided the standard to which they appealed. Even today, Americans are obsessed with the British royal family. Over 30 million Americans watched Prince Harry, who is unlikely to ever inherit the throne, marry Meghan Markle, a mixed-race American actress, but now Her Royal Highness, the Duchess of Sussex.[55] The worthy rich come from good old families, have grace and manners, dress properly, show good taste and appreciate fineries like vintage wines. They may display precious jewelry whose primary use is to be able to say, "I am rich enough to spend money on something useless." Once established, they are beyond pecuniary pursuits and can spend their time in elegant leisure. Some among the worthy rich work, but they do so voluntarily, not because they need the money, but because as the chosen, they are guardians of society, who do their duty.

Post-Civil War Gilded Age political economist Thorstein Veblen proposed a Theory of the Leisure Class[56] who, once establishing themselves, focus on proving their worthiness for their status through leisure, conspicuous consumption and elegant entertainment. Despite the contempt the European or American bourgeoisie may have expressed for the aristocracy, the aristocracy remained the bourgeoisie's model as the capitalists tried to emulate the lords and dukes. There was no such contempt among ante-bellum Southern slave owners who ran their plantations to openly replicate European feudal manors. In the Gilded Age, Northern industrialists and financiers, having defeated the South, now tried to prove their worth did not come from mere money, but they too had grace and elegance, and were a true aristocracy.

The codes of dress, style and behavior among the worthy rich are deliberately so subtle that when they are followed, they may not be recognized by outsiders. They are signals to the fellow worthy rich that

"I am one of you." If you cannot realize when the code is being followed that is proof that you do not have the right stuff. Again, if you have to have good taste explained to you, that proves you do not have it. New money, who do not fully understand the code, can be too conspicuous in trying to imitate old money. If you can be detected, that is an indication that you are among the unworthy rich. The worthy rich travel in an exclusive circle for which mere money does not qualify you. There are clubs, resorts and communities for which your whole background must be examined before you can be admitted. Outsiders may not even know they exist.

In a generation, there could be a shift from new to old money. Cornelius Vanderbilt, the Commodore, who built the New York Central Railroad, was a crude vulgar uneducated sea captain, who made blunt remarks like, "What I care about the law? Hain't I got the power."[57] His children and their descendants became the epitome of "high society." Amy Vanderbilt wrote one of the definitive guidebooks on etiquette.[58] Even if the Commodore's son, William, ran the railroad from his office in Grand Central Station, his family entertained the worthy rich with lavish elegant parties in the "cottages" of Newport RI, which were deliberately built to imitate European aristocratic palaces like Versailles. Sensing the emotional allure of royalty and feudal glory, capitalists turned themselves into aristocrats. Traditionalists, whose material interests are hurt, feel culturally redeemed and part of the great chain of being symbolized by the capitalist glorious nobility.

Give Us Our King

In *White Trash*, Nancy Isenberg questions if the United States was ever truly a democracy. She notes that from the very moment the first white colonists landed on the shores of Jamestown, there were enormous disparities in wealth and status, and ever since they rebelled against the British monarchy, there has been a "subliminal desire of all Americans have for kings. JFK had Camelot; Reagan was Hollywood royalty."[59] In Oliver Stone's movie *JFK*, Kevin Costner's character, Louisiana District Attorney Jim Garrison, pleaded that democracy requires the American people to "Not forget your dying king."[60]

Kennedy, Reagan and Trump imitated feudal aristocrats. In fact, Trump named his son Baron. In absolutist feudalism, nation and king are synonyms, as proclaimed by Louis XIV: *"I am the state."* In similar language Trump declared "I am your voice" and "I alone can fix it."[61] Nixon asserted he was above the law, or actually he was the law: "Well, when the president does it, that means that it is not illegal."[62] However, if anyone represented the urban capitalist coastal elite, it was Kennedy. His most famous call was "And so, my fellow Americans: ask not what your country can do for you — ask what you can do for your country"[63] – a rally cry not that different from the Nazis. To many, as president, Kennedy embodied the nation, although in a more subtle way than Louis XIV. His underlying message was that he owed nothing to the citizenry; rather, they owed him. Yet this is often cited as the supreme charge for patriotism and sacrifice.

Kennedy uttered these words at the ultimate moment of American prosperity and domination, but he needed to rally support for a cold war, which included a nuclear arms race that endangered the survival of the planet. It required making the Russian communists seem so evil that it might be necessary to destroy the world to save it from them. In the midst of all this affluence, there was an improvised *"Other America,"*[64] hidden in direct view, but uncovered by Michael Harrington. As we pointed out before, to feudal peasants living in squalor and, more recently, to many – especially "white trash" – trapped in the "other America," there was a sense that if my king is great, my nation is great and hence I am great. My lord may plunder me, leave me in poverty, conscript me to kill and die in his wars, even behead me, but he is *my* lord, not the representative of some alien people. To people left anxious and insecure by feudalism or neoliberal militaristic capitalism, an ostentatious ruler can provide a sense of order and stability. Everyone's place is clear, even if people low on the hierarchy receive little rational material benefit. Louis XIV's building Versailles may have bankrupted France, but it was a shrine to national greatness. During Trump's presidency, visitors observed the luxury within his Trump Tower penthouse dwarfed the White House. "By moving into the White House, will The Donald actually be *downsizing* – settling for digs way less awesome than his current gold-plated ones?"[65]

In times of anxiety, when people feel disrespected, face a deteriorating standard of living and increasing uncertainty about their place within society and their society's place within the world, Stephen Kinzer proposes:

> Cosmopolitanism. . . . has produced results that disturb people in many societies. This leads them back toward the ruling system that primates instinctively prefer: A strong chief protects the tribe, and in return tribe members do the chief's bidding. . . . Most people want to belong to groups. Strong leaders strengthen group identity. Submission gives people a clear place in a hierarchy, while disorder and free will make them anxious and uncertain . . . They are demanding a new kind of leadership, which is actually the old kind: autocratic, atavistic, and unbound by strictures of prudence, truth, or reason.[66]

Whatever is the origin of this craving for authority, which is found among parts of the population throughout history, we cannot say, but we can say that without it, hierarchies would not be stable. The number one thing elites need is a critical mass that is deferential to authority, in fact grateful for it, and willing to kill and die for it. Accordingly, in virtually all hierarchical societies – capitalist, feudal, earlier – elites will strive to cultivate a desire for authority.

Elites will want to build the attitude that the triumph of a leader, with whom I can identify, is my triumph, even if I am personally left behind. Group identity can trump personal rational benefit. When Obama ran for reelection in 2012, he carried 93% of the black vote[67] despite the fact that when he left office, "the wage gap between blacks and whites [was] the worst it's been in nearly four decades."[68] According to black philosopher Cornell West, Obama was "reluctant to target black suffering – be it in overcrowded prisons, decrepit schools or declining workplaces."[69] Nevertheless, in Obama's very first words as president-elect, he presented his victory as a vindication of the American Dream, something which all – regardless of race or background – have achieved, perhaps vicariously, through him.

> If there is anyone out there who still doubts that America is a place where all things are possible; who still wonders if the dream of our founders is alive in our time; . . . tonight is your answer . . . It's the answer spoken by young and old, rich and poor, Democrat and Republican, black, white, Latino, Asian, Native American, gay, straight, disabled and not disabled . . . I will never forget who this victory truly belongs to – it belongs to you.[70]

People, who have not met with much personal success, who often must struggle to make ends meet, can find meaning and purpose by feeling they are part of some larger cause, that they can share in the victory of a dominant nation or a master race and that they too can glow in its glory. When enemies appear, we know we will prevail. Through this, Southern whites could feel the aura of belonging to the superior race, even if they were as poor as blacks. Hitler rallied ordinary Germans by assuring them they were part of the master race.

In rust belt cities, where factories close and jobs are exported, sports teams can build identification with community and nation. Professional athletes are often paid millions of dollars and have little in common with most people living in the city but when the local team wins, often a billion-dollar corporation, many ordinary residents will cheer, "We won." Indeed, sports is regularly used as a way to galvanize patriotism and militarism. Many sports championship games began with soldiers marching into the arena, waving colors and flags, and sometimes fighter planes flying overhead. Cheering crowds would celebrate the team's victory or the army's victory as their victory. As William Astore, himself a retired Air Force Lieutenant Colonel, observed:

> These days, you can hardly miss moments when, for instance, playing fields are covered with gigantic American flags, often unfurled and held either by scores of military personnel or civilian defense contractors. Such ceremonies are invariably touted as natural expressions of patriotism, part of a continual public expression of gratitude for America's "warfighters" and "heroes." . . . Those same pre-game festivities included a militaristic montage narrated by

Bradley Cooper (star of "American Sniper"), featuring war scenes and war monuments while highlighting the popular catchphrase "freedom isn't free." Martial music accompanied the montage along with a bevy of flag-waving images.[71]

Freedom to Blindly Obey

The conservative tradition morphed across the Atlantic Pond. Even if Americans secretly yearned for a king, America never knew feudalism. Feudal residues bring Europeans to view the state as their protector, but American conservativism treats the state as a foe of freedom. The United States was born in rebellion against a British state which the American proto-capitalist elite did not control. Hence, the idea of the state as adversary whose powers must be limited was embedded into American political culture since inception. It makes America a more fertile ground than Europe for neoliberalism, Trumpian promises to "drain the swamp" in Washington, and hostility to welfare. In Europe, socialism was never a dirty word and even the right accepts state social services.

America anointed itself the "land of the free." That is what makes America exceptional; that is what makes America great. America has a mission, assigned by some higher force, perhaps divine, to bring freedom to the rest of the world, at the point of a gun if necessary. Liberty is something to kill and die for. By becoming an American, you acquire freedom, but there is seldom a real discussion of what freedom means. When Magrass asks his students what is freedom, almost none can answer. Virtually all American presidents, commanders-in-chief, present themselves as defenders of freedom, as does the American military which demands unquestioning obedience from low ranked soldiers. America is the world police force, the guardian of freedom. According to former four-star US Navy Admiral and Supreme Allied Commander of NATO, James Stavridis, later Dean of the Fletcher School of Law and Diplomacy at Tufts University: "Our military exists to protect our nation and our allies from those forces who threaten our values: democracy, liberty, freedom of speech and religion, racial and gender equality."[72]

Freedom or liberty are vague terms, with contradictory meanings. In American political culture, it is often interpreted as the ability to do what you want without interference, especially from the government. Under American capitalism, people with property are free to do with it as they chose. The American dream says you can become what you chose, but that ignores the fact that this is only available to people with resources. As Obama put it, this amounts to the freedom to "Pull yourself up by your own bootstraps, even if you don't have boots."[73] In *West Side Story*, male and female Puerto Ricans debate the meaning of the American Dream.

> GIRLS
> Free to be anything you choose
> BOYS
> Free to wait tables and shine shoes[74]

Before the Civil War, the freedom to use your resources as you chose included the freedom to own slaves. Today, it includes the freedom of corporations to close factories and throw workers out on the street. Liberty for the rich and powerful is the right to deny freedom for the vast majority. Many traditionalists invoke religious freedom to justify denying freedom for gay people.

The words "freedom" or "liberty" can be used to mean very different things. Carved on the wall in a courthouse in Worcester, coastal Massachusetts, is the sentence: "Obedience to Law is Liberty." [Worcester is actually inland from Boston.] The Christian New Testament charges: "Live as people who are free . . . living as servants of God . . . Fear God. Honor the emperor."[75] Forged in iron on the gate of the Auschwitz death concentration camp was the slogan "Arbeit Macht Frei; Work will set you free."[76] A free nation does not necessarily have free citizens. Rather, its leader can be free to rule without restraint, without fear of being forced to account to another master, except perhaps a god who has chosen his nation and is superior to all other gods.

General William Boykin – former head of the Green Berets and Deputy Secretary of Defense for Intelligence under President George

W. Bush Jr. – certainly sees himself as a defender of freedom, yet he suggests presidents get their authority through something almost identical to the feudal divine right of kings.

> Why is this man [George W. Bush Jr.] in the White House? The majority of Americans did not vote for him. Why is he there? I tell you this morning he's in the White House because God put him there for such a time as this. God put him there to lead not only our nation but to lead the world in such a time as this . . .
>
> [Speaking about Islam] I knew my God was bigger than his. I knew my God was the real God and his was an idol. Because we are a Christian nation and our roots are Judeo-Christian . . . We are in the army of God, in the house of God; the kingdom of God has been raised for such times as these.[77]

Other leading Republicans described Trump in language similar to how Boykin praised Bush.

> "God raised up, I believe, Donald Trump," said former U.S. Rep. Michele Bachmann after he won the GOP nomination. "God showed up," the Rev. Franklin Graham said to cheers at a post-election rally . . . "For me, that has to be providence. That has to be the hand of God," said Paula White, an evangelical pastor Trump has tapped to pray at his inauguration.[78]

As he reminisced about feudalism, de Maistre declared that it too valued liberty. He was talking about a kind of freedom similar to one alluded by the Bible and General Boykin: "Liberty has always been the gift of kings, for all free nations were established by kings."[79]

The lower classes are usually told they are part of a nation and, as such, share in its bounty, honor and security, along with their leaders, with whom they rise or fall. The enemy of the nation is the enemy of all of its people – rich or poor; anyone who threatens their rulers threatens them. Their nation must dominate others or at least be free of outside oppression.

A free people can be hung by their own king. In the 1925 operetta *The Vagabond King*, Louis XI faces a rebellion by the Duke of Burgundy. The king summons poet and thief Francois Villon, asking him to rally the Paris mob to defend the crown. As a reward, Villon will hang. During his reign, Louis XI intensified the misery of the peasants by paying for his wars through increasing the taille, a tax imposed upon commoners, while nobles were exempt. But he is the poor's king and Villon tells them that being ruled by Louis, even dying for him, is liberty and honor. With Villon's inspiration, the mob defeats Burgundy, but they are outraged when they see the gallows waiting for Villon. Villon is reprieved when the king's cousin Katherine De Vaucelles volunteers to hang in his stead. The king spares both lives, but Katherine is demoted to a commoner when she marries Villon. As Villon led the crowd against Burgundy, they sang:

> Come all you Beggars of Paris town,
> You lousy rabble of low degree . . .
> Well spare King Louis to keep his crown
> And save our city from Burgundy . . .
> You and I are good for nothing but to die
> We can die for Liberty.
>
> Sons of toil and danger,
> Will you serve a stranger
> And bow down to Burgundy . . .
> Sons of shame and sorrow,
> Sons of France around us,
> Break the chain that bound us.[80]

We can ask how much freedom the dead have, but as we saw in pre-capitalism, obedience and service to God and king equals freedom. In a sense, willingness to abandon all material possessions, including your life, is the supreme statement of freedom. You may die, but you can feel secure you are dying for something. Convicted murderer Jody Arias said, "Death is the ultimate freedom."[81] In pre-capitalist societies, war for war's sake was often seen as an intrinsic good, a way to achieve honor and glory and prove valor. Islam and pre-Christian Norse paganism both promised slain warriors a special place in paradise. As Christian aristocrats and knights led armies of peasants, they certainly sought plunder and booty, but they saw victory in battle as proof they held a special essence and were above the common lot. Courage and willingness to die showed worthiness. Reminiscing about feudalism, romantics accused capitalists of destroying the sense of honor and virtue. Capitalists are cowards. They may send the young or the poor off to war, but in search of profit, not for some ultimate moral purpose.

War: Irrational Liberation

Contemporary traditionalists accuse cosmopolitans of shunning war because they are incapable of understanding heroism and higher calling. As they display Confederate flags, Southern rural rock band Lynyrd Skynyrd charge coastal urbanites cannot appreciate "God and guns"[82] and know nothing about life in the hunting lodge. Traditionalists upheld late Vietnam bomber pilot John McCain or Navy Seal Chris Kyle- the hero of the immensely popular 2015 movie *American Sniper*,[83] who is credited with personally killing a record number of 160 Iraqis and Afghanis, as paragons of virtue for everyone to emulate or at least admire. Early in the movie, Kyle's father, who gave him a hunting rifle when he was eight years old, lectures him that there are three kinds of people: sheep, wolves and sheep dogs. He warns "We ain't raising no sheep in this house . . . and if you become a wolf," as he shows Chris his belt. Sheep need sheep dogs to protect them from wolves who are everywhere. In the eyes of General Boykin and perhaps Kyle's father, urban cosmopolitans are sheep, who shun guns and seldom know how to defend themselves or their country. As a traditionalist, disgusted by cosmopolitans, Boykin praised Kyle and the movie about him:

> I think Americans are so fed up in terms of what they see as a lack of leadership in the Congress and the White House and every sector of our society that they are drawn to a movie like this because it shows a real hero, a real leader, a person who understands what their transcendent cause is, what's worth fighting, sacrificing and even dying for . . . That's a very strong and powerful message, and

I think it attracts Americans to it . . . When you make heroes out of people that are clearly patriots . . . I think it's just too much for the left. But who cares?[84]

Honor and valor elude rational definitions. If you have to have them explained to you, you don't understand them. Traditionally, honor can be valued above life itself. As late as World War I, Prussian officers, usually with Junker aristocratic backgrounds, would duel over some minor insult. Dueling is something that has virtually died out in modern capitalism but, in American history, rural hero Andrew Jackson was famous for his duels. Even early members of the New York elite Andrew Hamilton and Aaron Burr dueled to the death. They fought in New Jersey because by 1804, dueling was already illegal in New York. Movies romanticizing the nineteenth century untamed rural West are full of duels. Often, there was a woman pleading to the men that it was stupid. In the 1952 Western movie *High Noon*,[85] the bride (Grace Kelly) of retiring Marshal Will Kane (Gary Cooper) threatens to leave him if he insists on trying to capture or kill a freed outlaw, whom he had previously arrested. In the Western movie *The Man Who Shot Liberty Valance*, a restaurant owner (Vera Mills) begs a lawyer from the East (Jimmy Stewart) who barely knows how to fire a gun but whom she loves, not to fight, for she knows: "When two men go out to face each other, only one returns."[86]

To cosmopolitans, who do not share traditional values, acts of honor and valor may appear completely senseless. They often amount to suicidal blind obedience. That was not a problem for romantic Poet Laureate of Great Britain, Baron Alfred Tennyson, when he composed a tribute to British cavalry who charged into cannon fire – with none returning – during the Crimean War.

> Theirs not to reason why,
> Theirs but to do and die.
> Into the valley of Death
> Rode the six hundred . . .
>
> Boldly they rode and well . . .

When can their glory fade?
O the wild charge they made!
All the world wondered.
Honour the charge they made!
Honour the Light Brigade,
Noble six hundred![87]

In the movie *Gallipoli*,[88] British officers during World War I order Australian troops to leave the trenches and run into machine guns on a futile mission. Knowing none will return, they nonetheless obey.

Soldiers who ride into the "shadow of death" without "reasoning why" give up their individual identity. From an irrational point of view, they have merged with some higher force, perhaps the nation, to which their life is secondary. If they do not reason why, they will not ask who or what the nation really is? Whom does it serve? The rich and powerful elite or the ordinary citizen? The elite can benefit from much of the population forgoing its rational interests and blindly obeying. As they enter the battlefield, frontline soldiers must not ask who is the true enemy of the lower classes: lower class people from other countries whose lives may be little different from theirs, or their rulers, who live much better than they do, control the government and the economic institutions, make the laws, can subject them to a wide range of punishments, and can send the ordinary citizen to fight the elite's wars.

Citizens enter the military and allow themselves to be sent to the frontline where they may not return for a variety of reasons, sometimes for a combination of motives: desire for adventure and glory, hope to prove honor and valor, need for economic security which they could not find in civilian life, being forced to go through a draft. No matter why they went there, once in combat, some sacrifice themselves. Again, there could be many motives. Some may truly believe they are part of some greater cause, beyond their individual identity – perhaps the nation – and they should give their lives for it. It is their destiny; what they are meant to do. In Frederick Wiseman's 1968 *High School*, a former student about to be dropped from a plane in North Vietnam donates his GI insurance to school. He writes to the principal, implying it does not matter if he is killed, and assures her, "I am only a body doing a job."[89] However, not everyone who sacrifices sees themselves as so lacking in individuality and simply merging with some higher force. Not all soldiers are driven by glory. In 1949, Samuel Stouffer published a study of American World War II soldiers. He found many had no idealistic motive. They simply fought to "get the war over so that they could go home." According to Brigadier General Samuel Lyman Atwood Marshall, 70% of World War II combat soldiers never fired a weapon.[90] Apparently for the majority, the moral and psychological inhibitions against killing were too powerful. Marshall concluded army training failed to produce sufficiently compliant cannon fodder and recommended reforms in training practices, school curricula and pedagogy – and cultural values and institutions. By his criteria, the changes were successful; in Korea, Vietnam, Iraq and Afghanistan, the majority shot.

Soldiers may or may not have been inspired by patriotic exhortations, but they bonded with their fellow frontline troops in the same predicament as them. They fight not for an abstraction or for their country, but for their "buddies." In a more recent study of American troops in Iraq, Dr. Leonard Wong found they care most about the members of their unit. One soldier told Wong:

> That person means more to you than anybody. You will die if he dies. That is why I think that we protect each other in any situation. I know that if he dies, and it was my fault, it would be worse than death to me." Another explained: "You have got to trust them more than your mother, your father, or girlfriend, or your wife, or anybody. It becomes almost like your guardian angel."[91]

In war, soldiers may identify with whomever they perceive as having a background similar to theirs, no matter what nation they come from. In *The Grand Illusion*,[92] another movie about World War I, the head of a German prison camp learned that downed French pilots were officers, and therefore likely to have aristocratic backgrounds. As fellow members of his caste, he invited them to lunch before imprisoning them. Members of the elite caste may kill each other, but that is part of the honor code. Caste solidarity appears to override national solidarity. That may true of the lower caste as well.

Early in World War I – Christmas 1914 – British and German soldiers heard people singing "Silent Night" on opposite sides of the trenches. They waved bottles at each other, climbed over the barbed wire, shook hands, starting drinking, singing, dancing and playing games together. If they continued, the war might have ended and both empires could have collapsed – something clearly detrimental to officers, aristocrats and capitalists, but possibly beneficial to ordinary people forced into fighting for a cause they did not understand. The officers of each side threatened to court martial their own troops for treason – an offense for which they could be shot by their own country's guns. The soldiers were ordered to return to their trenches and resume killing each other. They obeyed, but the question remains: were their fellow soldiers, who wore different uniforms, their real enemy?[93] Dying for your country would be especially difficult to understand for cosmopolitans who consider themselves citizens of the world, not necessarily a nation or a community.

When the United States entered World War I, labor leader Eugene Debs was sent to jail for telling the working class their real enemy was the rulers of their own nation, not fellow workers born in a different country:

> The poor, ignorant serfs had been taught to revere their masters; to believe that when their masters declared war upon one another, it was their patriotic duty to fall upon one another and to cut one another's throats for the profit and glory of the lords and barons who held them in contempt . . . the working class who fight all the battles, the working class who make the supreme sacrifices, the working class who freely shed their blood and furnish the corpses, have never yet had a voice in either declaring war or making peace. It is the ruling class that invariably does both. They alone declare war and they alone make peace . . . You need at this time especially to know that you are fit for something better than slavery and cannon fodder.[94]

Despite all the attention the culture wars have gotten recently, they were more intense during the American Civil War, post-World War I Weimar Germany and the American invasion of Vietnam. We will discuss these in more detail in later chapters. Perhaps nothing better epitomizes the cultural rift between traditionalists and bohemian cosmopolitans than the moral values they each attach to joining the military. As the war in Vietnam raged, there was a ballad telling of a dying Green Beret who hopes his son will follow in his footsteps and his wife will "[p]ut silver wings on my son's chest; Make him one of America's best."[95] On the other end of the spectrum, Arlo Guthrie confronted the sergeant during his draft interrogation: "You want to know if I'm moral enough to join the army, burn women, kids, houses and villages.[96]

Although there is hostility to the military among bohemian cosmopolitans, many sympathize with low-rank soldiers, seeing them as victims – often inundated with propaganda or driven into such poverty by capitalism that the military seems like an attractive alternative. Antiwar protestors mourned the deaths of American soldiers in Vietnam. In 1969, there was "A March Against Death" from Arlington National Cemetery to the White House in which each participant held a placard with the name of a soldier killed in Vietnam. Each soldier's name was read in front of the White House. It took two days to read all 45,000 names.[97] The demonstrators would say supporting the troops means bringing them home to safety. However, the slogan "Support the Troops!" is more commonly chanted among traditionalists. They follow that demand with "Don't Let Them Die in Vain! Don't Deny Them Victory!" People who see war as meaningless carnage would respond that amounts to a desire to have more die in vain. This dispute could be heard from the wars in Iraq and Afghanistan, through Vietnam, at least back to World War I, if not much earlier. World War I was full of pleas to stop the carnage:

> Ten million soldiers to the war have gone,
> Who may never return again . . .
> For the ones who died in vain . . .
> I didn't raise my boy to be a soldier . . .

> Who dares to place a musket on his shoulder,
> To shoot some other mother's darling boy? . . .
> It's time to lay the sword and gun away.[98]

On the other hand, there were also poems like the one written in 1915 by British Lieutenant Colonel John McCreae, which on first reading might seem like a call to end senseless deaths. However, it is actually a cry from the dead to have more join them in the graves.

> In Flanders fields the poppies blow
> Between the crosses, row on row,
> That mark our place: and in the sky
> The larks still bravely singing fly
> Scarce heard amid the guns below.
>
> We are the dead: Short days ago,
> We lived, felt dawn, saw sunset glow,
> Loved and were loved: and now we lie
> In Flanders fields!
>
> Take up our quarrel with the foe
> To you, from failing hands, we throw
> The torch: be yours to hold it high
> If ye break faith with us who die,
> We shall not sleep, though poppies grow
> In Flanders fields.[99]

National Globalism

Anti-cosmopolitan attitudes are not uniquely rural. In both urban and rural communities, working class whites see their standard of living deteriorate, their jobs and educational opportunities usurped by other races, and their children conscripted into wars, opposed by unappreciative, unpatriotic, ungodly cosmopolitans. Many traditionalists feel that although the ungrateful cosmopolitans avoided fighting in these wars, they received wealth and privileges from their country's greatness, benefits denied the people who sacrificed to protect them, but they held in contempt. In Sacramento on June 26, 2016, violence broke out when about thirty members of a self-proclaimed white nationalist group, the

Traditionalist Workers Party, held a rally. The party claims to defend "faith, family and folk" against "economic exploitation, federal tyranny, and anti-Christian degeneracy."[100]

There is no conflict between nationalism and globalism. A great nation is an empire which asserts its dominance over the rest of the world. It has been chosen by some higher force – nature or God – to rule. "Rule, Britannia! Britannia rule the waves!" Britain bore the "white man's burden" to bring civilization to savages across the globe. They proudly proclaimed, "the sun never sets on the British empire." The Nazis believed Germans were a master race destined to control the world. The United States had a "manifest destiny" to extend from "sea to shining sea" and beyond. It has a duty to bring America's ideal of freedom, especially free enterprise, and democracy to the rest of the world, by any means necessary, possibly including nuclear holocaust. The marines pledge "to fight our country's battles" "from the halls of Montezuma to the shores of Tripoli."[101] By appealing to this sense of national greatness, the elite gets the lower class to fight and die in their battles, even if they are of little rational benefit to the poor and oppressed.

Cosmopolitans can strive to create community where everyone looks out for each other – including themselves, their local and global neighbors, trying to build the best world for everyone, without sacrificing their individual identity. To quote the Talmudic sage Hillel: "If I am not for myself, who will be for me? But if I am only for myself, who am I?"[102] They might live cooperatively but not blindly obey their bosses and generals, certainty not die for them. When capitalist elites destroyed feudal irrationality, they discovered they had to resurrect it. Traditionalism did not go extinct, but persisted as it simultaneously served and undermined capitalist modernity. As the carriers of modernity, cosmopolitans – both capitalist and Left-bohemian – found themselves, in different ways, waging a culture war against traditionalists which has raged for centuries. In subsequent chapters, we shall see how this conflict, both economic and cultural, unfolded in the old and new American South, the World Wars, fascism, the counterculture of the Vietnam era, the counter-counterculture and the presidencies of Ronald Reagan and Donald Trump.

2

THE SOUTH SHALL RISE AGAIN

FINDING GLORY IN DEFEAT

> Swanee!
> How I love you, how I love!
> My dear ol' Swanee
> I'd give the world to be
> Among the folks in
> D-I-X-I-E
> Even now my mammy's
> Waiting for me
> Praying for me
> Down by the Swanee
> The folks up north will see me no more
> When I go to the Swanee Shore![1]

"Swanee" (above) was written by George Gershwin, a Russian Jewish immigrant, raised in New York and sung in black face by Al Jolson, another Russian Jewish immigrant, raised in Washington, DC. Al Jolson also sang along with Paul Robeson:

> Gone are the days when my heart was young and gay,
> Gone are my friends from the cotton fields away;
> Gone from the earth to a better land, I know,

> I hear their gentle voices calling, "Old Black Joe."
> I'm coming, I'm coming, for my head is bending low;
> I hear those gentle voices calling "Old Black Joe."
> Why do I weep when my heart should feel no pain?
> Why do I sigh that my friends come not again?
> Grieving for forms now departed long ago,
> I hear their gentle voices calling, "Old Black Joe."[2]

This song was written by Stephen Foster, composer of many songs yearning for the old South, including *Swanee River*. Foster spent his entire life in the North, only making one brief visit to the South.

Black Marxist Paul Robeson was hardly someone who would sentimentally sing in the cotton fields. In the 1950s, he was one of the actors and singers purged for Leftist tendencies. He linked the struggle against fascism in Europe to the struggle for black rights in America – they were both waged against racism – and he founded "The American Crusade Against Lynching." He proudly declared:

> My father was a slave and my people died to build this country and I am going to stay here and have a part of it just like you . . . I refuse to be a slave in my own country . . . I'll never turn my back on my comrades and my friends. The poor and the dispossessed.[3] . . . I shall take my voice wherever there are those who want to hear the melody of freedom or the words that might inspire hope and courage in the face of fear. My weapons are peaceful, for it is only by peace that peace can be attained. The song of freedom must prevail[4]. . . . I do not hesitate one second to state clearly and unmistakably: I belong to the American resistance movement which fights against American imperialism, just as the resistance movement fought against Hitler.[5]

Ante-Bellum

The legacy of the old South may be slavery and lynching, but if there is one region of the United States where traditionalism thrived and capitalism and feudalism merged, it was the South. The antebellum South, before the Civil War, remained agrarian as the North industrialized. It reeked with contradictions for it maintained a pre-capitalist, essentially feudal, mentality, as it created more millionaires than the rest of the country by growing cotton for the nascent capitalist factories in the North and in Britain. Slaves were actually antebellum America's most valuable commodity.

> In 1860, the economic value of slaves in the United States exceeded the invested value of all of the nation's railroads, factories, and banks combined.[6]

> In the upper South the selling of slaves became more profitable than the growing of tobacco. Slaves vary widely in value from fifty dollars to two thousand dollars depending on who they are, how old they are, but the valuable ones are very, very valuable . . . Cotton became the key crop, the key cash producer in the life of the nation . . . This is a terribly profitable crop that we're talking about. By 1840 the value of cotton exports was greater than everything else the nation exported to the world combined! And that made slaves the most valuable thing in the nation beside the land itself.[7]

The wealth slavery produced was matched by poverty, with not only blacks, but also "White Trash," or "Crackers," whites without slaves – the vast majority of the Southern white population – living in greater misery than Northern urban factory workers. There was even a song: "I'd rather be a nigger than a poor white man."[8] In 1856, South Carolina Governor James Hammond reported many poor whites obtained "a precarious subsistence by occasional jobs, by hunting, by fishing, by plundering fields or folds, and too often by what is in its effects far worse – trading with slaves, and seducing them to plunder for their benefit."[9]

Hammond himself was far removed from the poor whites. He owned 22 square miles of land and over 300 slaves. He coined the phrase, "Cotton is king" and, as a religious traditionalist, declared slavery to be a Divinely sanctioned virtue: "American slavery is not only not a sin, but especially commanded by God through Moses, and approved by Christ through his apostles."[10]

In wealth, Hammond was an outlier among Southern whites. It is estimated that less than 8% of Southern white families owned slaves, that few families owned more than 10, but the majority of slaves lived on large plantations with at least 100. Fewer than 3000 families owned that many.[11] Yet when the Civil War came, over a million Southerners marched off to defend the "glorious cause" – Southern rights, including the right on slaves or at least maintain an apartheid system – with over 200,000 never returning.[12] Crackers could preserve a sense of self-worth from the mere fact that they were white, and could identify with rich plantation owners as part of a superior race. The Civil War offered them an opportunity to prove their valor by fighting to assert their Southern pride and white rights, especially the right to own slaves, even though economically, they never could.

According to black historian William Brewer:

> The enslavement of the Negro determined the position of poor whites of ante-bellum days . . . To these lowly people, slavery offered what they considered a defense of self respect. On the other hand, this class was literally excluded from the labor market . . . The plantation organization overshadowed everything else in the South and Negroes, in monopolizing skilled and unskilled occupations, deprived poor whites of industrial opportunity. This class might resign itself to a sordid existence in the slave regions, or migrate to the frontier and the Ohio Valley . . . These refugees from the plantation carried with them a deep and abiding hatred of Negroes. The institution of slavery deprived the majority of poor whites of wealth, culture, and political power . . . The poor whites understood that slavery was responsible for their hopeless economic condition. Slavery imposed upon this class nearly three hundred years of ignorance, inertia and peculiar prejudice.[13]

Poor whites are "free." That makes them superior to slaves and they can glow in their "whiteness." No matter how poor and miserable they are, they are part of a higher order of being, something whose worth is proven by their willingness to kill and die for it. Although they may dream of owning slaves, they are sacrificing for a cause beyond pecuniary avarice, unlike philistine Yankee capitalists, and can share the glorious civilization with rich plantation owners. The existence of freed blacks is a challenge to that civilization for freedom is a privilege that comes from being part of the superior race. White Trash could either see freed blacks as allies in opposition to the neo-aristocracy or as enemies threatening their superior status. If they saw them as rivals, they could hate them even more than the planters would for they may have a use to planters, but for crackers, they are a challenge to their very identity.

The Civil War was not the first war of succession to preserve the "glorious cause." According to black historian Gerald Horne, slavery was at the core of the creation of the United States. As early as 1772, the cosmopolitan–traditionalist conflict was beginning to emerge. Early cosmopolitan "Londoners were beginning to see slavery and slaveholders as an American phenomenon that sophisticated metropolitans disdained as uncivilized."[14] The abolition of slavery in London provoked fear that the British might eradicate it on the other side of the ocean. "If slavery were to be deemed null and void in London, then why not in Charleston?"[15] Horne suggests that at the time of the American Revolution, not only Southern planters had an interest in maintaining slavery, but so did the wealthy Northern merchants who evolved into capitalists. The New England shipping industry depended upon the slave trade. Their profit came from the "Middle Passage" through which white armies would attack African villages. As many as 20,000,000 Africans were seized, with half dying before they crossed the ocean.[16] Here is how one survivor described the experience of being cargo on a Middle Passage ship.

> I now saw myself deprived of all chance of returning to my native country . . . The stench of the hold while we were on the coast was so intolerably loathsome, that it was dangerous to remain there for any time . . . But now that the whole ship's cargo were confined together, it became absolutely pestilential. The closeness of the place and the heat of the climate, added to the number of the ship, which was so crowded that each had scarcely room to turn himself, almost suffocated us. . . . This produced copious perspirations so

> that the air became unfit for respiration from a variety of loathsome smells, and brought on a sickness among the slaves, of which many died – thus falling victims of the improvident avarice, as I may call it, of their purchasers. This wretched situation was again aggravated by the galling of the chains, which now became insupportable, and the filth of the necessary tubs [toilets] into which the children often fell and were almost suffocated. The shrieks of the women and the groans of the dying rendered the whole a scene of horror almost inconceivable.[17]

Once survivors reached the Americas, they were transformed into commodities to buy and sell and stripped of their identity, their religion, their language, their culture, their history.

As unbearable as this may have been for black victims, it was certainly beneficial to wealthy whites – both commercial and industrial Northerners and agrarian Southerners. "This enormous influx of Africans laid the foundation for the concomitant growth of capitalism."[18] Although the American Revolution had many causes, fear that the British might, one day, restrict the freedom to own slaves inspired both Northern and Southern "founding fathers" to fight for independence. They even feared the British might arm blacks to attack their former masters. Among the charges, Jefferson made against the British in the Declaration of Independence is that they "excited domestic insurrections (slave revolts) amongst us."

> It was also in Boston in 1768 that John Hancock and other eminent petitioners accused the redcoats of encouraging slaves to "cut their masters' throats and to beat, insult and otherwise ill treat said masters"; it was felt that with the arrival of more redcoats, the Africans surmised they would soon "be free [and] the Liberty Boys slaves." . . . James Madison speculated in late 1774, "if America & Britain should come to a hostile rupture, I am afraid an Insurrection among Negroes may & will be promoted. In one of our Counties lately a few of those unhappy wretches met together & chose a leader who was to conduct them when

the English Troops should arrive – which they foolishly thought would be very soon & that by revolting to them they should be rewarded with their freedom."[19]

The heroes of American history who created the republic were as invested in the "peculiar institution" or "glorious cause" of slavery as the Confederates who fought to dismantle the union "four score and seven years" later. Both fought for freedom: the freedom to own slaves. At the time of the revolution, slavery may have made George Washington the richest man in America.[20] In 2017, when people, who deciding that the "glorious cause" should not be glorified, wanted to remove public monuments to Confederate heroes, President Trump reacted:

> This week it's Robert E. Lee. I noticed that Stonewall Jackson is coming down. I wonder is it George Washington next week, and is it Thomas Jefferson the week after? You know, you really have to ask yourself, where does it stop?[21]

Trump may not have realized how accurate he was. Robert E. Lee's slaves were the direct descendants of Washington's. His wife inherited them from her great grandmother – Martha Curtis Washington.[22]

Southern planters became rich by producing cotton and selling it in capitalist markets to Northern and British factories. It may appear that capitalism united Southern slave owners and Northern industrialists but their interests, culture and visions collided, culminating in the most brutal war in the history of the world up to its time – the American Civil War. To prevent competition from Britain and other emerging European capitalist powers, Northern industrialists wanted high tariffs while Southern planters wanted low tariffs, precisely because they could buy cheaper goods from the North's rivals. Despite the ideological claim, expounded by neoclassicists like Ayn Rand and Allan Greenspan that capitalists prosper when allowed to fend on their own without interference from the government, Northern businessmen wanted federal subsidies for infrastructure projects of minimal benefit to Southern interests, like the transcontinental railroad. Before the Civil War when they dominated, Southern planters expected the federal government to capture and return escaped slaves over the objection of many Northerners. After the war when the South was relatively weak and the North controlled the federal government, Southern elites would call for "states' rights."

Even though participating in the capitalist market was making many Southern planters rich, often richer than Northern capitalists, the North and the South were developing into two distinct societies – one industrial and unambiguously capitalist; the other, agrarian and neo-feudal – which would have difficulty coexisting under the same federal government. Although slavery and the slave trade may have produced large fortunes, there is a contradiction. Capitalist ideology promises laborers the freedom to choose where they work. With slaves tied to the land even more than feudal serfs, Southern planters often came to see themselves more like pre-capitalist aristocrats than Northern businessmen. The movie *Gone With the Wind* describes the plantation as the last vestige of feudalism, a romantic reconstruction of an idyllic harmonious world, filled with grace, valor and glory, where everyone accepted their national place. It does not hint at the misery slavery produced.

> There was a land of Cavaliers and Cotton Fields called the Old South . . . Here in this pretty world Gallantry took its last bow. Here was the last ever to be seen of Knights and their Ladies Fair, of Master and Slave . . . Look for it only in books, for it is no more than a dream remembered. A Civilization gone with the wind.[23]

Despite the enormous wealth generated for elite planters, in the long run, the plantation system probably would not have been able to compete economically with Northern industry. Even without the Civil War, it may have been doomed. According to historian Eugene Genovese,[24] by the 1850s, slavery was, in purely market terms, beginning to approach a liability. The planter, unlike the Northern industrialist, was forced to assume total responsibility for maintenance of his labor force, including their feeding, clothing, lodging, medical care, support for the aging, child rearing, moral indoctrination and recreation. He could not simply dismiss his excess slaves, forcing them to fend for themselves in a pool of unemployed. The paternalistic system failed to generate sufficient surplus to allow for agricultural capital improvements. The planter could not afford newly developed agricultural technology, including chemical fertilizers; he could hardly waste potentially productive land by allowing it to remain fallow or practice crop rotation. Because slaves had little incentive to do anything beyond the minimum they could get away with, the planter expected them to abuse his equipment and animals. Therefore, the planter felt forced to buy heavy crude plows and hoes and rely upon mules rather than horses. The land was becoming rapidly depleted; the older areas of Virginia and the Carolinas could no longer sustain cotton. Despite the non-profitability of plantation agriculture, the planter consistently refused to reinvest his capital in the industrial sector. Railroad construction was minimal (what there was primarily was built by Northern capitalists); factories barely existed. Whatever surplus was generated was either conspicuously consumed or reinvested in commodities that would yield prestige among his fellow planters – land and slaves. It has sometimes been suggested the Civil War should have rationally been averted for the planter, whom these critics considered essentially a capitalist, should have realized the higher profitability of industrialization and accordingly abandoned plantation slavery.

The all-crucial flaw, at least according to Genovese,[25] in this argument about the non-profitability of slavery, is that the planters hardly conceptualized themselves as capitalists, but rather were antagonistic to the crass avarice, competition and individualism of bourgeois culture. The plantation approximated the feudal manor; with the planter acting as the would-be aristocratic lord, assuming guardianship of "his people." It was an imperfect feudal system, diffused with contradictory capitalist elements, for it existed in a larger predominantly capitalist world, and had to generate sufficient profit to compete (at which it was not, as demonstrated, all that successful). In any event, the logic of bourgeois subordination of all other considerations to maximizing profit could hardly be translated into the language of the planter. The planter was a sophisticated class-conscious pseudo-aristocrat, acutely aware of his class enemy, or at least was his spokesman, George Fitzhugh, selected by Genovese. Like Hammond, Fitzhugh insisted slavery was biblically sanctioned. If "slavery be morally wrong, be a violation of natural rights, the Bible cannot be true."[26]

Fitzhugh maintained a coherent internally consistent ideology, closely approximating the world view adopted by the European aristocracy when forced to definitively formulate their picture of reality as they were confronted by an antagonistic rising bourgeoisie. Man (they would use "man" to refer to people in generic sense) rather than being a free agent, who enters society to maximize utilitarian rational personal interests, is a social being whose humanity stems from his dependence upon others; individual freedom must be sacrificed for protection and security. Accordingly, it is possible to be the property of someone else, but the person who assumes ownership of another is a mere representative of a higher purpose because society, as a unified entity, supersedes any component individual. Like the "great chain of being," the plantation is an organic community of interdependent pieces, with each having an assigned purpose and striving to maintain and enhance the system through which all attain meaning. The planter assumes care of his slaves. He is their guardian, their benevolent father, who might occasionally have to discipline them, but only for their own ultimate benefit. All true value emanates from land, blood and labor. The plantation constitutes an end in itself; it could not be conceptualized as a means to some utilitarian purpose, such as profit. Slavery is the ideal state for the laborer; he is provided for, protected, and given a sense of integral membership in an organic community. Without a care in the world, without have to worry food or shelter, Fitzhugh claimed, no one was better off than the Southern black slave.

> The Negro slave is free, too, when the labors of the day are over, and free in mind as well as body; for the master provides food, raiment, house, fuel and everything else necessary to the physical well-being of himself and his family.
>
> The Negro slaves of the South are the happiest, and, in some sense, the freest people in the world. The children and the aged

and infirm work not at all, and yet have all the comforts and necessaries of life provided for them. They enjoy liberty, because they are oppressed neither by care nor labor. The women do little hard work, and are protected from the despotism of their husband by their masters. The Negro men and stout boys work, on the average, in good weather, not more than nine hours a day. The balance of their time is spent in perfect abandon.[27]

The alternative, the wage slave of the industrial North, would force the laborer to fend for himself, leaving him a helpless victim of blind market forces, which only benefit the avaricious who strives to extract as much from his worker with as little in exchange as possible. Accordingly, industrial capitalism produces ever-increasing immiseration and unemployment for the unprotected working class.

When the day's labor is ended, he is free, but is overburdened with the cares of family and household, which makes his freedom an empty and delusive mockery . . . The free laborer must work or starve. He is more a slave than the Negro because he works longer and harder for less allowance than the slave, and has no holiday, because the cares of his life with him begin when its labors end. He has no liberty, and not a single right.[28]

Even the capitalist suffers for he fails to receive the true meaning found in land and organic social relations. This was hardly a world which the planter would wish to enter.

Interestingly, Fitzhugh's critique of the "free" Northern worker's condition resembles Karl Marx's. Marx called the relationship between the capitalist and his employee "wage slavery" although in the midst of the American Civil War he wrote in a letter to President Abraham Lincoln:

We congratulate the American people upon your re-election by a large majority. If resistance to the Slave Power was the reserved watchword of your first election, the triumphant war cry of your re-election is Death to Slavery.[29]

Marx's collaborator, Frederick Engels, made a comparison which resembles Fitzhugh's even more.

> The slave is sold once and for all; the proletarian [factory worker] must sell himself daily and hourly. The individual slave, property of one master, is assured an existence, however miserable it may be, because of the master's interest. The individual proletarian, property as it were of the entire bourgeois class which buys his labor only when someone has need of it, has no secure existence.[30]

During an 1836 strike, young female factory workers in Lowell, Massachusetts sang a song comparing their situation to slavery.

> Oh! isn't it a pity, such a pretty girl as I
> Should be sent to the factory to pine away and die?
> Oh! I cannot be a slave, I will not be a slave,
> For I'm so fond of liberty,
> That I cannot be a slave.[31]

Southern neo-aristocrats presented their plantations as harmonious communities, like romanticized feudal manors, where the slaves happily sang in the fields. This image of the antebellum South persisted in tales, movies and songs long after slavery was abolished. It is still presented today by advocates of "Southern pride." Indeed, the slaves did sing in the fields, but they were often songs of defiance, rebellion and even hints of how to get away. One such song was *Follow the Drinking Gourd*. The "drinking gourd" was actually the big dipper which points to the North Star. It was a code used by the Underground Railroad – a network organized to guide escaping slaves- to indicate which stars and rivers to follow.

> When the sun goes back and the first quail calls
> Follow the drinking gourd
> The old man is a-waitin' for to carry you to freedom
> Follow the drinking gourd . . .

Now the river bed makes a mighty fine road
Dead trees to show you the way
And it's left foot, peg foot, traveling on
Follow the drinking gourd.[32]

There were ex-slaves who remembered plantation life nostalgically like Clara Davis who recalled in 1937:

> I want my old cotton bed and the moonlight shining through the willow trees, and the cool grass under my feet while I run around catching lightening bugs. I want to feel the sway of the old wagon, going down the red, dusty road, and listening to the wheels groaning as they roll along. I want to sink my teeth into that old ash cake.
>
> White folks, I want to see the boats passing up and down the Alabammy river and hear the slaves singing at their work. I want to see dawn break over the black ridge and the twilight settle over the place spreading an orange hue. I want to walk the paths through the woods and see the rabbits and the birds and the frogs at night.[33]

We get a very different image from Solomon Northrup, a free black musician who was living a middle-class lifestyle in New York state until he was kidnapped and forced into twelve years of slavery.

> The hands are required to be in the cotton field as soon as it is light in the morning, and, with the exception of ten or fifteen minutes, which is given them at noon to swallow their allowance of cold bacon, they are not permitted to be a moment idle until it is too dark to see, and when the moon is full, they often times labor till the middle of the night. . . .The day's work over in the field, the baskets are . . . carried to the gin-house, where the cotton is weighed. No matter how fatigued and weary he may be – no matter how much he longs for sleep and rest – a slave never approaches the gin-house with his basket of cotton but with fear. If it falls short in weight – if he has not performed the full task

appointed him, he knows that he must suffer. . . . It is an offense invariably followed by a flogging, to be found at the quarters after daybreak. Then the fears and labors of another day begin; and until its close there is no such thing as rest.[34]

Throughout the southern United States, there were armed militias, recruited to capture escaped slaves. Slaves lived in constant fear of being sold and removed from their families. If they were assertive or "uppity," they could be whipped. Even on "nice" plantations, they were in fear of being sold to a more vicious master. Slaves were deliberately kept ignorant. In many states, it was a crime to teach them to read, partially out of fear they might revolt. When Nat Turner led a slave revolt, about 60 whites were killed, but 56 blacks were hung as rebels and possibly as many as another 200 were killed by white militias and mobs.[35] Throughout the South, there were armed patrols checking for escaped slaves. These were the "well regulated militias" that the second Amendment to the Constitution says makes "the right to keep and bear arms" necessary.[36]

Despite this reality, the Southern planter saw himself as benign lord, caring for his charge unlike the avaricious Northern industrialist. The planter could hardly, while pursuing his interests, abandon his manor for seemingly more financially lucrative activity because in doing so, he would cease to be an aristocrat, and accordingly would abandon his class as he identified it. In fighting to maintain the paternal hierarchy, he fought to retain the world which he controlled. The bourgeoisie as a rival ruling class would formulate problems in a completely different way. He would establish a culture with little appreciation for all that the planter treasured. The planter's class interests lay in preserving the manor. Industrialization could only serve the bourgeoisie.

Bellum

Like European aristocrats, Southerner slave owners saw themselves as noble fighters. Northern capitalists focused more on building their industries than fighting for fighting's sake. If Southern gentry had a profession, other than managing the plantation, it was most often military officer. If they went to college, it was typically West Point (located in New York) or

Annapolis (located in border state Maryland). If the South seceded and fought the Civil War to preserve Southern culture, Alexander Hamilton Stephens, Vice President of the Confederacy was clear what that meant.

> Our new Government is founded upon . . . the great truth that the negro is not equal to the white man; that slavery, subordination to the superior race, is his natural and moral condition. This, our new Government, is the first, in the history of world, based upon this great physical, philosophical, and moral truth.[37]

When the Civil War broke out, civilians on both sides treated it like a football game and came to watch with picnics as they cheered their team on. In spring 2011 **Hallowed Ground** *Magazine* (our emphasis) reported that during the first major battle, Bull Run (also called Manassas):

> London Times correspondent William Howard Russell observed, "On the hill beside me there was a crowd of civilians on horseback, and in all sorts of vehicles, with a few of the fairer, if not gentler sex . . . The spectators were all excited, and a lady with an opera glass who was near me was quite beside herself when an unusually heavy discharge roused the current of her blood – 'That is splendid, Oh my! Is not that first rate?'"[38]

Adjusting for inflation, *Gone With The Wind* is the highest grossing movie of all time;[39] the novel has sold 30 million copies.[40] At the movie's 1939 premier in Atlanta, 300,000 people came to watch a seven-mile long parade, wave Confederate flags, and attend costume balls. Clearly the movie and the book resonated with how Southerners wanted to remember Old Dixie.[41] *Gone With The Wind* portrays the Southern elite as would-be aristocrats, gentlemen, who seek war for war's sake, as a matter of pride, honor and glory. They prove their worth through fighting. Dueling persisted among the Southern neo-aristocracy, long after it became illegal in the North. War provides an opportunity to show Southern valor, especially because they are sacrificing for some higher collective cause – beyond some individual purpose, even if that purpose is personal honor rather than profit. They had some inherent quality –"Southernness" – which eludes rational explanation but made them superior to Yankees. Like feudal aristocrats, they understand land, blood and spirit; all Yankees understand is money. They deserve their station because they were born to it. It is part of their being. Even Yankees who are born rich do not understand the Southern and aristocratic essence. Capitalism calls for individual advancement, not accepting your assigned place. They will willingly disrupt the "great chain of being" not caring that it is sanctified by God and nature.

These cavaliers held Yankees in contempt for violating the laws of chivalry. They were envisioning a war where armies charged each other and soldiers fought each other, one-to-one; not one where battalions got mowed down with Gatling guns. Generals, brandishing their swords on horseback, would lead the charge; not watch the battle from a safe distance through binoculars. They were confident Southern valor would defeat Northern technology. They were outraged at Rhett Butler (Clark Gable) who, although from Charleston, South Carolina, thought like a cosmopolitan Yankee. They were also confused by Ashley Wilkes (Leslie Howard) who, although an army officer, was reluctant to go to war.

Gerald O'Hara (Thomas Mitchell):	The situation is very simple. The Yankees can't fight and we can . . .
Man:	One Southerner can lick twenty Yankees . . .
Frank Kennedy (Carroll Nye):	Yes, gentlemen always fight better than rattle . . .
Man:	But Ashley, Ashley, they've insulted us!
Charles Hamilton (Rand Brooks):	You can't mean you don't want war!
Ashley:	Most of the miseries of the world were caused by wars. And when the wars were over, no one ever knew what they were about . . .
Charles Hamilton (addressing Rhett Butler):	What do you mean, sir?
Rhett Butler:	I mean, Mr. Hamilton, there's not a cannon factory in the whole South.

Frank Kennedy:	What difference does that make, sir, to a gentleman?
Rhett Butler:	I'm afraid it's going to make a great deal of difference to a great many gentlemen, sir.
Charles Hamilton:	Are you hinting, Mr. Butler, that the Yankees can lick us?
Rhett Butler:	No, I'm not hinting. I'm saying very plainly that the Yankees are better equipped than we. They've got factories, shipyards, coalmines . . . and a fleet to bottle up our harbors and starve us to death. All we've got is cotton, and slaves and . . . arrogance.
Man:	That's treacherous!
Charles Hamilton:	I refuse to listen to any renegade talk![42]

While the war left most of his compatriots ruined, Rhett Butler, who spent most of it profiteering like a capitalist, found himself immensely rich as it ended. As Southern defeat became apparent, he deplores the irrational vision of glory that drove so many to succumb to war, even though he personally prospers. (The following quote is from the novel, not the movie.)

> "All wars are sacred," he said. "To those who have to fight them. If the people who started wars didn't make them sacred, who would be foolish enough to fight? But, no matter what rallying cries the orators give to the idiots who fight, no matter what noble purposes they assign to wars, there is never but one reason for a war. And that is money. All wars are in reality money squabbles. But so few people ever realize it. Their ears are too full of bugles and drums and the fine words from stay-at-home orators. Sometimes the rallying cry is 'save the Tomb of Christ from the Heathen!' Sometimes it's 'down with Popery!' and sometimes 'Liberty!' and sometimes 'Cotton, Slavery and States' Rights!'[43]"

Despite the fact that he came from the South, Rhett Butler is again thinking here like a Northern cosmopolitan capitalism, rejecting Southern traditionalist neo-feudalism. As Karl Marx, Max Weber and even Ayn Rand point out, capitalism undermines the sacred and prides itself on destroying myths. To quote Marx (from the Communist Manifesto), it replaces glory as a virtue with "naked self-interest, callous cash payment." There will still be wars, but they will be fought to advance the rational economic interests of the elites. For all the glorious rhetoric behind pre-capitalist wars, the victors could expect booty and plunder, but had to invent some moralistic justification for why they are entitled.

Rhett is convinced lower class people can be seduced to sacrifice their lives for valor but not to provide riches for someone like him. His assessment of the ordinary soldier applies to both the North and the South. While Northern capitalists and Southern neo-aristocrats may view war very differently and have different motives for fighting, the lower classes are not going to volunteer to kill and die for their master's money. Accordingly, another language must be found to inspire them and that is not provided by the capitalist "cash nexus." Hence, even capitalists will turn to earlier moral codes with stronger concepts of honor to galvanize the population. Butler may be overstating his case; there were wars fought for war's sake. Partially, the Civil War was one of them; World War I may have been an even more extreme and disastrous a case, although in the end, there was money to be made for the victors, especially the Americans.

Other white Southerners, who undoubtedly lost family and friends, are appalled by Butler's attitude toward the dead. As traditionalists, they insist death sanctifies a cause; it makes it noble, whether or not it serves a rational purpose, and whoever sacrifices his life is a hero. Although the other white Southerners dreamed of preserving slavery, the rational meaning of the cause is far less important than its glory: "Do I understand, sir, that you mean the Cause for which our heroes have died is not sacred?" They are convinced "To die for one's country is to live forever."[44]

For all his rejection of rejection of militaristic jingoism, in the movie, Rhett Butler does join the Confederate army when defeat is certain but, as a result, he becomes even richer and later, as a civilian, donates money to decorate the graves of the "glorious dead."

The wealthy would fill the Confederate officer corps, but most of the killing and dying would fall on poor White Trash. Although few would ever own slaves, they had to be recruited to sacrifice themselves for the "glorious cause." These posters, designed to inspire enlisting in the Confederate army, emphasized that the South is separate and assumed potential volunteers identify with their state more than the nation as a whole. In one poster, all Yankees were labeled as "abolitionists" – evil provocateurs who wanted to destroy harmonious Southern culture, turning slaves against their masters and protectors. Whether white Southerners owned slaves or not, it was assumed they would perceive abolitionists as enemies. They not only wanted to free blacks, they planned to violate Southern homes and families and defile their wives, daughters and even graves. This poster also implied that the Confederacy was the true heir of the American revolution and it must be defended against Yankees who sought to undermine it. It quoted Virginia governor Patrick Henry when he declared liberty is more valuable than life. We must ask what liberty they thought he was referring to. Clearly, it included, as Abraham Lincoln described it, "That perfect liberty [Southern whites] sigh for [is] the liberty of making slaves of other people."[45]

MEN OF VIRGINIA, TO THE RESCUE!

> **Your soil has been invaded by your Abolition foes, and we call upon you to rally at once, and drive them back. We want volunteers to march immediately to Grafton and report for duty. Come one! Come ALL! and render the service to due to your State and Country . . . Action! Action! SHOULD be our rally motto and the sentiment of Virginia's inspired orator, "Give me Liberty or Give me Death" animated every loyal son of the Old Dominion! Let us drive back the invading foot of a brutal and desperate foe, or leave a record to posterity that we died bravely defending our homes and firesides – the honor of our wives and daughters – and the sacred graves of our ancestors.**[46]

A similar poster from Tennessee suggested that raping beautiful Southern women was among the primary motives for Yankee mercenaries to invade their serene Southern land-steal, rape and plunder. Yankees were ruffians – fighting for pay, not for honor or glory – who had no appreciation for Southern graces. Northerners were ruffians, but the implication was that poor white Southerners were not. The poster appealed to potential recruits by calling them "Freemen," suggesting they were a separate order of being from black slaves. White men of Tennessee, whether rich or poor, must prove they were not cowards, must prove they had valor by enlisting in the Confederate army.

> *FREEMEN of TENNESSEE!*
>
> The Yankee War is now being waged for "beauty and bounty." They have driven us from them, and now say OUR TRADE they must and will have. To excite their hired and ruffian soldiers, they promise them our lands and tell them our women are beautiful-that beauty is the reward of the brave.
>
> Tennessee! your country calls! Shall we wait until our homes are laid desolate; until sword and rape have visited them! NEVER! Then TO ARMS!
>
> And let us meet the enemy on the borders. Who so vile, so craven as not to strike for his native land!
>
> The undersigned proposes to immediately raise an infantry company to be offered to the Governor as part of the defense of the State and of the Confederate States. All those who desire to join us in serving our comment country will report themselves immediately.[47]

When we (Magrass and Derber) investigated archives of Confederate and Union recruitment posters, we noticed a decided difference in emphasis. Promises of glory and valor through protecting Southern innocence against Northern ruffians was rampart in Confederate posters. Union posters certainly appealed to patriotism, honor, glory and valor. They were full of eagles and flags. However, almost all their posters also promised each soldier utilitarian pecuniary rewards, including bounties and pensions. This is something we seldom saw in Confederate posters.

> **CHRUSH THE REBELLION! PRESERVE OUR GLORIOUS UNION!**
>
> Recruits, Look at this! $25.00 WARD BOUNTY! Take It!
>
> $225 Bounty! Rally 'round the Flag, Boys! COME ONE! COME ALL

UNITED WE STAND! DIVIDED WE FALL

Our Capital is yet menaced by the enemy, and you are again called upon to **ENROLL YOURSELVES UNDER THE STARS AND STRIPES.**

Pay and Rations Commence upon Enrollment . . .

Good Quarters, Good Pay, And $100 Bounty when honorably discharged.[48]

The semi-official Northern army marching song "Battle Hymn of the Republic" has the chorus "Glory! Glory! Hallelujah!" and the verse "let us die to make men free." However, we did not find a single recruitment poster that mentioned abolishing slavery as a motive joining for the Northern army. They did speak of punishing the rebels and preserving the union, with a sense that the Union was a higher cause than the individual. Abraham Lincoln himself considered the war as essential for preserving the Union, with slavery as a secondary issue.

> My paramount object in this struggle is to save the Union, and is not either to save or to destroy slavery. If I could save the Union without freeing any slave I would do it, and if I could save it by freeing all the slaves I would do it; and if I could save it by freeing some and leaving others alone I would also do that. What I do about slavery, and the colored race, I do because I believe it helps to save the Union.[49]

Very few whites, anywhere, believed blacks and whites were equal. Certainly, not Lincoln:

> I am not, nor ever have been, in favor of bringing about in any way the social and political equality of the white and black races, [applause] – that I am not nor ever have been in favor of making voters or jurors of negroes, nor of qualifying them to hold office, nor to intermarry with white people; and I will say in addition to this that there is a physical difference between the white and black races which I believe will forever forbid the two races living together on

terms of social and political equality. And inasmuch as they cannot so live, while they do remain together there must be the position of superior and inferior, and I as much as any other man am in favor of having the superior position assigned to the white race . . . I will add to this that I have never seen, to my knowledge, a man, woman or child who was in favor of producing a perfect equality, social and political, between negroes and white men . . . I will to the very last stand by the law of this State, which forbids the marrying of white people with negroes. [Continued laughter and applause.][50]

Abolitionists were a small minority in the North and almost non-existent in the South. They were shunned everywhere, North and South. William Lloyd Garrison, editor of the abolitionist newspaper *The Liberator* and founder of the New England Anti-Slavery Society, faced a mob of several thousand in Boston who tied a rope around him and prepared to tar and feather him until the mayor had Garrison arrested, perhaps for his own protection.[51] As we shall discuss in more detail later, New Yorkers rioted in protest against the draft and attacked freed blacks whom they blamed for the war.

Inspired by some higher glorious cause or not, the North crushed the South by fighting like ruffians, using the most advanced technology of the time. As General William Tecumseh Sherman, who led the march through Georgia – bitterly remembered by Southerners to this day – said, "War is Hell!" not a medieval game of chivalry and glory. He used a "scorched earth" policy, with the Union army destroying Georgia's infrastructure including its industry and transportation network. Sherman's troops were expected to supply and feed themselves by plundering farms and other Southern property. Sherman believed he inflicted about $100 million dollars (about $1.6 billion in 2017 dollars) in damage. In an ultimatum to Confederate General William Hardee, Sherman warned

> should I be forced to resort to assault, or the slower and surer process of starvation, I shall then feel justified in resorting to the harshest measures, and shall make little effort to restrain my army –burning to avenge the national wrong which they attach to Savannah and other large cities which have been so prominent in dragging our country into civil war.[52]

Sherman's union troops displayed attitudes not that different from Confederate soldiers, treating victories as something to celebrate and sing about while waving flag.

> Hurrah! Hurrah! we bring the jubilee!
> Hurrah! Hurrah! the flag that makes you free!
> So we sang the chorus from Atlanta to the sea
> While we were marching through Georgia.[53]

Another tactic the union adopted was blockading Southern ports. It destroyed the Southern economy but violated the chivalry code by attacking civilians. It produced a 95% decline in cotton exports and resulted in severe shortage of food, medicine, weapons, and luxuries. Food riots broke out in Richmond. Once the Union gained control of the Mississippi, it became virtually impossible to ship work and food animals into the eastern Confederacy.[54]

The Confederate army was not always chivalrous. Confederate President Jefferson Davis ordered that any black captured while fighting for the Union should be treated as an escaped slave and handed over to the states where they would most likely be executed as slaves in revolt.[55] At Fort Pillow Tennessee, Confederate General Nathan Forrest, who later became the first Grand Wizard of the Klu Klux Klan, killed black and white prisoners, along with civilians, as soon as they surrendered. In Shelton Laurel, North Carolina, Confederate Lt. Colonel James Keith had his men burn homes and barns, hang and whip women and round up 15 men and boys, take them into the woods and shot them. In Saltville, Virginia, Champ Ferguson led a band of Confederate guerillas who killed wounded Union troops when they found them lying on the field and then entered hospitals to kill even more of the sick.[56] Chivalry itself, the idea of a medieval code on how to morally and honorably conduct war and not harm civilians, was a myth. We noted before the brutality of the crusades including the massacre of tens of thousands of Moslems, Jews and Christians. Feudal armies callously burned fields to starve the civilians whom they fed into submission.[57] Medieval knights would catapult dead bodies over castle and city walls in the hope of provoking plagues.[58] The American Civil War has been called the first modern war because it showed how utilitarianism and technology can overwhelm honor and valor. That may be true but self-anointed cavaliers who honored valor were certainly capable of atrocities.

Post-Bellum

Northern deaths in Civil War actually exceeded Southern. Conservative calculations say 360,222 Northerners and 258,000 Southerners died with two-thirds of these deaths, coming from the disease, not battle wounds. However, recent estimates put the death toll at over 750,000.[59] As a percent of the population, on the other hand, Confederate deaths were nearly double Union: 2.8% vs. 1.6%. For the North, the war was an economic boon, stimulating its factories to produce weapons, uniforms and supplies. War profiteering sparked the growth of the great robber baron fortunes including Morgan, Rockefeller, Carnegie and Vanderbilt. The North finished the war as the world's second largest economy, a serious rival to Britain. On the other side, the war destroyed the plantation system, the core of the Southern economy. It ravished homes, farms, towns, and whatever meager infrastructure the South had. It reduced the South to an impoverished, virtually third world, shell which took about a century to recover.

After the Confederacy surrendered, the federal government faced the problem of how to rebuild the South, reintegrate it into the union, and prepare former slaves for freedom. This would be especially difficult because the Southern economy – or as Southerners themselves called it, Southern civilization – was grounded in slavery which was now illegal.

Traditionalist white Southerners and their opponents, especially blacks, remember "Reconstruction" – the period when the Northern army occupied the South – very differently. Blacks were granted citizenship and the right to vote. For a brief period, there were more than 1500 blacks holding political offices in the South including 600 state legislators, 16 members of Congress, black US Senators Hiram Rhodes and Blache Bruce from Mississippi and black Governor Pickney Pinchback of Louisiana.[60] From the point of view of rational economic interests, poor whites, along with blacks, had reason to support reconstruction, although for many, their sense of whiteness trumped that. The occupying army rebuilt roads, bridge and hospitals. There were plans to distribute confiscated plantations among ex-slaves and poor whites, but in the end, most were restored to their former wealthy owners. Reconstructionist policies called for opening nearly 46 million acres for purchase at low prices by freed blacks and poor whites with tax abatements, but that never happened.[61] On the other hand, the Freedman's Bureau did feed 15 million blacks and 5 million poor whites.[62] The bureau tried to unite families that had been separated. Before the war, the South lacked a public-school system. Such a system was created during reconstruction with 1000 schools, which educated both former slaves and virtually illiterate poor whites. During reconstruction, black colleges, which are still considered outstanding institutions, were created, like Howard and Fisk.[63]

Although much of what reconstruction attempted to achieve may seem laudable, white supremacy was too ingrained in Southern society for it to win sufficient Caucasian popular support. Hatred of blacks may explain part of the hostility of White Trash toward reconstruction, but they legitimately feared blacks were receiving services denied them. Perhaps with a more dedicated program to rebuild the Southern economy and keep the promise to distribute the benefits throughout the entire economy, ensuring that everyone receive them – black and white, lower class as well as upper class – poor whites might have become more sympathetic and possibly even overcome their racial resentment.

As the American invasions of Vietnam, Iraq and Afghanistan demonstrate, a government imposed by conquest is likely to fall as soon as the occupying army leaves. Once white Southerners regained the right to vote, barely 20% would accept leaving reconstructionist reforms in place.[64] The federal government would not permit the former Confederate states to restore slavery, but Southerners created an apartheid system, also called segregation but nicknamed "Jim Crow," which stripped blacks of almost all of their civil rights. Although the fifteenth amendment guaranteed blacks the right to vote, most were prevented from doing so by poll taxes and literacy tests. Jim Crow had a long series of laws, but here are a few of them: 1) Black and white children must attend separate schools; 2) Blacks and whites had separate bathrooms and drinking fountains; 3) Blacks could not be served in the same section of restaurants as whites; 4) Blacks could not initiate handshakes with whites because that might imply racial equality; 5) Blacks had to sit at the back of buses; 6) Black men must not approach white women.[65] Deprived of the land they were promised during reconstruction, blacks typically became "share croppers," something comparable to feudal serfs. These were tenant farmers who could not afford to pay their rent in cash but would instead pay with a percentage of their produce. Often, they lived on the very plantations where their families had been slaves. Their former masters would guarantee they were heavily in debt and could not escape.

White Trash, also unable to own land, likewise found themselves being share croppers. This would imply a rational common class interest between ex-slaves and poor whites, but poor Caucasians were encouraged to assert their membership in the master race and identify with their landlords and employers over "racial inferiors." One thing that was unforgiveable was for blacks to be "uppity" – act above their station by speaking in educated language, doing better than some whites economically, or holding a position with authority or prestige.

The apartheid system was instituted to insure uppity blacks did not advance beyond their naturally or Divinely established station and did not attempt to reassert the rights they had temporarily gained during reconstruction. Traditionalist white Southern memories of reconstruction bears little resemblance to the way it is recalled by blacks and their cosmopolitan allies. To many traditionalist white Southerners, it provokes even more bitterness than the Civil War itself. From the very beginning, President Andrew Johnson, who came from Tennessee, fought the Freedman Bureau's plan. Speaking like an Ayn Randian neoclassicist, he suggested it would do ex-slaves a disservice by denying them the American Dream – the incentive to uplift themselves by their bootstraps. He declared:

> The idea on which the slaves were assisted to freedom was, that on becoming free they would be a self-sustaining population. Any legislation that shall imply that they are not expected to attain a

self-sustaining condition must have a tendency injurious alike to their character and their prosperity.[66]

In the early 1870s, a mini-civil war broke out in Louisiana, resulting in hundreds of deaths. Two enemies each claimed to be the state government – one endorsed Reconstruction, won the Black vote and was supported by the occupying Union army; the other opposed Reconstruction with force of arms, organized White leagues, won the Caucasian vote, and controlled the country side.[67] In 1901, when Reconstruction would be within living memory in Louisiana, the *New Orleans Times-Picayune* proclaimed: "No people were ever so cruelly subjected to the rule of ignorant, vicious and criminal classes as were the southern people in the awful days of reconstruction."[68]

One of the most hated insults in the South became the word "carpetbagger." White Southerners did not believe most Northerners came to their communities to reconstruct a devastated region. Rather, as capitalist fortune hunters without honor or graces, they came to exploit by buying up cheap land that rightfully belonged to Southern aristocrats, or as the *Voice of the South* website put it, "scooping up grand plantations at near-avaricious prices."[69] Using the black vote at a time when whites who had supported the Confederacy were disenfranchised, the carpetbaggers got themselves elected to office, and then raised taxes to the point where they were so exorbitant that they drove former slave owners off their own land. Dixiecrats were convinced that carpetbaggers used the bloated treasuries of the "prostrate States"[70] to line their own pockets, but more sympathetic historians claim they built railroads, factories, infrastructure, hospitals and schools.[71] Building railroads may have helped industrialize the South, but it certainly filled carpetbagger wallets. "In 1870, Northerners controlled 21% of the South's railroads (by mileage); 19% of the directors were Carpetbaggers."[72] Yankee domination actually intensified after the occupying army left. "By 1890, they controlled 88% of the mileage and 47% of the directors were Carpetbaggers."[73]

Whether or not the carpetbaggers sincerely cared about blacks and poor whites, ex-confederates saw them as Yankee cosmopolitans who had little appreciation for Southern traditionalist civilization and riled up ex-slaves to challenge their betters, when before, blacks acknowledged their inferiority and were content with their station. They were convinced blacks were merely pawns used by the carpetbaggers to control the South.

The carpetbaggers were, in fact, largely well-educated cosmopolitans including teachers, newspaper editors and lawyers.[74] Some Southerners, mainly from the border regions, including veterans who fought for the Union, supported the carpetbaggers. Called Scalawags and considered traitors "who turned against their brothers in order to support the Northern cause"[75], they may have been even more hated than carpetbaggers.[76] We hear from *The Voice of the South*:

> These white, Southern Republicans were mostly non-slaveholding farmers prior to the war who, according to Confederates, gloated about the shift in power and fattened upon the disadvantage of their former superiors.[77]

The 1915 movie *Birth of a Nation*, acclaimed as the greatest silent movie ever made, but actually a tribute to the Klu Klux Klan (KKK), has the leading carpetbagger Austin Stoneman (fictionalized but probably based on Pennsylvania Congressman Thaddeus Stevens) promise "We shall crush the white South under the heel of the black South." Now that the reconstructionist government has legalized interracial marriage, or what traditionalist Southerners called "miscegenation," Stoneman is pleased when his mulatto lieutenant Silas Lynch plans to marry a white woman. Stoneman assures him: "Don't scrape to me. You are the equal of any man here." It is Stoneman's daughter (Lillian Gish), to whom he proposes: "See! My people fill the streets. With them I will build a Black Empire and you as a Queen shall sit by my side." She is horrified by the suggestion and replies that Lynch deserves "horsewhipping for his insolence." Now that Stoneman realizes his own daughter is the target of Lynch's lust, he too is horrified, but Lynch has her gagged and tied up until she is rescued by the Klan.[78]

Many ex-Confederates responded violently to reconstruction. Believing Southern defeat must be revenged, Southern valor must be redeemed, white supremacy must be restored, and they were God's chosen, they formed the Klu Klux Klan on December 24, 1865. It was a virtual revival of the Confederate army, but with a few differences. Knowing if caught by the reconstruction government they faced the gallows, they replaced the gray uniforms with white sheets, both to cover their faces and mask their identities, but also to look like ghosts, whom they assumed superstitious blacks feared. To terrorize their victims, they added rituals like burning crosses. They acted not only as an army but also as a police force, not restrained by civil liberties, and enforcing a very different law code in opposition to the Yankee imposed government. Forty years after reconstruction ended, Woodrow Wilson, who was not only president but also the leading American historian of his time, said: "The white men were roused by a mere instinct of self-preservation . . . until at last there had sprung into existence a great Ku Klux Klan, a veritable empire of the South, to protect the Southern country."[79] He also praised *Birth of a Nation*, the first movie ever shown in the White House: "It is like writing history with lightning. And my only regret is that it is all so terribly true."[80] One of the most important duties of the Klan was to protect the virtue of white women against the uncontrollable lust of black savages who were now free to maraude. In the book version of *Gone with the Wind*, we are told:

> It was the large number of outrages on women and the ever-present fear for the safety of their wives and daughters that drove Southern men to cold and trembling fury and caused the Ku Klux Klan to spring up overnight. And it was against this nocturnal organization that the newspapers of the North cried out most loudly, never realizing the tragic necessity that brought it into being. The North wanted every member of the Ku Klux hunted down and hanged, because they had dared take the punishment of crime into their own hands at a time when the ordinary processes of law and order had been overthrown by the invaders.[81]

Southerners praised the Klan, not only for controlling blacks, but also Yankee invaders. We read in a letter from Monroe County, Mississippi written on March 30, 1871:

> My beloved Sister: I will endeavor to answer your joyfully received letter. I must tell you something about the Ku Klux, they are raging on the other side of the River. They have whipped several white men, whipped and killed several Negroes.
>
> They whipped Colonel Huggins, the Superintendent of the free schools nearly to death, and everybody rejoiced when they heard it, for everybody hated him. He squandered the public money, buying pianofortes, organs, sofas, and furniture for the Negro School house in Aberdeen.
>
> The people are taxed beyond endurance. The Ku Klux gave him seventy lashes, and then gave him ten days to leave the country. He left and went to Jackson.
>
> There was a Regiment of Militia came into Aberdeen Friday. They are sent here to put down the Ku Klux. Huggins has come back with the Militia, but I wouldn't give a straw for his life, for he will be killed.
>
> It is the opinion of most everybody there will be war. The Yankees coming here will make the Negroes more insolent.
>
> With a Country full of Yankees, things are going too far, for the free whites of the South are determined not to put up with it.
>
> A Negro can kill a white man, take it in Court, get a Negro jury, clear him and then turn him loose, things can't go on this way. We are in a most peculiar situation.
>
> Give my love to all the Connections and write soon. Yours, Jennie.[82]

Towards the end of *Birth of a Nation*, wealthy ex-slave owners are trapped in the same little cabin with poor white former Northern soldiers while being attacked by black Union troops. Until they are rescued by the Klan, they use whatever weapons are at their disposal for, as the film script says: "The former enemies of North and South are united again in common defense of their Aryan birthright." Aryan is the same name the Nazis used. It is not enough that they are white; they must be born Christian and of Northwest European decent. A birthright is a privilege you are literally born with. It is not earned. It is part of your being and marks you as inherently superior. Like kings or feudal lords, the Aryan birthright is assigned by God or Nature. It is your place within the great chain of being. You have it because of who you are, not what you do. Union or Confederate, rich or poor, they share in this common Aryanness. It is their heritage; it cannot be undermined by cosmopolitans, who do not appreciate ultimate irrational reality, or racial inferiors, who try to usurp a place which belongs to Aryan masters. This evokes not only the specter of fascism but glorious feudal nobles carrying out God's mission.

In one of the last scenes of the movie, all is vindicated. Rows of Klansmen in white hoods and robes stand with guns and baronets between blacks and the voting booths. The Nation is reborn; The Klan is the real government; blacks and their Yankee cosmopolitan allies cannot seize the state and challenge traditional Southern white authority. Immediately after this, there is another scene in heaven. A beast, most likely the Devil, on horseback wields a sword but he is overcome by an unarmed Jesus, who presumably blesses what is going on earth below. David Griffith, director of the movie, offered this subtitle "Dare we dream of a golden day when the bestial War shall rule no more . . . But instead – the gentle Prince in the Hall of Brotherly Love in the City of Peace." As the Klansmen maintain order, Divine peace has been attained.

Fast forward 100 years. Today the Klan envisions its members as true patriots, the true defenders of America – all of America. A man of valor who fights for his country will join. Its website shows Confederate and Union flags flying together.[83] America is now united and what was once the Union as well as the Confederacy must be protected from vermin who seek to undermine it. It must be steadfastly Christian for there are communists everywhere, within and without, out to destroy it.

> Stand up and be counted, show the world that you're a man!
> Stand up and be counted go with the Ku Klux Klan!
> We are a sacred brotherhood, who love our country too.
> We always can be counted on, when there's a job to do.
> We serve our homeland day and night, to keep it always free
> Proudly wear our robes of White, protecting liberty.
>
> Survival cause for vigilance, the symbols of our land.
> The sword and water, robe and hood, betrayed our noble plan.
> In search for peace and liberty, we pledge our hearts in hands.
> We must defeat the communists to save our Christian land.[84]

Communism is evil; it divides people by class. It suggests that slaves and their masters, workers and their bosses are enemies, but blacks and exploited non-rich whites should be allies. It is ungodly. The modern Klan is here to protect America – all of it: North and South – from communism. North Carolina evangelist Billy Graham, who befriended presidents and was considered a moderate was clear: "Communism is a religion that is inspired, directed and motivated by the Devil himself who has declared war against Almighty God."[85] In ante-bellum times, evangelists preached that the South was an interconnected whole, like the "great chain of being" where everyone had their divinely assigned place – not based on their achievements, but on their essence. This required no rational explanation; it simply was and must be accepted one faith. To demand an explanation was a sign of lack of grace and faith; something that a Yankee atheist might do. As early as 1850, leading Southern preacher James Henley Thornwell, editor of the *Southern Quarterly Review*, equated the plan to abolish slavery with communism. He warned if the abolitionist agenda were

> fully and legitimately carried out, would condemn every arrangement of society, which did not secure to its members an absolute equality of position; it is the very spirit of socialism and communism. . . . The parties in this conflict are not merely Abolitionists and Slaveholders; they are Atheists, Socialists, Communists, Red Republicans, Jacobins on the one side, and the friends of order and regulated freedom on the other. In one word, the world is the

battle ground, Christianity and Atheism the combatants, and the progress of humanity the stake.[86]

After Thornwell and the Civil War, leading Southern Evangelists continued to preached the same message: that the Bible teaches slaves are to defer to their master; all blacks are to defer to whites; children are to defer to parents; wives are to defer to husbands; the poor of any race are to defer to those whom God has endowed with wealth. Having faith – accepting your place – will be rewarded, if not in this world, then in the world to come. As humiliating as defeat in the Civil War must feel, it can only be a momentary setback. Vindication will come. Righteous Southerners shall overcome Godless Yankees. The South shall rise again and all faithful White Southerners shall share in its glory.

For over a century, this message of glory proclaimed that cosmopolitan Northerners used the federal government to try to impose their socialist schema on traditionalist Southerners. They not only manipulated blacks to turn against their natural superiors, they brought atheism in the school by teaching lies like evolution and calling it science. As cosmopolitans in the federal government sought to impose an end to apartheid or segregation, Alabama Governor George Wallace warned:

> Today I have stood, where once Jefferson Davis stood, and took an oath to my people. It is very appropriate then that from this Cradle of the Confederacy, this very Heart of the Great Anglo-Saxon Southland . . . and I say . . . segregation today . . . segregation tomorrow . . . segregation forever.
>
> Hear me Southerners! . . . your heart has never left Dixieland . . . you are Southerners too and brothers with us in our fight . . .
>
> We [America] are become government-fearing people . . . not God-fearing people . . . in reality, government has become our God. It [America] is, therefore, a basically ungodly government and its appeal to the pseudo-intellectual and the politician is . . . to play at being God . . . without faith in God. It is a system that is the very opposite of Christ for it feeds and encourages everything degenerate and base in our people . . . Its pseudo-liberal

spokesmen and some Harvard advocates have never examined the logic of its substitution of what it calls "human rights" or individual rights . . . including the theory that everyone has voting rights without the spiritual responsibility of preserving freedom . . . It is degenerate and decadent.[87]

For all his preaching moral purity, Wallace's tenure as governor has been characterized as "an era of unparalleled corruption that operated through a crony system", earning his brother's company over a million dollars in state contracts with an initial investment of $1000.[88] Early in his political career, he sponsored laws which would attract multinational corporations to Alabama by offering an ununionized badly educated white labor force with wages below the national average. Social services would be kept to a minimum to insure low corporate taxes. Alabama state policy was orchestrated to benefit an alliance of industrialists and agribusinesses, descending from antebellum plantations, at the expense of the majority – black and white.[89] Thus did Southern glory continue to divide and conquer, as it always has.

Ever since Reconstruction as the "new South" industrialized somewhat, low black wages produced a "race to the bottom," pitting whites against blacks as they competed by seeking low salaries and agreeing not to unionize. Southern states often have what are euphemistically called "right to work" laws that restrict the power of labor unions and prohibit "closed shops" which strengthen unions by requiring all employees to join. In the midst of depression, President Franklin Roosevelt made a deal for the support of Southern Democrats. To ensure share croppers and black workers did not have enough security to challenge their employees, he exempted agribusiness from New Deal programs and put welfare policies under the control of the states rather than the federal government. This depressed benefits for white trash as well as blacks and these rules remained in effect until they were further weakened by President Bill Clinton. Capitalists played their own divide and conquer politics, feeding off glory sentiments in the South that had resonance in many traditionist, conservative areas of the North as well.

White anger, in the South especially, but across America, tended to be directed against blacks rather than the corporate elite. Many saw welfare as designed to serve blacks and wanted to minimize it, if not abolish it, even though poor Whites benefited as well. This helped depress wages for all races. Evangelism may encourage many white Southerners to accept their station. Consequently seven of the ten states with the lowest median family income are in the old Confederacy. Alabama is fourth from the bottom.[90] As President Lyndon Johnson, Wallace's nemesis, who grow up poor in Texas, put it:

> I'll tell you what's at the bottom of it. If you can convince the lowest white man he's better than the best colored man, he won't notice you're picking his pocket. He'll give him somebody to look down on, and he'll empty his pockets for you.[91]

White evangelical Southerners rallied behind Reagan whose policies served the corporate elite more than the 99% and whose personal life hardly met the standards of fundamentalist morality. Likewise, Trump received 81% of the white evangelical vote.[92] Cosmopolitan Berkeley sociology professor Arlie Hochschild spent five years, off and on, among white residents of the Louisiana bayou, a state with the fifth lowest median family income, among people whose lives and health had been undermined by oil companies. She felt great empathy for their plight, but showed that the narrative of Southern traditionalism and glory persists to sustain their identity and pride.

> We vote for candidates that put the Bible where it belongs. We try to be right-living, clean-living people, and we'd like our leaders to live that way and believe in that too. Republicans are for big business. They won't help us with the problems we got here ... But Republicans put God and family on their side and we like that.[93]

She also found resentment towards blacks, whom they believed were receiving benefits from government programs denied them. Sponsored by cosmopolitan liberals, these policies made blacks overly entitled as it sheltered them from their own immorality.

> I've had enough of "poor me." I don't like the government paying
> unwed mothers to have a lot of kids, and I don't go for affirmative
> action. I met one black guy who complained he couldn't get a
> job. Come to find out he'd been to private school. I went to local
> public school like everyone else I know. No one should be getting
> a job to fill some mandated racial quota or getting state money
> not to work.[94]

Evangelicals and other Southerners who voted for Trump were inspired by his pledge to "Make America Great Again," a slogan also used by Reagan. As he embraced the heroes of Southern succession, George Wallace ran for president with a promise to "Stand Up For America." In the Civil War, many Confederates saw themselves as the real Americans, the heirs of the American Revolution. They went to war to preserve the rights the founding fathers fought for. Wallace presented himself as both the heir of Jefferson Davis and standing up for the real America. Until protests demanded their removal, Confederate flags flew along with Union throughout the South. The South is patriotic. Southerners join the United States military in numbers disproportionally above their percent of the population.

Although Southerners are 36% of the American population, they constitute 44% of US military recruits.[95] Undoubtedly part of the explanation is poverty and lack of economic opportunity, but another part may be that violence and guns are more ingrained in Southern culture than other parts of the country. Southern sense of justice requires retribution, not restitution or rehabilitation; punishment for punishment's sake, with or without any rational purpose. Although there is no evidence that the death penalty reduces crime, executions are regular occurrences in the former Confederacy, but since the mid-1960s, there has only been one in New England and New York. Some 36% of the Southern population own guns, but only 16% in the Northeast.[96] The gun is more than an instrument; it is a badge of Southern identity.

> "They're fixing to change this whole bidniss" as the man at the
> Charleston gun show had said – to take away the last vestige of

Southern manhood... The gun show was the one place they could be themselves, like a clubhouse, with strict admission and no windows... The gun show wasn't about guns and gun totin'. It was about the self-esteem of men – white men mainly – the dominant ethnic group of the South, animated by a sense of grievance ("the heart of Southern identity," according to one shrewd historian) – who felt defeated and still persecuted, conspired against by hostile outside forces, making it a symbolic last stand.[97]

Although the North may have defeated the South through chicanery, squeamish Yankees, who do not know how to handle a gun, need courageous Southerners to protect them honorably. As Chris Kyle's father told him in Odessa Texas, when he received a hunting rifle at age eight, sheep need sheep dogs to protect them from wolves. To show you are a worthy Southerner, you must show you are willing to fight. Victory in recent battles will prove that the defeat in the Civil War was a fluke that should not have happened. The Confederacy was "stabbed in the back" and that must be avenged through the United States military.

Now that the country is reunited, the US armed services represent all Americans – South as well as North, if anything more South than North. It may seem contradictory that you display your Southern valor by joining the very forces that reduced the South to a wasteland, but again, Southernness must be part of your inner being. It is something you must feel. If you require a rational explanation, that shows you do not understand it. The Confederacy's heroes from the Civil War offer an inspiration to join the US military for those born afterwards. They must follow in their ancestor's path. A Navy recruitment poster from World War II shows a big picture of Robert E. Lee overshadowing a smaller image of a sailor carrying a baronet. Lee dictates: "I fought for Virginia. Now **** it's your turn!"[98] The poster gives no explanation of the cause for which the Virginian will be fighting (although World War II may be the most rationally understandable of all wars). As a Southerner, you fight for fighting's sake. You are merging with some force higher than yourself; it could be collective – not individual – freedom; Southernness, with slavery and apartheid as glorious causes; your state – Virginia or wherever; the nation as a whole. America cannot and must not steamroll Southernness.

While the Civil War was an overwhelming victory for the North and an utter defeat for the South, it is celebrated in the South far more than the North. There are regular Civil War battle reenactments in the South, with people putting on vintage uniforms, carrying vintage flags and replicas of vintage weapons, pretending to charge and shoot each other. Some even pretend to be dead. These are rare in the North. In 2018, the Southern Poverty Law Center counted 718 statues and monuments honoring Confederate heroes throughout the South and about another 800 roads, schools, and other public buildings named in tribute to them. Most of these were built at least a generation after the war, beginning in the 1890s, around the time that Jim Crow apartheid laws were being firmly established. According to North Carolina historian Karen Cox[99], most of these were sponsored by the United Daughters of the Confederacy who were trying to ingrain, in the Southern mind, a conviction that their men sacrificed for a "glorious cause." There was a second building boom for Civil War monuments during the civil rights movement of the 1950–60s. It was to make clear that "the South shall rise again" and there will be "segregation today . . . segregation tomorrow . . . segregation forever."

Recently blacks and their cosmopolitan allies have demanded that these monuments be taken down from public spaces for they insist the "glorious cause," is slavery – something to be ashamed, not proud, of. Many of them have been removed, but that is not something that traditionalist Southerners passively accept. There has been violence and reactions like the one offered by Florida Lawyer Leonard Rabon Poe:

> The Civil War is not over. The Northern Mind is still fighting the Civil War with political correctness and public shaming. Southern heroes and iconography are attacked as mementos of a vile, Southern slave-based aristocracy. The flags carried by our honored dead are removed, monuments to our great men are razed, and streets honoring our patriots are renamed. And we are shamed into silence. To those of us with a Southern Mind, we sense that a

great injustice has been done. We feel like it's a matter of Southern pride. "Proud of what, fighting for slavery?" the Northern Mind asks. No! We are proud of a Southern heritage that pre-existed the conflict. We are proud of Southern men who lived with personal honor and individual courage. We are proud of Southern women who were beloved for their charm and grace. We are proud of a Southern society founded on hospitality and Christian values. Pride, honor, gentility, and faith: the pillars that support the Southern Mind. Then and now. But the Northern Mind won the War, and glorified its Northern values: a classless society where anyone can be President, a strong centralized government that can dictate policy to the world, economic interests that are the measure of national morality, and victory in all things by any means necessary.[100]

In the heart of cosmopolitan Harvard, a white student hung a Confederate flag from her window. A black student asked her to remove it saying it was a symbol of slavery and genocide but she refused and insisted it represented pride in her Southern heritage. In response, the black student hung a swastika, declaring it to be the equivalent of the Confederate flag.[101] As we shall discuss in a later chapter, arguably, this is true, but a Native American could say the US flag represents genocide and a Southerner could say it represents Sherman's brutal rampage through Georgia. Who is to decide what is offensive to whom? If we simply remove offensive symbols, we are simply denying history and as Karl Marx warned: "History repeats itself – first as tragedy, second as farce."[102] The far right could rise again. If we are to prevent another "glorious cause" with nostalgia for the Confederate South or Nazi Germany, we must remember what they really were – slavery and genocidal xenophobia.

South Boston

As noted before, we do not want to give the impression that the traditionalist–cosmopolitan conflict or the clash between glorious neo-feudalism and profitable capitalism we have been describing is uniquely

Southern. As there are demands to remove monuments honoring Confederate heroes in the South, there are demands to rename buildings named for supporters of slavery in the North. Called the "Cradle of Liberty" and popular with both tourists and residents, Faneuil Hall in downtown Boston is a sight for civic celebrations, music and small shops. Its founder, Peter Faneuil, was a merchant who made a fortune in the slave trade. In 2018, the largely black "New Democracy Coalition" threatened to boycott the landmark unless it was renamed. Although sympathetic, Boston Mayor Martin J. Walsh legitimately worried about the consequences of erasing Peter Faneuil's memory. He said: "We can't erase history, but we learned from it." He pointed out that escaped slave Frederick Douglass called for slavery's abolition from the Faneuil podium,[103] but this is the same Faneuil Hall where Jefferson Davis declared "servitude is the only agency through which Christianity has reached that degraded race, the only means by which they have been civilized and elevated."[104]

In the North as well as the South, military recruiters assume many will be attracted with promises of glory with slogans like, "The few, the proud, the brave, the Marines" and "It's not just a job, it's an adventure." Indeed, as noted in previous earlier, capitalists routinely turn to the rhetoric of glorious causes to recruit their own soldiers, since money, the grubby currency of capitalism, lacks the inspirational Godly power of glory. However, recruiters in New York and Alabama also made utilitarian promises of scholarships and job training that will lead to a secure well-paying career once the soldier returned to civilian life. That assumed he returned alive and the promises were often lies. Nonetheless they would be attractive to people who see little opportunity in their community, perhaps because of poverty or failure in school, something which for many had been an alienating experience.

If glory or promises of economic opportunity failed, in both the South and the North, there was the draft until the 1970s. During the Civil War, both sides blatantly assumed the poor would kill and die and the rich would benefit. "The 1862 Confederate Conscription Act provided draft exemption for educated elite, slaveholders, office holders and man employed in valuable trades."[105] A draft was instituted in the North, but it was openly a draft for the poor. Anyone who could find a substitute or pay $300 was exempt. Poor northerners did not passively accept being forced to fight in what they perceived to be a rich man's war. Riots broke out, especially in New York. Even though freed blacks had nothing to do with the enactment of the draft, many poor white New Yorkers blamed them for their risk of being carted away through involuntary conscription and freed blacks were targeted in riots. Victims, virtually powerless to challenge their oppressors, often turn their anger against people below them. Their rulers may convince them that the source of their misery is aliens – outsiders from another race or nation. Through this technique, they can rally the subordinate classes to fight in their wars. Unable to directly attack the rich, subjugated whites turned against blacks, many of whom were freed slaves. However, the riots were actually successful for the draft was repealed.

Fast forward over 100 years: The cosmopolitans live in wealthy neighborhoods in the coastal urban centers, but they support integrated public schools as long as their children can go to private schools. They can provoke provincial traditional reactions among people who feel left behind in Northern cities as well as the rural South. In Massachusetts in the 1970s, working class Irish rioted when blacks were bused by the government to attend schools in their neighborhood, South Boston. That busing was supported in wealthy suburbs like Brookline, where there was no busing.

To protect the "vanishing rights" of white citizens, which they felt was being undermined by forced busing, Irish Whites in South Boston formed ROAR (Restore Our Alienated Rights). As they sang "Southie is My Home," a member asked "Why can't poor white kids be bused to your suburban schools?"[106] One commentator observed:

> The women in the anti-busing movement are not rejecting their own values – instead, they believe they are reaffirming them, fighting for what their parents, their schools and their church have taught them.[107]

ROAR's leader Congresswoman Louise Day Hicks declared:

> It is now up to the people to decide through whatever means at their disposal what steps they will now take to save themselves from the apostles of urban neglect . . . NO PEOPLE anywhere at anytime can be expected to live with the injustice that has been heaped time and time again on the good parents of Boston. They have been had, and they will respond.[108]

As she attacked "radical agitators" and "pseudo-liberals" of the counterculture, she asserted:

> "[A]t least one hundred black people walking around in the black community . . . have killed white people during the last two years" . . . "white women can no longer walk the streets [of Boston] in safety" and that "justice [had come] to mean special privileges for the black man and the criminal." She attacked "black militants [who] tyrannize our schools, creating chaos and disruption."[109]

Around the same time, a new integrated high school opened in West Roxbury – another mostly Irish neighborhood, then somewhat wealthier than South Boston, but still heavily working class. A large graffiti was painted on an underpass near the school demanding: "Niggers go home!"

Forty years later still, South Boston is gentrifying. As housing costs rise, cosmopolitans are pushing out traditionalist working class Irish. They can longer afford to live in their own community. Their alienated rights are being eliminated, not restored. They have all the more reason to be angry than in the 1970s, but they no longer have the resources or the will to fight back. The blame lays with housing policies and wealthy cosmopolitans, not blacks who are also victims as their neighborhoods likewise are being gentrified. In Boston, real estate agents have renamed the old black neighborhood, Roxbury. So cosmopolitans will be willing to pay higher housing costs and feel they living in a prestigious predominately white address, it is now called the South End. As long as the 90%, in the North as well as the South, is divided against itself by race and other factors, their quality of life will continue to degenerate.

The same capitalist elites who close factories and eliminate jobs in the North, only to move them to the South and then to Singapore, gentrify Northern neighborhoods and undermine any community solidarity among families who may have lived there for generations. Cosmopolitans breed resentment as they displace traditionalists but the transformation is orchestrated to profit millionaire and billionaire real estate developers. As elites preach glory and "America First," traditionalists focus their anger on people, who – they come to believe – do not wear the badge of true Americanism, perhaps because of skin color, ethnic origins, or values that question American greatness. Through this process traditionalists are turned against cosmopolitans, whites are turned against blacks, native-born are turned against immigrants, and the real elite, who bear most of the responsibility, remains hidden, unchallenged and free to rule as they chose, to their benefit, but at everyone else's expense.

The South is more than a region. It is a state of mind. It transcends geographical boundaries. It may have withdrawn from the union and attacked the federal government, but it is the true America for many millions of traditionalists in the South and around the country. Since the Civil War, even when traditionalists like Reagan lived in the White House, cosmopolitans occupied Washington and used it to undermine the American spirit. Southernness (or whiteness) is needed to restore national glory, valor and greatness. Reviving Americanism required war against the Yankee pretenders. For the common good, all must accept their place within a Divinely sanctioned chain: white over black, rich over poor, male over female. The reward may not be personal; individuals may have to sacrifice, perhaps on the battlefield, but they can know they are part of some great mission that cosmopolitans, especially Yankee cosmopolitans, can never appreciate. Traditionalism may be prominent in the South but it is pervasive throughout America. Appealing to traditionalists, Trump carried Pennsylvania, Michigan and Wisconsin and there are cosmopolitan enclaves in the South including Chapel Hill and Asheville, North Carolina, Austin, Texas and the French Quarters of New Orleans. The United States is hardly unique in having traditionalists and cosmopolitans at war but living side to side. In the next chapter, we shall look at how the traditionalist cosmopolitan conflict reached even greater intensity in Europe, fueling an even more catastrophic glorious cause, especially in Germany.

3

STABBED IN THE BACK

THE MASTER RACE SHALL BE THE MASTER

Nazis once proudly marched through the streets of Germany chanting these verses:

> The rotten bones are trembling,
> Of the World for [because of] the Great War.
> We have smashed this terror,
> For us it was a great victory
>
> We will continue to march,
> When everything shatters;
> Because today Germany hears/recognizes us,
> And tomorrow the whole World.
>
> They don't want to understand the song,
> They think of slavery and war.
> Meanwhile, our acres ripen,
> Flag of freedom, fly!
>
> We will continue to march,
> When everything shatters;
> Freedom rose in Germany,
> And tomorrow the world belongs to it[1]
>
> Germany awake from your nightmare!
> Give foreign Jews no place in your Reich!

We will fight for your resurgence!
Aryan blood shall never perish!

All these hypocrites, we throw them out,
Judea leave our German house!
If the native soil is clean and pure,
we united and happy will be![2]

The Great War: Oh! That's What Great Means

World War I was essentially a family quarrel among Queen Victoria's grandchildren. King George V of Great Britain and Kaiser Wilhelm II of Germany were her grandsons, and Empress Alexandra Feodorovna, wife of Czar Nicholas II of Russia, was her granddaughter. The Kaiser may have been the queen's favorite grandson and she is rumored to have died in his arms.[3]

The only way to understand World War I may be to assume there was a contagious craving for glory and war for war's sake – a desire to show your country's greatness by crushing its rivals, even if there was little rational reason for them to be enemies – throughout Europe. It defies rational comprehension, even more than the American Civil War. Nobody could explain what they were fighting about – then or now. In retrospect, we can discern rational motives, but they could not have inspired the euphoria that accompanied the break-out of the war: Britain's desire to contain Germany as a potential rival; Germany's hope to equal or surpass Britain; France wanting to reclaim Alsace-Lorraine, which it lost to Germany in the Franco-Prussian War; Russia, the Ottomans and Austria–Hungry struggling to stem the disintegration of their empires; and, of course, everyone's greed for colonies. Hardly anyone cared about Archduke Franz Ferdinand of Austria–Hungry, whose assassination sparked the explosion.

As the soldiers marched off in 1914, most sides expected a glorious little war, which would last a few months, give an opportunity to show honor and valor, possibly cost a few hundred deaths, and bring lots of booty to the winners. Hardly anyone saw a four-year cataclysm with a death toll possibly in the tens of millions that would leave Europe in shambles – something even more devastating than the American Civil War was to the South. There were a few exceptions like British Foreign

Secretary Sir Edward Grey, who mourned, "The lamps are going out all over Europe and we shall not see them lit again in our lifetime."[4]

In country after the country, the war was initially greeted with celebrations as excited young men, seeking adventure, ran to enlist and were cheered by their girlfriends, families and neighbors. The excitement resembled the early American reaction to the Civil War – when also, at first, everyone expected something short and glorious. In London, few harbored hostility towards Germans a few weeks earlier, but as the word spread that Parliament had declared war, one teenaged girl recalled:

> It was all very unreal of course, I mean all very exciting. I remember when war was declared going outside Buckingham Palace and cheering with all the crowds as the king and queen came out on the balcony and being frightfully excited and thinking it was *splendid that we were going into the war and all the rest of it*.[5]

Soldiers were thrilled with the opportunity to see action. One British cavalry officer remembered:

> When we heard that war was declared, everybody was delighted. And we thought it far more amusing to go and see some part of the continent than to go on manoeuvres. Literally cheers went up from each side of the barrack square, from the men, when somebody gave out that war was declared.[6]

Like in the American Civil War, young men were prodded to enlist with calls to defend the honor not only of their country but also their women. British young women handed white feathers, a symbol of cowardice, to young men still in civilian clothes. Recruitment pollsters emphasized that only a boy who enlists deserves his girlfriend's love.

> To the YOUNG WOMEN OF LONDON – Is your "Best Boy" wearing Khaki? If not don't YOU THINK he should be? If he does not think that you and your country are worth fighting for – do you think he is WORTHY of you? Don't pity the girl who is alone – her young man is probably a soldier – fighting for her

and her country – and for <u>YOU</u>. If your young man neglects his duty to his king and country, the time may come when he will NEGLECT YOU. Think it over – then ask him to JOIN THE ARMY <u>TO-DAY</u>.[7]

In Germany, there was a similar war fever as recalled by one school boy.

> I was in a small German garrison town in 1914 and I remember very well the tremendous enthusiasm. Of course, we schoolboys were all indoctrinated with great patriotism when war broke out. My father was an active infantry officer and I shall never forget the day when they marched out to the trains. All the soldiers were decorated with flowers, there was no gun which didn't show a flower – even the horses I think were decorated. And of course all the people followed them. There were bands playing, flags flying, and a terrific sort of overwhelming conviction that of course Germany now would go into war and win it very quickly.[8]

By the end of 1914, with the death tolls already in the hundreds of thousands, it should have been rationally apparent that the combatants were engaged in something far more brutal than a game of honor. As we saw by Christmas time, many soldiers on both sides were beginning to wonder what they were killing and dying for, and who their real enemies were. When the war began the German moderate Left – the Social Democrats – held a majority in the Reichstag (Parliament) and decided to mend class differences and unite together with the Bourgeoisie and Junkers (aristocrats who filled most of the officer corps) as Germans in support of the war. They approved the credits necessary to fight.[9] As the war dragged on, the Social Democrats split, with one side – the Communists, or the Spartacists – resolute in its opposition. Its strongest voice, Rosa Luxemburg – a Jewish immigrant to Germany from Poland – saw it as war for the rich and powerful against the working class, in language very similar to that used by American socialist leader Eugene Debs in the United States. Like Debs, she was imprisoned for this but, unlike him, she was assassinated by an alliance of social democrats and rightwing militarists, soon after her release. Neither the social democrats nor the far right could forgive Luxemburg for seeing the "Great War," not as great but as pointless carnage and destruction.

> Gone is the euphoria. Gone the patriotic noise in the streets, the chase after the gold-colored automobile. . . . The trains full of reservists are no longer accompanied by virgins fainting from pure jubilation . . . The cannon fodder loaded onto trains in August and September is moldering in the killing fields of Belgium, the Vosges, and Masurian . . . Cities become piles of ruins; villages become cemeteries; countries, deserts; populations are beggared; churches, horse stalls. International law, treaties and alliances, the most sacred words and the highest authority have been torn in shreds.[10]

By conservative estimates, the war caused 15 million deaths worldwide – 9 million military and 6 million civilian, not counting the flu of 1918–1919 – perhaps the most deadly epidemic in the history of the world with between 20 and 40 millions fatalities.[11] During the war, Britain lost around 750,000 military personnel, France 1.4 million, Russia 1.7 million, the United States 116,708, Austria–Hungry 1 million and Germany 2 million.[12] By 1917, the major European powers had exhausted each other. Germany had an advantage because Russia surrendered, which freed German forces to concentrate entirely on Britain and France, but then the United States entered the war. From an American point of view, this was a true capitalist war – fought to protect investments. The House of Morgan had lent so much to Britain that it would have been bankrupted by a German victory and the collapse of the House of Morgan would have destroyed the American economy.[13]

President Woodrow Wilson would not have been able to rally the American people with a promise to make the "World safe for the House of Morgan," so he adopted more lofty rhetoric like making the "World safe for Democracy" as he suspended the Bill of Rights and jailed members of Congress and Leftists like socialist leader Eugene Debs for speaking out against the war effort. Like Britain, America had little quarrel with Germany before the war. But now, British and American propaganda denounced Germany as the Hun, insatiable savages out to destroy all that was pure and holy since the beginning of civilization. There were enlistment posters of a gorilla-like monster (dark, possibly black) in a German army helmet carrying in one arm a virginal blonde bare-breasted girl. In the other arm he carried a bloody club with the German word "KULTUR" as he walked over America.[14] Both the American and British war departments used German behavior in Belgium as evidence of barbarism. Civilians were killed and buildings, including libraries, were destroyed, but stories were invented including babies "speared on a Hun's bayonet" and the Kaiser's troops cutting off 4000 children's hands.[15] Although it had nothing to do with the German invasion and does not justify German attacks on civilians, innocent little Belgium had committed a genocide in the Congo with 10 million victims, more than the number of Jews the Nazis killed in the Holocaust.[16] Part of the reason why the Congo genocide has gotten so much less attention may be that the dead were not white.

While, in World War I, Germany was no innocent, it was no worse than any other country at the time. The Kaiser was not a symbolic monarch like in Britain. He was a militarist with limited, but real, powers similar to the President of the United States. The Reichstag was elected and represented a much wider spectrum of opinions than the American Congress. Social services in Germany were among the best in the world and civil liberties were comparable to the United States and Britain. As exaggerated as the lies made up about World War I Germany were, they were dwarfed by the reality of World War II Germany. The public memory of stories created about Germany in World War I made it difficult for the American and British War Departments to convincingly publicize the Holocaust and other Nazi atrocities in World War II.

Like in Europe, America's entry into the war divided the country and provoked two very different reactions. With voices like Debs, there was a massive anti-war movement, which has been virtually erased from memory. Some 300,000 resisted the Draft. True to Marxist predictions, the anti-war movement had substantial working-class support. The International Workers of the World (IWW, or Wobblies), many of whom were later jailed, organized among Seattle longshore and provoked a general strike throughout the city soon after the war ended.[17] On the other hand, the American Federation of Labor urged lining up behind the government as 50,000 marched in Seattle in support of military "preparedness." Once the United States declared war, millions of American rallied in war fever. There were public celebrations to get people to buy liberty bonds and enlist. Vigilantes "ostracized, harassed, and sometimes violently attacked those whom they charged with refusing to show respect for the flag, the military, and/or the mission to save democracy."[18] German Americans who had previously had cordial relations with their neighbors found themselves shunned and bullied. In *East of Eden*, Mr. Fenchel, a local German tailor who had lived peacefully in the community for 20 years, is mocked because of his accent and met with taunts like "Hail the Kaiser." When he says he is sorry when told of the death of a local boy in the war, the response is "he's not sorry enough." Shortly afterwards, his shop gets burned down.[19]

To inspire patriotism, George M. Cohan wrote the song "Over There":

> Johnnie, get your gun
> Get your gun, get your gun
> Take it on the run . . .
> Every son of liberty
> Hurry right away . . .
> Make your daddy glad . . .
> Send the word, send the word over there
> That the Yanks are coming . . .
> And we won't come back till it's over
> Over there . . .
> Johnnie show the Hun.[20]

Unlike for Europe, for the United States World War I was a short war with relatively few losses. Ironically after victory and peace was declared, America suffered "burn out," or malaise, but while Americans were in Europe, it was called the "Great Adventure," an opportunity to see the world and taste "the good life," with songs like:

> How ya gonna keep 'em down on the farm
> After they've seen Paree?[21]

They not only saw Paree, but also the trenches only a few miles north. Those might keep them down on the farm. However it also gave them a sense that they were part of some greater cause, helping America save the world or at least the "good" part of the world, pay its debt to France for the revolution with the slogan "Lafayette, We are here." What is striking about that slogan is that Britain was a more important ally than France, especially to American policy makers and corporations. The war bred a sense that all Americans were together in this Great Adventure, this great crusade, and class differences did not matter. Of course, anyone who said they did matter could find themselves in jail. As long as young men were off to war, they would not be striking, demonstrating or interfering with corporations, who would then be free to profit from the war.

Although the war brought total devastation to Europe, it was a boon to America, a stronger stimulant for economic growth than the Civil War had been for the North. While the war destroyed the infrastructure of every major country in Europe, it left America's more than intact. To arm, supply and feed its troops along with its allies, the United States built an industrial base which overwhelmed the rest of the world. And its industrial base permitted it to transform a modest military into the world's largest within a year. "By 1920, the United States national income was greater than the combined incomes of Britain, France, Germany, Japan, Canada, and seventeen smaller countries."[22] In 1918, Germany found itself facing 2 million fresh American troops, when it had so few surviving men of military age that it was fighting with 12 year-old boys. At home, people were lucky to eat rats as a result of the blockade by the British navy. There were food riots. The German fleet at Kiel mutinied and refused to leave port. However, German troops were still in France and Germany had not yet been invaded. A battlefield map would give the impression that Germany was still capable of winning. However, the reality was they would not be able to resist once America and their allies crossed the Rhine.

Assessing the situation, General Erich Ludendoff informed the Kaiser that Germany's predicament was hopeless and the Kaiser abdicated. It is important to emphasize that the Kaiser was a militarist with a big ego and a temper, but he was no Hitler and was capable of working within German democratic institutions, although he personally held them in contempt. Prior to the war, he displayed no overt anti-Semitism and he counted many Jews – including Walter Rathenau, Albert Ballin, Maximllian Harden and Theodor Herzl – among his personal friends, but at the surrender he remarked, "I shall not leave the throne to please a couple of hundred Jews and several thousand workers."[23] While Germany agreed to an armistice on November 8, 1918, the formal signing ceremony took place on November 11. In those three days, soldiers on both sides continued to kill each other.

On the frontline and in the home front, the announcement that the war was over would be met with at least two very different reactions among Germans: 1) relief that years of pointless death and destruction were over; and 2) fury at being denied the one thing that would make the sacrifices meaningful – victory. Without that there would be no glory, no vindication; all the deaths, all the suffering would be in vain. Germans were Aryans – a master race, ordained by some higher force – God or nature – to rule the world. Like the South in the Civil War, Germany was destined to win. The only people who could defeat Germans were other Germans, or alien vermin within Germany's midst. Defeat was drawn from the jaws of victory. Germany was betrayed, "stabbed in the back." Even Ludendoff, the very general who advised surrender, was convinced Germany lost only because it was "stabbed in the back."[24] Those in the new government – the Weimar Republic – which surrendered in November 1918 were traitors – "November Criminals." In the Treaty of Versailles, the victors forced Germany to confess to full responsibility for causing the war, even though it was emphatically untrue since almost every major country involved was equally guilty. Germany's army could not be larger than 100,000 troops or its navy no larger than six battleships. Germany, now impoverished, would have to pay reparations, assume the cost of their former enemies' reconstruction-something that could bankrupt Germany for generations.[25]

To many on the Right, these terms were extreme humiliation and anyone who agreed to them was an enemy of the real Germany.

Soldiers in the hospital, recovering from injuries, might be pleased that they would not be sent back to the frontline or they might feel betrayed. One obscure corporal was disgusted at the news of surrender, which he learned about in the hospital while recuperating from a gas attack. He was a failed artist and an Austrian immigrant with a modest middle-class background, but he was destitute enough to have to live in a homeless shelter before he enlisted in the German army. His name was Adolf Hitler. He could be considered a bohemian cosmopolitan as an aspiring artist, but like Trump and Reagan, he found himself leading traditionalists. Psychologists have suggested he conceived of the Nazi ideology because he was mentally ill, most likely a sociopath. However, as Derber has shown in another book, sociopathology is not necessarily an individual phenomenon, but rather something that can pervade an entire society.[26] Whatever his mental health, Hitler could be considered among the most brilliant politicians who ever lived for he rose from nowhere to rule one of the most developed countries in the world. For better or worse – using methods that could be considered reprehensible but brilliantly exploited glory – in a few years he restored Germany's prosperity and rebuilt its military to the point that it could again seriously threaten its enemies from the first war. If he was a madman, then the question is: how could a madman gain control of one of the world's most sophisticated countries?[27] Could his millions of followers also be insane?

Weimar Germany: Two Worlds In One Country

In the immediate years after World War I, when its government was called the Weimar Republic, Germany was a polarized country torn by culture wars which dwarfed anything the United States experienced since the Civil War, though we shall see the US was going through its own cultural wars in the aftermath of WWI. It may not be an accident that Wolfgang Streeck, who sees a world divided between cosmopolitans and traditionalist, is German, where traditionalism resonated to the most horrific outcome of the twentieth century.

Traditionalism is the cultural seedbed of fascism and nationalist glory while cosmopolitanism is the cultural hurdle against them. Traditionalists define submission to the authority of God and nation as sacred. Cosmopolitans reject submission to authority which erases individual expression in the service of God and glory. The Nazis would exploit traditionalism to build their political base after WWI. Urban German cosmopolitans would reject Hitler and the fascists but were destroyed by the traditionist followers of Hitler's glorious cause.

Before turning to Weimar, let us look briefly at the roaring war between cosmopolitans and traditionalist in the US 1920s, a weaker yet striking parallel to the German experience. The aftermath of the Great War provoked confusion, questioning and identity anxiety on both sides of the Atlantic as people tried to figure what the cataclysm was all about and whether it was worth its costs. In the United States, this was the Roaring Twenties, an era for urban cosmopolitans of new bohemianism and hedonism, culture experimentation, sexual liberation, flappers, partying, listening to jazz, the Harlem Renaissance, dancing the Charleston, smoking, speakeasies and drinking, despite, or perhaps because of, prohibition. The war provoked a feeling that the sacrifice was futile, there is no ultimate purpose, and life should simply be enjoyed. Despite the overwhelming victory, the dominant political mood among ordinary citizens was isolationism – little to be gained by being engaged in the affairs of the rest of the world other than being trapped in wars. However, with the world's now unqualified dominant economy, American corporations heavily invested abroad, confident that the British and French armies would protect their interests, as the United States voluntarily reduced its military forces to pre-war levels. In fact, it was American loans which permitted Europe to begin to recover from the Great War and Germany to pay its reparations to France, Belgium and Britain.

The twenties did not roar for all Americans. Wages grew at a much slower pace than profits and stocks. There were severe culture wars on the west side of the Atlantic. In reaction to the cosmopolitan challenge to conventional values, there was a retrenchment of traditionalism and racism, especially in rural communities. Many considered prohibition, outlawing liquor, a godsend – literally. The Ku Klux Klan reemerged with a vengeance. In 1921, over 10,000 whites descended on the black neighborhood in Tulsa, Oklahoma, resulting in a riot possibly killing 200 blacks and 50 whites. When the whites invaded the black community, "[m]achine-guns were brought into use; eight aeroplanes were employed to spy on the movements of the Negroes and according to some were used in bombing the colored section."[28] The 1920s experienced increased xenophobia, with new laws restricting immigration, written so people from Aryan countries would have an advantage. In the Palmer raids, aliens suspected of Leftist tendencies, especially sympathy for the Bolshevik Russian Revolution, were deported.

One of the most well-known victims was Emma Goldman, a Russian Jewish anarchist who urged draft resistance during World War I, preached sexual freedom, but actually turned against the Russian Revolution when she witnessed it first-hand, seeing it as repressive of freedom as the capitalism it was trying to overthrow – perhaps more so – and famously saying "If I can't dance, I don't want your revolution." But that does not mean she embraced American militaristic capitalism. Goldman was prophetic. In 1908, even before the Great War and only five years after the Wright brothers' first flight, she described the desolation aerial bombings could deliver as she denounced patriotism:

> We Americans claim to be a peace-loving people. We hate bloodshed; we are opposed to violence. Yet we go into spasms of joy over the possibility of projecting dynamite bombs from flying machines upon helpless citizens. We are ready to hang, electrocute, or lynch anyone, who, from economic necessity, will risk his own life in the attempt upon that of some industrial magnate. Yet our hearts swell with pride at the thought that America is becoming the most powerful nation on earth, and that she will eventually plant her iron foot on the necks of all other nations . . . Such is the logic of patriotism.[29]

In the 1920s, fundamentalist Christians flocked to hear Billy Sunday at tent revivals. In the South, there were laws banning teachings that contradict the Bible, especially evolution. Bohemians, artists and educated blacks found America so puritanical and racist that many fled to "Gay Paree," where in reaction to the war's devastation, there was a similar, maybe stronger, bohemian response. This was the "lost generation." It included such prominent writers and artists as Gertrude Stein, Ernest Hemmingway, F. Scott Fitzgerald, Cole Porter, Josephine Baker and Ada "Bricktop" Smith.

The song "How ya gonna keep 'em down on the farm after they've seen Paree?" continues:

> How ya gonna keep them away from Broadway,
> Jazzin' around,
> And paintin' the town?
> How ya gonna keep 'em away from harm?
> That's the mystery!
> They'll never want to see a rake or plow,
> And who the deuce can parlez-vous a cow?
> How ya gonna keep 'em down on the farm
> After they've seen Paree.[30]

The "harm" the song is referring to is not death and the horror of war, but the temptation of urban cosmopolitan life, which will destroy the innocence of rural traditionalist boys. Cosmopolitan life is so attractive that it will undermine traditionalism and traditionalists will be attracted to it like a magnet, once exposed. This song, of course, is written as a parody mocking traditionalism and implying that cosmopolitanism is superior.

Returning now to the German culture wars of the 1920s, the "gayest," the city, in multiple senses of the word, in the world was probably Berlin. For many, it was proudly decadent and despite its post-war poverty and misery – or perhaps because of it, since it made prostitutes, restaurants, cinema, cabarets, jazz club and nightly entertainment, cheap – it attracted cosmopolitans, seeking avant-garde culture, from around the world. LGBT people (Lesbian, Gay, Bisexual and Transsexual) felt welcome, not shunned. The world's first sex change operations were performed there. Both women and men, gay and straight, felt free to express themselves sexually, with sex no longer tied to family and procreation. Weimar cinema was not shy about sexuality with films like *The Blue Angel*[31] telling of a rigid aging professor, who is enraptured by a seductive nightclub singer Lola Lola, played by Marlene Dietrich. Although married, Dietrich herself was known for her multiple affairs with both genders. To people born later, Weimar Berlin's decadence was made famous by Christopher Isherwood's memoir *Berlin Stories*,[32] the basis of Bob Fosse's Broadway musical and movie *Cabaret*. The attitude of character Sally Bowles was common. It was an attitude shared by many American and British flappers, which Sally was: all politics has led to is misery; let's withdraw from the world and celebrate hedonism-relish life as a "cabaret". Sally sang about her dead roommate Elsie:

> She wasn't what you'd call a blushing flower
> As a matter of fact she rented by the hour . . .[33]

Berlin and other major German cities were centers for new art forms like Expressionism, Surrealism and Dadaism, which interestingly embraced their own brand of the irrational, drastically different from the traditionalist German form, and one repudiating mainstream organized religion and visions of glory.[34]

> For many, Dada protested the bourgeois nationalist and colonialist interests, believed to be the root cause of the war, and against the cultural and intellectual conformity – in art and more broadly in society – that corresponded to the war. Hence, the movement rejected the logic and SELF-DEFINED reason of bourgeois capitalism, and embraced irrationality. The movement after the war quickly spread to Berlin and Cologne, and later to Paris.[35]

Although the Dadaist and other super-cosmopolitan German artistic communities believed in a reality which rationality could not reach, they shunned glory. They did not seek to renounce their individual identity, sacrifice themselves and merge with some higher cause. Rather they saw their art as way to reach their inner being and express their uniqueness. As Tristan Tzara, a Romanian Jew living in Paris, made clear: "I speak only of myself since I do not wish to convince, I have no right to drag others into my river, I oblige no one to follow me and everybody practices his art in his own way."[36]

Dadaism, Expressionism and Surrealism were self-proclaimed avant-garde movements in art, literature, music and theater. Typically, they would juxtapose disparate things and ideas to suggest there exist relationships which logic cannot perceive. They essentially shared our critique of "capitalist irrational rationality" and valued feeling, the spontaneous, and non-sequential. Although we have argued the irrational is largely responsible for the Great War, they saw the conflict as stemming from irrational rationality run wild: capitalist tunnel vision, the pursuit of profit and domination for their own sake, without any concern for greater purpose or quality of life. Without irrational rationality, this utterly irrational catastrophe may never have happened. One Dadaist was so cosmopolitan, he commuted between Germany, Paris and Switzerland, and went by both a German and French name – Hans or Jean Arpt. Here is how he remembered spending the war in Switzerland:

> Revolted by the butchery of the 1914 World War, we in Zurich devoted ourselves to the arts. While guns rumbled in the distance, we sang, painted, made collages and wrote poems with all our might. We were seeking an art based on fundamentals, to cure the madness of the age, and find a new order of things that would restore the balance between heaven and hell. We had a dim premonition that power-mad gangsters would one day use art itself as a way of deadening men's minds.[37]

The Dadaists, Surrealists and other super-cosmopolitan artistic communities did not see art as apolitical. They usually identified with the German Left and a branch of Marxism which saw socialism as a path to personal freedom and self-expression, rather than submission to what Stalin and Lenin called the "dictatorship of the proletarian." The German Left and anti-war movement overlapped, almost coincided. Few German Marxists saw anything glamorous or admirable in World War I. It was a pointless waste of lives, infrastructure and physical comforts and necessities, which must never be repeated. They felt there was little honor in serving in the military and therefore no reason to feel any loyalty to a nation which willingly sacrifices their citizens for their glory and profit or any need to blindly obey leaders. They were proud of struggling to prevent carnage and rejected calls for victory, even if that could be called treason. Weimar communist artists and writers regularly produced pieces emphasizing the futility of war. Among the most famous was Bertolt Brecht, whose *Threepenny Opera* is still regularly performed on both sides of the Atlantic. In one song, the main character Macheath (or Mack the Knife) with best friend and enemy Tiger Brown, the chief of police, reminisce about their army days together.

> Johnny joined up and Jimmy was there and George got a sergeant's rating
> Don't give your right name the Army don't care
> And the life is so fascinating . . .
> Johnny is missing Jimmy is dead and George went crazy shooting
> But blood is blood and red is red
> And the army is still recruiting.
> Let's all go barmy, live off the Army
> See the world we never saw
> If we get feeling down we wander into town
> And if the population should greet us with indignation
> We chop off your bits because we like our hamburgers raw.[38]

Unlike the Russians, German communists during Weimar were deeply committed to civil liberties and most believed communism could only flourish under democracy. When Rosa Luxemburg heard of Lenin's Bolshevik revolution, here is how she reacted:

> Freedom only for the supporters of the government, only for the members of one party – however numerous they may be – is no freedom at all. Freedom is always and exclusively freedom for the one who thinks differently. . . . Decree, dictatorial force of the factory overseer, draconian penalties, rule by terror – all these things are but palliatives. The only way to a rebirth is the school of public

life itself, the most unlimited, the broadest democracy and public opinion. It is rule by terror which demoralizes. . . . Let the German Government Socialists cry that the rule of the Bolsheviks in Russia is a distorted expression.[39]

Not everyone in Weimar Germany who worked to insure the Great War was never repeated was a communist. Erich Maria Remarque was not, but he was a veteran. His best-selling book *All Quiet on the Western Front* has been acclaimed as the greatest novel about war ever written. It tells how boys growing up in Germany were raised to think of war as something glorious, adventurous and fun, only to endure a brutal trauma, from which only the lucky return alive, for a cause which no one understood. It suggests the typical French or British soldier was no different than the average German, with whom they might have been friends had they met somewhere other than the battlefield. The book is written as reflections by the main character, a young soldier in the trenches.

> I know nothing of life but despair, death, fear, and fatuous superficiality cast over an abyss of sorrow. I see how peoples are set against one another, and in silence, unknowingly, foolishly, obediently, innocently slay one another . . . But now, for the first time, I see you are a man like me. I thought of your hand-grenades, of your bayonet, of your rifle; now I see your wife and your face and our fellowship. Forgive me, comrade. We always see it too late. Why do they never tell us that you are poor devils like us, that your mothers are just as anxious as ours, and that we have the same fear of death, and the same dying and the same agony – Forgive me, comrade; how could you be my enemy? . . . there are hundreds of thousands in Germany, hundreds of thousands in France, hundreds of thousands in Russia. . . . Any noncommissioned officer is more of an enemy to a recruit, any schoolmaster to a pupil, than they are to us. And yet we would shoot at them again and they at us if they were free.[40]

Soon after Remarque's novel was published, it was transformed into a movie. We can appreciate the intensity of the culture wars within Weimar Germany by observing in 1930, before the Nazis seized power,

Nazi Minister of Propaganda Joseph Goebbels stormed a theater where the film was showing with about 150 young SA Brown Shirts. Shouting that the film was Jewish and communist [Remarque was Catholic and not a communist] and celebrated cowardice and treason, they threw stink bombs and sneezing powder as they released snakes and white mice into the theater.[41] Despite the pacifist tendencies of many communists, the Nazis, as they rose to power, regularly engaged them in street brawls, which the Nazis were more likely to win.

Triumph of the Will

Until the late 1920s, most political analysts would dismiss the Nazis as part of the "Right lunatic fringe" – very unlikely to ever assume power and one of many similar rightwing movements. However, we can ask how different they were from groups like the KKK, who never attained official state power but were a major political force in the American South. Whether the Nazis should then be taken seriously or not, as early as 1923, General Ludendorff joined with Hitler in an attempt to overthrown the Bavarian government during a beer hall putsch. Given the hierarchical values of the Junker class, it is striking that the Kaiser's second highest general would ally with an ex-corporal, who could easily be dismissed as rabble.

While the communists were "international socialists" with slogans like "Workers of the world, unite" and "The working man has no country",[42] Hitler's Nazis were "National Socialists." The German communists – on the Left – were generally cosmopolitans who saw socialism as a movement to transcend, if not dissolve, national borders, abolish corporations, minimize private property, and free the vast majority from the oppression of the capitalist class and the remaining aristocracy. Appealing to traditionalists, with vehement racist and anti-Semitic tones, the Nazis – on the Right – defined socialism as sacrificing personal interests for the nation, abandoning class differences, with everyone –rich and poor – working together, and corporations intact, but coordinated by the state. Hitler contrasted his version of socialism to that of the communists':

> A Socialist is one who serves the common good . . . Our adopted term "Socialist" has nothing to do with Marxist Socialism. Marxism

is anti-property; true socialism is not . . . Socialism values the individual and encourages him in individual efficiency, at the same time holding that his interests as an individual must be in consonance with those of the community . . . It is charged against me that I am against property, that I am an atheist. Both charges are false.[43]

These differences made the Nazis seem less dangerous to the German elites than the communists. The Nazis saw communists or Bolshevists as predominantly Jewish enemies of the German "volk"[44] – a spiritual quality, not really amenable to rational definition – shared by all true Germans, regardless of class or position, which binds them together into some higher unified force. As part of the volk, a German is more than an individual. The volk is something Bolsheviks and most other cosmopolitans have trouble understanding – a sign of their inferiority. The idea that Germans are unified through the volk can be traced back at least to the romantic reaction to the French Revolution, if not medieval feudalism, but it was intensified and transformed by the Great War and its aftermath. The Nazis believed truth stemmed from the irrational, from instinct, the soul, the spirit, not reason or the intellect.

> What the intellect of the intellectual could not see was grasped immediately by the soul, the heart, the instinct of this simple, primitive, but healthy man. It is another one of the tasks of the future to re-establish the unity between feeling and intellect; that is, to educate an unspoiled generation which will perceive with clear understanding the eternal law of development and at the same time will consciously return to the primitive instinct.[45] . . . What we suffer from today is excess of education. Nothing is appreciated except knowledge. The wiseacres, however, the enemies of action. What we require is instinct and will.[46]

Although the Nazis were heavily organized in Munich and other major cities, and attacked the communists in street fights in Berlin, they considered cities centers of decadence, vice and sin, while the country was offering peace, harmony, purpose and meaning. Like the communists, they used the word "bourgeois" as a pejorative; however, to them, it did not mean capitalist, but rather overly materialistic, complacent comfortable middle class, with little sense of higher values. They regarded the art movements that flourished under Weimar as the epitome of bourgeois decadence, something unGerman, which undermines the volk spirit and leads to debauchery and pacifism.

Hitler favored heroic classical nudes sentimental German landscapes, or painting of wholesome blond German farmers tilling the native soil.[47] In Hitler's own words:

> Before National Socialism acceded to power, there was a so-called "modern" art in Germany, i.e., just as the word itself indicates, a new art every year. National Socialist Germany, in contrast, wishes to re-establish a "German art," and this art shall and will be eternal, just as is every other creative merit of a people. If it lacks such eternal merit for our Volk, then it is today without significant merit as well.[48]

The Nazis denounced the sexual liberation of Weimar as communist- and Jewish-inspired depravity, intended to undermine German purity. As traditionalists, they called for restoring women's function to residing within what the Kaiser's regime had called "the three K's" – in German: Kinder, Kuche, Kirche; in English: Children, Kitchen, Church. The purpose of women and the family is to serve the state, through breeding children, especially boys, who will grow up to be valiant soldiers. SA commander Josef "Sepp" Dietrich (who later switched to the SS and help liquidate the SA) declared:

> The family is the most important cell of the state. Whoever disturbs the family acts against the well-being of the state. National Socialism has restored the family to its rightful place. We do not want the petty-bourgeois ideal in the family, with its plus-sofa psychology and walking manikins, with its contempt for and degradation of the woman and effeminization of the children. We know that the wife has a heavy burden to bear. The National Socialist stands behind her because she lends him a helping hand. The wife is a comrade, a fellow combatant.[49]

Hitler was clear it was preferable that women breed and raise families than have professional careers and be involved in politics and economics.

> If today a female jurist accomplishes ever so much and next door there lives a mother with five, six, seven children, who are healthy and well-brought up, then I would say: From the standpoint of the eternal value of our people the woman who has given birth to children and raised them and who thereby has given back our people life for the future has accomplished *more* and does *more*! . . . The so-called granting of equal rights to women, which Marxism demands, in reality does not grant equal rights but constitutes a deprivation of rights, since it draws the woman into an area in which she will necessarily be inferior.[50]

Convinced the irrational captures a higher reality, the Nazis did not believe democracy satisfies people's – certainly not true Germans' – needs. Democracy rests on weakness – a cancer stemming from bourgeois, especially Jewish, degeneration. It fails to provide unity and a sense of sacrifice, that the individual is part of some greater cause. The Nazis' goal was to rebuild the commitment to authority found in feudalism. They wanted to create a Thousand Year Third Reich, which would restore the glory of the Holy Roman Empire (the First Reich) and the Kaiser's empire (the Second Reich). As Führer, Hitler is more than an elected representative; he is the embodiment of the German volk. The German people is more than the sum of individuals; it is a unified force binding individuals together, culminating in the Führer. As Deputy Führer Rudolph Hess proclaimed when he introduced Hitler at rallies, "Hitler is Germany, just as Germany is Hitler."[51] This is almost a modern reestablishment of the feudal or post-feudal absolutist mentality, the rule of monarchs ruling through Divine right. It is virtually identical to Louis XIV's declaration "I am the state" (even though he was French, not German). Hitler was clear that greatness and progress come when there is authority, not democracy, or perhaps rule by the Führer is German democracy – true democracy.

> The Jewish doctrine of Marxism rejects the aristocratic principle of Nature and replaces the eternal privilege of power and strength

with the mass of numbers and their dead weight . . . As a contrast to this kind of democracy we have the German democracy, which is a true democracy[52] . . . The so-called democratic freedom to live to the full according to one's persuasions and instincts leads not to an evolutionary advancement nor to a freeing of exceptional forces or values.[53]

Germany is a single unified organic entity with individuals like cells in the body. As the cell exists for the body, so the individual exists for the sake of Germany. To preserve the health of the body, cells routinely sacrifice themselves. Sacrifice brings purification and gives meaning even at the cost of death. Willingness to die for Germany, for the Führer shows you are a true German. Upon joining the SS, the initiate must swear:

> I swear to you, Adolf Hitler, as Fuehrer and Reichschancellor of the German Reich, loyalty and bravery. I swear to you, and those you have named to command me, obedience unto death, so help us God.[54]

Hitler inspired his followers with calls like these:

> Our aim is the dictatorship of the whole people, the community. I began to win men to the idea of an eternal national and social ideal – to subordinate one's own interests to the interests of the whole society . . . Our future is Germany. Our today is Germany. And our past is Germany. Let us take a vow this morning, at every hour, in each day, to think of Germany, of the nation, of our German people. You cannot be unfaithful to something that has given sense and meaning to your whole existence . . . Our love towards our people will never falter, and our faith in this Germany of ours is imperishable. Deutchland ueber Alles [Germany over all] . . . fills millions with great strength, with that faith which is mightier than any earthly might. . . . boundless, all embracing love for the Volk, and, if necessary, to die for it.[55]

War is an intrinsic good, not a tragedy, for it provides an opportunity to sacrifice. It erases the self and promotes the nation or master race as far more important than the individual. The individual simply exists to submit his will to the higher authority of the master race that he can never question. Moreover, war erases the self and promotes the nation or master race as far more important than the individual. The individual exists and gains glory simply by submitting his will to the higher authority of the master race that he can never question. Deaths are to be expected, even welcomed. Richard Koenigsberg, director of the Library of Social Science, proposed that Nazi ideology can lead to deliberately provoking war to provide an opportunity for sacrifice with war deaths being not a tragic cost of war, but its goal. It is something that the Nazis intentionally sought as a means to purify the people, especially men, unify the nation, and build identification with the Reich. If Koenigsberg is right, then many of Hitler's campaigns were orchestrated not for their strategic value but to offer the chance to be heroic and court death for its own sake. If so, then the irrational was built into Hitler's war planning.

To sacrifice is to merge with the volk, to achieve your destiny. As a German or Aryan, you are part of the master race, chosen by some higher force – be it God or nature – to rule the world, to bring inferior peoples to beg for your mercy. Although the Nazis were more technologically sophisticated than the Confederates, they too believed that valor overrode technology. If you are chosen, you must win. A German has his race in his being, in his spirit. He is guaranteed victory by his essence, by his willingness to fight, sacrifice and die. There is no substitute for victory; without it, the sacrifice would be in vain. Nothing can defeat Germany except Germans or alien vermin within Germany's midst. Triumph in the Great War was guaranteed until the leaders in the new government, pacifist cowards – the "November Criminals," particularly Jewish criminals – betrayed the Reich, "stabbed it in the back." Weakness cannot be forgiven. The weak deserve to be destroyed. This ideology requires winning, and even suggests you can win with death, but it does not say what you win. It may not matter. The ideology does not require a concrete material rational objective. Honor, glory and valor are their own rewards. This is a call for war for war's sake; victory for victory's sake. Hitler was convinced there was no excuse for Germany's losing the Great War. If he had been Führer then, it would not have not have happened. He promised his people that never again will Germany lose a war.

> It was no pacifist conviction that caused me to enter this hall in those days. I was still a soldier at that time, a soldier in body and soul! That which brought me here then was my protest as a soldier against what today can be called the greatest humiliation of our people. In a war which lasted four years this people had withstood twenty-six nations and it was defeated only by means of lies and deceit. If there had not been Germans in those days who destroyed the confidence in their own regime, England and France would never have won. If in those days a certain Adolf Hitler had been Chancellor of the German Reich instead of a musketeer in the German Army, do you believe that the capitalist idols of international democracy would have won?[56]

Morality is irrelevant or perhaps immorality is moral. Hitler proudly compared himself to Genghis Khan for his brutality. Cruelty is a virtue; blood purifies; compassion is weakness. The future, the world, belongs to the strong and ruthless. It is striking how Ayn Randian capitalism, which sees itself as the epitome of rationality, and Nazism, with its worship of the irrational, converge here in their glorification of brutality which they essentially treat as a moral virtue.

> Our strength consists in our speed and in our brutality. Genghis Khan led millions of women and children to slaughter – with premeditation and a happy heart. . . . It's a matter of indifference to me what a weak western European civilization will say about me . . . I'll have anybody who utters but one word of criticism executed by a firing squad – that our war aim does not consist in reaching certain lines, but in the physical destruction of the enemy. . . . Truly, this earth is a trophy cup for the industrious

man ... He who does not possess the force ... must step aside and allow stronger peoples to pass him by.[57]

The Jewish Question

The Nazis were convinced that the November Criminals, who did not have the will to prevail, who surrendered Germany when it was on the brink of victory, who replaced the Kaiser's Reich with the cowardly decadent Weimar Republic, were communists and Jews. The reality is different. Jews were prominent in the founding of the Weimar Republic, including Hugo Haase, Otto Landesberg and Hugo Prues, but they were a minority within the government. The dominant party were the Social Democrats, who were influenced by Marx, but believed socialists should participate in democratic capitalist governments, not try to overthrow them. They opposed the communists. In fact, Weimar Chancellor Friedrich Ebert, a Catholic Social Democratic who insisted his party support the First World War when it began, joined with far-right storm troopers to assassinate Jewish communist Rosa Luxemburg. Jews were clearly influential within the Communist Party, but the Jews were barely 1% of the population and the Communists received 17% of the vote in 1933 election – the third highest vote among 14 parties – so the Communists must have had substantial non-Jewish support.[58]

The Jewish were believed to orchestrate an insidious world-wide plot to dominate the world using whatever tactic was convenient and available with no concern for principle. There was a life or death struggle between the Aryan and Jewish races with Jewish vermin, essentially germs, infecting the Aryan body. Hitler warned: "What are the aims of the Jews? They aim to expand their invisible state as a supreme tyranny over the whole world. The Jew is therefore a destroyer of nations."[59]

Just as curing a disease requires destroying the germs, so the Jews must be killed.

Jewish lies claimed that Communism and monopoly finance capital were enemies, but they were actually both part of a unified international Jewish conspiracy. Although the Nazis embraced national capitalism, just as they were the representatives of National Socialism, they must resist internationalism in any form and preserve national traditionalism.

The Jews were the ultimate international cosmopolitans, who wandered the world without a state for 2000 years. When most Europeans were rural farmers, they were urban money-lenders. International finance capital brought urbanization to destroy the serenity of the rural village, to undermine tradition, and dedication to race, community and nation. The German peasant felt a communion with nature such that he and it were inseparable. The Aryan, ingrained with the dark cold forests of Northern Europe, experienced depth, intensity, a yearning for the sun. His physical make-up, light skin, blonde hair, blue-eyes reflected this yearning. All Germans in sharing in this essence constituted an organic community.

The responsibility for the disruption of the natural order brought on by industrialization and urbanization could not lie within the volk. It must have been an alien imposition. No one could have been more obviously responsible than the representative of the trans-European nation, the Jews, within Germany's borders. The Jew was seen as violating volkish norms in having no organic ties; he was always primarily concerned with the pecuniary and commerce. The transiency of urban life was a reflection of his transiency. German volkish identity became reinforced in contrast to him. The Gentile German bourgeoisie benefited all the more from the volkish ideology because the disruptions produced by industrialization were blamed on the Jews rather than them.

As Hitler rose to power, he blamed any of his failures on resistance from the international Jewish communist capitalist conspiracy.

> However, every proposal which came from me sufficed to agitate a certain Jewish-internationalist, capitalist clique immediately, just as had been the case in Germany, my Volksgenossen, where any reasoned proposal from us National Socialists was rejected primarily because we had made it.[60]

The Nazis were hardly alone in fearing the world could be ruled by a cabal of international Jewish capitalist communists. In Russia, the Czar's government distributed the *Protocol of the Learned Elders of Zion*, a forged document that proposed such a conspiracy. Although Henry

Ford was one of the world's richest capitalists, he also distributed the Protocols.[61]

As traditionalists, appalled but what they perceived as the immoral decadence of Weimar, the Nazis claimed the Jews were responsible. In his 1938 study sponsored by the Institute for Studies of the Jewish Question, Dr. Karl Wiehe concluded

> The decay of moral values in all areas of life – the period of deepest German degradation – coincided exactly with the height of Jewish power in Germany . . . Every single sphere of major influence had now fallen under Jewish control . . . No account of the Jewish Question in Germany can be complete without some mention of the tidal wave of sexual immorality that was to engulf the country . . . Well before 1933 the Jews had taken possession of the film industry . . . In revue and burlesque – frivolity and lasciviousness were to rear their ugly heads, so much so that during these years Berlin was correctly considered the most immoral city in the world . . . It was the Jews who introduced this pornographic "art form" to Germany, a debased genre completely unknown before the Great War, and so it is the Jews who can be held responsible for the general decline in morals.[62]

Dr. Wiehe's ideas should not be dismissed as a historical anomaly. In 2013, it was favorably cited on an American website that calls itself *Veterans Today*. Dr. Wiehe's critique of the Weimar German film industry resembles claims within the American traditionalist Right, who are convinced cosmopolitan Hollywood is Jewish controlled and the source of American moral decay.

The Nazis were certain that although Jews don't care about glory, they encourage wars because it brings them profits. But Jews are cowards who have others do their fighting for them. They were accused of avoiding military involvement in World War I, but Jewish veterans responded by insisting that 12,000 died fighting for Germany.[63] Although many Jewish voices felt the war was nothing but meaningless carnage, these veterans did not dare to appear disloyal to Germany.

Ironically, one tactic some Jews used to fit into the German ideal of the volk was to argue that they constituted a separate volk with an identity of their own and their identity should be respected as such. In response to the charge of urban transiency, there was a movement among Jews to return to the land, out of which grew Zionism and the kibbutz movement. This may seem contradictory but it seems they felt the way to prove they were German was to form a separate nation and leave Germany. Although ancient Israel, the kingdoms of David and the Maccabees, were aggressive warrior states, the Jews, especially the Ashkenazic Yiddishkeit Jews of Germany and Eastern Europe, evolved, during two thousand years of wandering in the diaspora, into a culture which regarded soldiers as the "scum of the earth." Their very existence would challenge the militaristic ideals the Nazis wanted for Germany. Yiddishkeit values – intellect, critical thinking, gentleness – developed as a means to survive in a hostile environment when you lack power. They would be especially offensive to Nazis. Yiddishkeit regarded softness as a virtue and admired intellectuals more than warriors. Finding it was an advantage to seem unthreatening when doing business with Gentiles, Ashkenazic Jews developed a self-effacing style. Humor was a weapon they would resort to far more readily than arms. Behind this seeming passivity was something Walter Waskow calls "God-wrestling."

> [S]keptical and angry. It shrugged its shoulders a lot, distrusted all authority, and learned to laugh at the absurdity of things ... Its heroes are the angry mockers of authority who conform reluctantly because they have to.[64]

Ashkenazic Jewry was particularly successful in finding pleasure, richness and meaning in the face of adversity. It encouraged compassion, emotional expressiveness, tolerance of human frailty, love of learning, humor, revulsion to violence, independence of thought, unwillingness to blindly accept authority and identification with the community.

In America, this tradition evolved into the borscht belt, the archetype of cosmopolitanism, and may help explain Jewish prominence in Hollywood. It may persist today in Woody Allen, Mel Brooks and Sarah

Silverman. It was an attitude that many Zionists identified with "galut" – weakness and vulnerability – although it may have helped the Jews to survive under 2000 years of adversary which perhaps no other people have faced and produced a people whose prominence vastly exceeded its numbers. The desire to shun this image was one reason Israel replaced Yiddish with Hebrew. Here is a report of conversation between Yiddish novelist Isaac Bashevis Singer and Israeli Prime Minister Menachem Begin:

> "Vith Yiddish, you took a living language vhich vas alive for some eight or nine hundred years and managed to kill it."
>
> Machchem Begin, who had himself grown up in a Yiddish-speaking home, began pounding his fist on the glass coffee table . . .
>
> "With Yiddish, he shouted, "we could not have created any navy; with Yiddish, we could have no army; with Yiddish, we could not defend ourselves with powerful jet planes; with Yiddish, we would be nothing. We would be like animals."
>
> Isaac sat with hands folded in his lap and shrugged his shoulders. "Nu," he said sweetly to the hushed crowd, "since I am a vegetarian, for me to be like an animal is not such a terrible thing."[65]

The Zionists accepted much of the Nazi image of the Jew and consciously tried to reverse it. Modern Israel may be the most militaristic small country in the world today. It adopted that style largely as an attempt to show the world that they are no longer the mooshy wimps, *schlemiels*, who could be pushed around for 2000 years, only to march into the gas chambers. There is a sense that if old Jews were too weak or peace-loving to fight back, they deserved their fate. New Jews are now tough. No one better mess with them.[66] Israeli tourist pollsters show soldiers with machine guns praying at Western Wall, the surviving relic of the old Jerusalem temple.

The Israelis need to learn from the Holocaust, but we can dispute what should be the lesson. Upon entering Yad Vashem, the Israeli Holocaust museum, you will see this engraved on the wall: "The Holocaust teaches that I must be like a dart; silent, sharp and dangerous." The Holocaust could inspire very different Israeli governmental policies. For many Israelis "Never Again!" means "Get them before they get you." Another reaction could be: "We know what it is to wander the earth at the mercy of other nations. Let us take no path which would increase the misery of displaced peoples and make sure no one else goes through a holocaust even vaguely approximately ours."

We can agree with the Israelis that the Holocaust's victims should have resisted. Cooperatively waiting at the train stations may have been the worst strategy. But the question is: how to resist? There were violent uprisings in some of the ghettoes, but they left almost no survivors. Holocaust victims had legitimate reasons to fear taking up arms would only result in even more complete slaughter. Except for some war veterans, few had experience with weapons and armed struggle might make them too similar to the very enemy they were fighting. Perhaps the most lives would have been saved through non-violent civil disobedience, defying the orders to report and forcing the Nazis to search door to door when escape was impossible. The highest survival rate may have been in Denmark where the king himself allegedly wore a yellow star – although, in this case, it was non-violent civil disobedience on the part of the Christian secular state itself.

Ashkenazic Jewry had become accustomed to cycles of tolerance and persecution. Although they often expected the state to be ultimately hostile, they looked to it to create a space which would permit them to continue and occasionally even thrive as a distinct community. Their simultaneous faith and skepticism led them to doubt if anything, good or bad, could be permanent. Until the Holocaust, this attitude helped them to accommodate to more powerful people without sacrificing their identity. Under "normal persecution," this may have been one of the secrets to their survival. Being used to cyclical adversity may have made many of them unable to recognize Nazism's uniqueness. A survival skill which had proved adaptive in the past may have prevented millions to respond to the new situation until it was too late.

The Jews may not have known how to respond because the Nazis did not let them know what to expect. From a Nazi point of view, inefficiency may be efficient. Randomness and unpredictability were among the principal weapons through which the Nazis controlled the population. They were able to make others submit to their will by denying them a sense of continuity, by never letting them know which actions would be tolerated and which would bring destruction, by one moment giving the appearance of reasonableness and lawfulness and the next acting through random terror. Unable to plan, the victims would cease to be able to trust their own judgment, become dependent upon their keepers and even, to some extent, come to view the world through their eyes. This may be the vehicle by which a Jewish community known for its centuries of cosmopolitanism and rejection of glory could appear to paradoxically embrace the glorious cause of their persecutors

Confinement where enemies control resources and access to the outside world can, on some level, lead to accepting their definition of reality and recognizing their legitimacy. Unpredictability creates a need for someone knowledgeable who can be trusted. When you cannot trust yourself, you may come to rely upon authority, even an authority whose goal is to destroy you. A need for trust may bring you to doubt if the powerful are as vicious as the empirical evidence suggests. This may be why so many Jews waited at the train stations. Unconsciously, this need for legitimacy can infiltrate the victim's vocabulary. It can lead to reflexively accepting your oppressor values and worldview

One device for inducing Jewish cooperation was to create a sense that the Germans were their protectors as well as their destroyers. "The SS vacillated between extreme repression and the easing of tension; the torture of prisoners, but the occasional punishment of particularly inhuman guards."[67] Once the Nazis subjugated the victims to their will, they became the upholders of "law," their law which reeked with contradictions. With codes of behavior so ambiguous, inmates could no longer rely upon their fellow prisoners and were forced to turn elsewhere for protection and to create some semblance of law, even to the Nazis. Although their long-term goal may have been to annihilate their captives, in the short-run the Nazis could create rules which would prevent the victims from destroying each other. By fostering divisions among the prisoners, through such means as having them fight over rations, they could transform the victims into agents of their own destruction and have the inmates thus serve their objectives, as they made the inmate more dependent on them.

When they had no protector, they might actually hope the Nazi guards could be their defenders. One concentration camp survivor, interviewed by Magrass, had been particularly brutalized by his Kapo, his prisoner foreman. He was about to complain to the Nazis, as if they shared his definition of justice, when something came over him and stopped him. He realized that the Kapo's cruelty was what the Nazis wanted and that the Germans might inflict even worse consequences upon him for complaining. Jews, including Jewish leaders, did cooperate with the Nazis, perhaps with the expectation that it could lead to more surviving. Yehuda Bauer[68] and Hannah Arendt, both Jewish refugees from Nazi Germany, point out that the ghetto Judenrate, Ghetto Jewish Councils, would routinely select residents to hand over to the Nazis out of fear that if they resisted the Germans would advance into the ghetto and take everyone. As we know, this collaboration saved very few. The ghettos were liquidated and even most of the Judenrate ended up in concentration camps. Arendt went so far as to claim

> The whole truth was that if the Jewish people had really been unorganized and leaderless, there would have been chaos and plenty of misery but the total number of victims would hardly have been between four and a half and six million people.[69]

It may seem that the Nazis intentions for the Jews were too obvious. The Jews should have known the Nazis had no interest in their well-being; their only desire was to destroy them, but we have argued anxious insecure people crave authority to give them order and purpose, to tell them the world is alright. Soldiers march off, knowing they may never return, at the command of authorities who tell them obedience will give their lives meaning and allow them to merge with some greater cause. In order for the world to be good, authority must be benign. People sacrifice for causes they do not understand, maybe even for an unseen god. Inmates in institutions may know their guards are enemies, but they are so dependent and stripped of any means to defend themselves, that they may turn to them as protectors. For authority to protect you, it must be strong. As early as 1651, Thomas Hobbes argued in *Leviathan*,[70] the proof of its strength is its ability to destroy you. If you can challenge it, it is weak. Not just for Jews, but for all traumatized people, even Aryans, suffering from the aftermath of the Great War and the Great Depression, the more ruthless the Nazis were, the more security they could offer, a possible explanation of why many Jews failed to fight fascism beyond the reality that such rebellion would almost certainly be totally crushed.

A Final Solution-Not Just For Jews

The Nazis brought calamity, not just to Jews. In addition to 6 million Jews, another 5 million civilians were killed in the Holocaust.[71] As they abolished civil liberties, the Nazis briefly brought prosperity and glory for Aryan Germans, only to be followed by a disaster greater than the Great War. When the Nazis came to power, Germany was in an extreme crisis. It is doubtful the fascists could have prevailed otherwise. There were bitter memories of the devastating defeat and the misery that followed, along with very different answers to the question who was to blame. In the early 1920s, there was unprecedented rampart inflation, when life savings were wiped out in a matter of seconds, and a wheel barrel full of marks might buy you a loaf of bread. The inflation was partly the result of a deliberate government policy to make the mark worthless so the reparations bills could be paid with bogus currency. However, by the late 1920s Germany was showing signs of economic recovery, primarily because of American investment. But then in 1929, the American economy itself crashed. As the Great Depression spread its tentacles around the world, it ruined other countries dependent upon the United States even more than America itself, where it almost brought about a total collapse. Germany is the prime example of a country that fared even worse than America. The Weimar government was inadequate for dealing with the new crisis and it was clear that it was doomed. No centrist policies seemed sufficient and Weimar was likely to be replaced either by the Communists on the Left or the Nazis on the Right.

Elites – capitalists and Junkers – now faced the dilemma: whom to choose? Under ordinary circumstances, capitalists prefer democracy to fascism. Democracy offers an ideal of "limited government" which protects private corporate property, while interfering with it only minimally. It promises "freedom." For capitalists, this means the freedom to manage their investments as they chose and treat their employees as they wish. Also, democracy permits the rulers to rule invisibly; it creates the illusion that the ruling class does not exist, that everyone – the people themselves – rule. Ordinary people are more likely to identify with a government which they believe they created, that they think was designed to serve them. Whatever the reality, the image of democracy may legitimate itself more effectively than any other system of government, any other system of class rule that has ever existed. To quote Winston Churchill: "Democracy is the worst form of government, except for all the others, that have been tried."[72]

When democracy permits the rulers to rule, they will accept it, maybe endorse it, but when capitalists feel their wealth and power are seriously threatened, that may be another matter. They are then likely to turn to glory – the kind the fascists, but not the socialists – offer. Communism seeks to abolish private corporate property; fascism does not. When democracy no longer serves the corporate elite, fascism may become the more attractive alternative. In Chile in 1970, a Marxist, Salvador Allende, was democratically elected president. He nationalized the copper mines, which were mostly owned by Rockefeller-controlled Kennecott Copper and Anaconda Copper. He also antagonized the World Bank, multinational corporations like International Telephone and Telegraph, the American Central Intelligence Agency, along with much of the Chilean military. His enemies allied to replace him with a military junta, led by General Augusto Pinochet,[73] who gave a free hand to foreign investors, expanded the gap between rich and poor, produced rampart inflation, but was praised by American economist Milton Friedman – a neoclassicist like Ayn Rand and Alan Greenspan – for creating the "Miracle of Chile."[74]

Just as the international capitalists would prefer a fascist Chile to a Marxist one, they would prefer a Nazi Germany to a communist one.

In the movie *Cabaret*, a baron – who is also a very rich businessman and thus a representative of both the German Capitalist and Junker classes – assures a poor English scholar, with whom he is having a ménage à trois, along with Sally Bowles: "The Nazis will take care of the communists and we'll take care of the Nazis."[75] When capitalists support rightwing regimes, they assume they can control them. Usually they are correct, but the Nazis were an exception. Many readers of Hitler's *Mein Kampf* would dismiss it as either deliberate exaggeration or the ravings of a madman who could not possibly carry out his proposals, but Hitler did carry out his promised agenda, as much as he could, until he was crushed by the war he provoked.

Thinking they could control him, that he would bring stability, and convinced that he would crush the communists, much of the German upper class turned to Hitler – some reluctantly, some not so reluctantly. We saw as early as 1923, General Ludendorff allied with him, but many Junkers held the Nazis in contempt, thinking they were upstarts, lacking aristocratic blue blood and gentlemanly discipline and manners, almost not Aryan enough. The capitalist reaction was mixed. Jewish business leaders did what they could to prevent the Nazis from rising, only to see their wealth confiscated. However, enough wealthy Aryans became enthusiastic donors, so that the Nazis soon found themselves not lacking for funds as they rose to power, and formerly destitute Nazis, including Hitler himself, could live well. Their supporters included Dr. Hjalmar Schacht, President of the Reichsbank, Fritz Thyssen, Chairman of United Steel Works, wealthy art publisher Ernst Putzi Hanfstaengl, chemical factory owner Albert Pietsch, and banker Baron Kurt von Schroeder. Although initially opposed, the I.G. Farben Chemical Trust and Krupp Steal eventually became supporters. There is evidence that the Nazis received money from leading capitalists outside of Germany borders, who feared the spread of communism beyond the Soviet Union and believed Hitler offered an anecdote in Germany. Their assistance was usually clandestine. They include Sir Henri Deterding, director of Royal Dutch Shell Oil, Montagu Norman, Governor of the Bank of England and Harold Harmsworth, holding the title Viscount Rothermere and the publisher of the British newspapers the *Daily Mail* and the

Daily Mirror, but Hitler's most important foreign financier was probably Henry Ford, who also kept his support secret. Britain's King Edward VIII was forced to abdicate, officially because he married a divorced American commoner, but the real reason was probably his support of Hitler.[76] Although not an active supporter, Winston Churchill declared before the House of Commons in November 1938, less than a year before the outbreak of World War II: "I have always said that if Great Britain were defeated in war I hoped we should find a Hitler to lead us back to our rightful position among the nations."[77]

Now well-funded and with Germany in deep crisis, the Nazis received a plurality, but not a majority, in the March 5, 1933 federal election – 43.91%.[78] With many willing to die for Hitler, diehard Nazis now had a critical mass that would permit them to rule, even without a majority.

An alliance between the Social Democrats and the Communists probably could have stopped Hitler, but they had a long history of mutual distrust. Some communists interpreted the Marxist dialectic to imply "the worst things get, the better they get." There was a sense: "after Hitler, us." Let Hitler get in. He will prove to be so incompetent and exacerbate the crisis so severely, there will be a yearning for us to govern. Although distrustful of Hitler but more fearful of the Communists, Paul von Hindenburg – the only German general ranked higher than Ludendorff in World War I and now President of the Weimar Republic – appointed him Chancellor. Within days, there was a fire in the Reichstag. To this day, no one has definitively established what caused it. It is possible the Nazis themselves set the fire, but Hitler blamed the Communists. In response, Hitler was able to declare an emergency and pass the "Enabling Act," which suspended virtually all civil liberties and allowed him to issue degrees without the consent of the Reichstag. There is a resemblance between the Enabling Act and the US Patriot Act, passed after 9/11, but with one difference: the Enabling Act was fully enforced. Hitler was now completely in control.[79]

Many observers would consider Hitler in the first years of the Third Reich as brutal, but anything but incompetent. He was able to intimidate Germany's enemies from World War I to the point that he was able to negate the Treaty of Versailles. Although British economist John

Maynard Keynes opposed him, Hitler used military Keynesianism – that is, preparing for war to stimulate the whole civilian economy – to restore prosperity.[80] He built the autobahn, which is still considered one of the best highway systems in the world, and founded Volkswagen, which is still one of the world's leading car companies. By 1937, unemployment fell from 6 million to 1 million.[81] Jews, gypsies, Slavic peoples, other non-Aryans, people deemed mentally or physically incompetent, from inferior races, homosexual, or otherwise unfit and undesirable faced harassment, brutality, incarceration, effective slavery and even extermination. However, for those deemed Aryans:

> The Nazis also supported an extensive welfare state (of course, for "ethnically pure" Germans). It included free higher education, family and child support, pensions, health insurance and an array of publically supported entertainment and vacation options. All spheres of life, economy included, had to be subordinated to the "national interest" (Gemeinnutz geht vor Eigennutz), and the fascist commitment to foster social equality and mobility. . . . As Hitler once noted, the Third Reich has "opened the way for every qualified individual – whatever his origins – to reach the top if he is qualified, dynamic, industrious and resolute".
>
> Largely for these reasons, up till 1939, most Germans' experience with the Nazi regime was probably positive. The Nazis had seemingly conquered the Depression and restored economic and political stability. As long as they could prove their ethnic "purity" and stayed away from overt shows of disloyalty, Germans typically experienced National Socialism not as a tyranny and terror, but as a regime of social reform and warmth.[82]

The material benefits that Hitler delivered helped reinforce the glory that inspired so many of his German followers. Aryan Germans could reap benefits only because they were part of the true German nation, whose glory was reflected in economic prosperity as well as military splendor and power.

Much of the funds for Aryan social services came from wealth confiscated from undesirables and racial inferiors, especially Jews. Among the Aryan majority, the Nazis were popular, maybe even loved, until World War II was undeniably lost. In the early years of the Third Reich, as Germans began experiencing economic recovery, glory emerged as the most powerful seduction for ordinary Germans. Nazi rhetoric offered a promise of excitement and glory, especially for the young who barely remembered the Great War. Many adolescents

> enjoyed being in the Hitler Youth or the League of German Girls, and fondly recalled the fun they'd had sitting around the campfire or trampling over the hills. A number of them confessed later . . . they "wanted to help in the building of the new, third, thousand-year Reich and to carry responsibility." Some were completely swept away by the propaganda and considered it "good that the Nazis hold power" . . . "They help Germany regain the greatness it deserves."[83]

As in most capitalist countries, the United States included, the Nazis sought legitimacy or popularity through a two-prong strategy. On the one hand, they appealed to the irrational and promised "glory," being part of a master race that would always be victorious and no one would dare challenge. Although this reinforces legitimacy, it is not sufficient. The leader must be strong and a leader who cannot deliver the goods and provide prosperity is weak. The people may relish being a part of the glorious master race, but they also need to have their day-to-day rational needs met. Guaranteed income and social services, which provide economic security and some modicum of comfort must accompany the glory. Despite all the demands for sacrifice, there is a contradiction: a master race deserves to live well; otherwise, where is the evidence of its superiority? Hungry people may forget glory and turn against the regime, even riot and rebel. Of course, another proof of glory is victory in war and military defeat can bring economic disaster, as World War I demonstrated.

When you base your economy on armaments, the armaments will lose credibility unless they are eventually used. In order for saber rattling to be believed, you must stab somebody. Eventually, the Nazis self-destructed by provoking a "Good War" more devastating than the "Great War."

Stabbed In The Back – Again

The Nazis were proud self-proclaimed polarizers. Although Hitler may have been loved by rightwing Aryan traditionalists, he was despised among Jews, Leftists, cosmopolitans and bohemians. The lucky ones, who saw what Germany was becoming and had the resources to leave, emigrated. Some Junkers, who considered the Nazis vulgar low-class upstarts, lacking aristocrat grace and refinement, not representative of the true greater Germany (including Austria) – effectively not Aryan enough – also left. The most famous of these were the Von Trapp family, upon whom the *Sound of Music* is based. Two of their sons served in the US army, fighting against Germany, of which Austria was then part.[84]

Many of Germany's leading scientists – some Jews, some Leftists, some both – left. These included atomic physicists, who consequently denied Germany the expertise it needed to build the atomic bomb. The most famous, Albert Einstein, who had been a pacifist most of his life, signed a letter urging President Franklin Roosevelt to sponsor a nuclear bomb, something which Einstein subsequently deeply regretted.[85] Einstein, himself, did not work on the Manhattan Project which built the bomb but many fellow German refugees did. These include Hans Berthe, James Franck, Rudolf Peierls, Klaus Fuchs and Dieter Greun. Although they were convinced if the bomb were to exist, it was better for it to be in American rather than German hands, some of them, like Einstein, were later horrified by what they did, especially after the bomb was dropped on Japan.[86]

Jews and Marxists, who could, fled Germany. These include members of the Frankfurt School in the Institute of Social Research. Among them was Herbert Marcuse who, during World War II, worked for the US Office of War Information and the Office of Strategic Services (OSS), which evolved into the Central Intelligence Agency. Other members of the Frankfurt School working for the OSS include Franz Neumann and Otto Kirchheimer. Another, Leo Löwenthal, joined Marcuse at the Office of War Information.[87]

Prominent German actors and writers fled to Hollywood. Marlene Dietrich moved there before the Nazis came to power. She, along with Billy Wilder, a Jew and another German refugee who became a Hollywood writer, created a fund to help Jews and other dissidents escape Germany. During the war, she actively sold war bonds and entertained American troops with the USO. Erich Maria Remarque also became a writer for Hollywood and had an affair with Dietrich.[88] Another writer who moved from Germany to Hollywood was Bertolt Brecht, but he returned to Germany after the war when he faced a prison term as one of the "Hollywood 10" – writers and actors condemned by Ronald Reagan and Senator Joseph McCarthy in the 1950s for Marxist sympathies.[89]

Article 3, Section 3 of the US Constitution defines Treason as below:

> Treason against the United States, shall consist only in levying War against them, or in adhering to their Enemies, giving them Aid and Comfort.

If you substitute the name *Germany* for the *United States*, it appears that virtually everyone whom we just listed is guilty. Hitler referred to the leaders of Weimar who surrendered at the end of World War I as the "November Criminals." Presumably, their crime was treason. If preferring peace to victory in a hopeless and meaningless cause is treason, then clearly working with your government's enemies to assure its defeat is treason as well. Hitler's claim that German troops in World War I were "stabbed in the back" by their own government is dubious, but he could legitimately say that Germans who went to work for the American and allied war effort did "stab their country in the back." However, that raises the questions: what should you do if you believe your country's government is tyrannizing, maybe even massacring its own people, and posing such a threat to the rest of the world that it may destroy civilization? Is it morally obligatory or morally repugnant to support an immoral regime? Is treason moral if your country is immoral? And who is to decide what is moral? What are we to make of a white Southerner who opposed slavery, refused to fight for the Confederacy and maybe even supported the Union? In the South, they were called scalawags and were not forgiven for generations. In the wake of Germany's defeat (in World War II, not World War I), much of the German population regarded the American, British and Soviet armies as liberators. Had Germany won, they may have reacted very differently. The families of the 25,000-plus civilians who were incinerated in Dresden probably would wonder if that is liberation.[90]

"Treason," "crime" (including war crime) and "hero" are completely subjective terms. If treason is defined as turning against your country, throughout almost all of history, governments and leaders have defined themselves as the country. From their point of view, going against them – no matter oppressive you may perceive them to be – is treason. If we define country not as government or ruling class but as the people, then there is the question: who is the "people?" The Nazis were very clear that only those with pure Aryan blood were the people. If there are vast differences of values, cultures and interests within a population, which side do you have to choose in order to be a loyal citizen? After the Nazis' defeat, the leaders were tried as war criminals and those who fought against them, even if wearing the uniform of Germany's enemies, were applauded as heroes. How different the reaction would have been if Germany had won!

While World War I was called the "Great War," World War II was called the "Good War" – the war that had to be fought, the war for which there was no alternative, because Germany actually became the barbaric monster propagandistic lies said it was in World War I. World War II veterans have been proclaimed the "greatest generation." The "Good War" is continually cited as proof that war is inevitable, there are bad people out there and nations – the United States in particular – must be vigilant and perpetually prepared to fight. In America, potential enemies – whether or not they have the resources to seriously threaten the United States – get compared to Hitler, with the implication that the only appropriate response is military. Except in a few countries like

Britain, the Good War actually caused far more death and destruction worldwide than the Great one. World War II was considered unavoidable by some of the world's leading pacifists including Albert Einstein and Bertrand Russell, although both spent the rest of their lives fighting for disarmament. If ever there was a regime whose own people and the rest of the world needed to be rescued from, it was Nazi Germany. However, even if we acknowledge that World War II is the one war that makes rational sense, it would have never happened without perhaps the most irrational waste of lives and resources in the history of the globe: World War I. Much of the guilt for laying the seeds for the "Good War" rests with victors in the "Great War" as they imposed the vindictive self-destructive Treaty of Versailles. John Maynard Keynes left the Versailles conference with this reaction:

> If we aim at the impoverishment of Central Europe, vengeance, I dare say, will not limp. Nothing can then delay for very long the forces of Reaction and the despairing convulsions of Revolution, before which the horrors of the later German war will fade into nothing, and which will destroy, whoever is victor, the civilisation and the progress of our generation . . . The policy of reducing Germany to servitude for a generation, of degrading the lives of millions of human beings, and of depriving a whole nation of happiness should be abhorrent and detestable – abhorrent and detestable, even if it were possible, even if it enriched ourselves, even if it did not sow the decay of the whole civilized life of Europe.[91]

Any reasonable leader of Germany, not just Hitler, would insist the treaty had to be renegotiated. Germany's enemies in World War II were hardly innocent. Before the war, as we have seen, Hitler had sponsors among the British and American elites. Without their support, he might have never risen to power. When they fought him in the most destructive war in the history of the world, they were not solely concerned with liberating the world from a monster. Churchill struggled to preserve what he could of the British Empire. "I have not become the King's First Minister in order to preside over the liquidation of the

British Empire."[92] The United States expected to finish the war as the world's overwhelmingly dominant power and reduce Britain to a junior partner. Stalin signed a pact with Hitler to divide Poland and the rest of Eastern Europe between them, only to find Hitler attack the Soviet Union. Hitler's glorious cause would likely never have happened had not Germany's enemies fought for their glorious causes in World War I. Glory breeds glory.

Unlike World War I, in World War II, there is an unambiguous "bad guy," but that does make the other side good. Emma Goldman asserted: "Much as I loathe Hitler, Mussolini, Stalin and Franco, I would not support a war against them and for the democracies which, in the last analysis, are only Fascist in disguise."[93]

In World War I, there was an enormous anti-war movement. World War II is remembered as the war when pacifism was abandoned, but that is not true. Pacifist movements existed, but they were relatively small. There were debates over how to rescue the victims of fascism, with a minority convinced war was not the answer. One simple act that would have saved enormous numbers and did not require war was lifting immigration quotes but, for many, that would not be dramatic or glorious enough. Deeply admired in Israel, David Wyman condemned the British and Americans for not bombing Auschwitz and other concentration camps.[94] Some Zionists use the fact that the camps were not bombed as proof that the world abandoned the Jews, that Jews are on their own and Israel must build a military that nobody dare challenge. Bombing the camps might seem heroic but the most likely result would have been killing most of the victims whom it was supposed to rescue.

Since Hitler wanted to prove much of the world wanted to destroy Germany, some argued that war was an ineffective response to Nazi atrocities. In 1940, Arthur Ponsonby warned before the British House of Lords, "The Government took the one course which I foresaw at the time would strengthen Hitler: They declared war on Germany."[95] Novelist Vera Brittain wrote in *Humiliation with Honour*, "Nazism thrives, as we see repeatedly, on every policy which provokes resistance, such as bombing blockade and threats of retribution."[96]

Pacifists were not passive during World War II. The War Resisters International managed to peacefully negotiate freeing Jews and other prisoners from Dachau. Conscious objectors went to jails, or were sent to work in rural camps and hospitals, or found themselves part of controlled starvation projects. Other pacifists were busy getting refugees food, money, visas and hiding places.[97] They deserve at least as much admiration for resisting fascism as the soldier who fought with arms. We will always wonder if there was a way to stop fascism without over 60 million deaths.[98]

Hitler did not repeat the cowardly treachery of World War I. He made sure that Germany fought to the very end, with the Russian army in Berlin and the American and British armies on the other side, not far behind, but deep into German soil. Rather than surrender, Hitler himself committed suicide. His war brought death to 7 million Germans – both military and civilian – about 10% of the population,[99] with misery and destruction surpassing the first war – although this time, the peace terms would not be as vindictive. As the war concluded, few Germans openly expressed pride over how valiantly they fought. While they may have cheered it as it began, when it ended, the typical German publicly expressed horror over what was done to them and what they had done to other peoples – whatever their private thoughts. Unlike the American South after the Civil War or some Germans after the Great War, nostalgia for the glorious cause did not live on in post-World War II Germany. We will talk more about this in the next chapter. The very Aryans, who were convinced the Nazis' victims deserved their fate when Hitler brought prosperity and near victory, but denied knowledge of the Holocaust and other atrocities in the wake of defeat. Much of the barbarism was publicly performed with far too many participants for average Germans to claim ignorance without enormous self-deception. Euthanasia is one example.

> Selections [for euthanasia] took place in hospitals. Scholars agree that while Hitler gave the "OK," the program was developed by physicians – and executed voluntarily and enthusiastically. The procedure became quite ordinary. Hospital personnel were not

squeamish. In 1941, the psychiatric institution Hadamar celebrated the cremation of the 10,000th mental patient in a special ceremony. Psychiatrists, nurses and secretaries attended and everyone received a bottle of beer for the occasion.[100]

The Holocaust could not have happened without the willingness of the German people to carry out the war effort and appear loyal to the Nazi State. Although allegedly a secret, the Final Solution would be one secret difficult to keep. Hitler had hinted at it when he first published *Mein Kampf*. In 1938, many Aryan Germans participated in, or at least witnessed, "Kristallnacht," or the night of broken glass. The mob destroyed Jewish homes, businesses, schools, hospitals and synagogues, with the death toll likely in the hundreds. The massacre was well known. It got worldwide attention with London Times commenting:

> No foreign propagandist bent upon blackening Germany before the world could outdo the tale of burnings and beatings, of blackguardly assaults on defenseless and innocent people, which disgraced that country yesterday.[101]

As World War II approached, almost all German cosmopolitans who might have rejected its irrationality had been killed, exiled, pushed underground, imprisoned or otherwise silenced. Once the Holocaust was in progress, families would often know someone working in the death camps. They would see their neighbors waiting at the train stations. Dachau is so close to Munich that you can see the smoke stacks. Even without television, enough information was available to know, but it is probably true – most did not know. They did not know because they did not want to know. Americans could watch destruction of villages in Vietnam, Iraq and Afghanistan on television and not know because they too would, consciously or not, choose not to put the pieces together. Like America, Germany is good. Anything it does must be good and necessary. Germans would come to simultaneously believe the victims would deserve their fate and the atrocities are not happening. How could America? How could Germany do such things? Americans are told the United States only invades – no, liberates – other countries to give them a better life. Aryan Germans were told their neighbors waiting at the train stations were being sent to "nice" places. Even if it should be obvious that was a lie, it might be safer and more convenient to believe it. Moreover, the glorious cause had been so embraced through the Nazi era, Aryans might well have accepted the extermination of the enemies of Germany even if fully visible and undeniable in all its gory details. However, in the post-World War II years, most Germans were able to rebuild their lives and acknowledge that war and Nazism should not be repeated-more so than white Southerners were able to reject their "Glorious Cause" after the Civil War. America learned very different lessons from their wars than Europe, especially Germany. This will be discussed in more detail in the next chapter.

4

AMERICA BECOMES EXCEPTIONAL BUT EUROPE PROSPERS

> Although we've used the fascist name
> Communism is just the same
> It's plain to see these two are twins
> And freedom dies if either wins
>
> One billion conquered should reveal
> The danger that is very real
> The greatest fascist threat you see
> Is the communist conspiracy
>
> So rally now to freedom's call
> Unafraid we'll stand up tall
> With faith and courage we will find
> Peace shall rein for all mankind.[1]

The collapse of fascism established the United States as the world's most glorious power. In order to proclaim itself the global police force, it needed a criminal. The Nazis were gone, so the Soviet communists who bore the overwhelming burden of defeating the Third Reich, were proclaimed their equivalent. Leftwing folk singers like Pete Seeger, Joan Baez and Bob Dylan denounced the Cold War with Russia, but Janet Greene, whom the Christian Anti-Communists crusade called "the rightwing Joan Baez", sang "rally now to freedom's call" for rightwing champions.

Denazification

After two world wars, Europe was decimated while the US became the glorious global hegemon. In this chapter, we first look at how Germany came to renounce glory – and the contradictory means and consequences of the process of denazification imposed largely by the Anglo-American victors. The overwhelming European destruction discredited the glorious fascist cause among many Germans, while also enabling the Anglo-American victors to impose punitive sanctions against Nazi leaders through war crime tribunals at Nuremberg and a number of other ways of condemning German fascism and preventing it from reemerging. Meanwhile, the US itself was embarking on its own self-proclaimed destiny of world transformation in which America would impose its own glorious cause on peoples everywhere as a form of moral salvation.

In the first section of this chapter, we look at denazification largely through the efforts made by the Anglo-American coalition to purge fascism from the minds and hearts of the German people and their politics. The enormity of German destruction already had discredited fascism to a large degree among many of the German people, who faced economic ruin and psychological humiliation, with seven million Germans dead, cities burned, and countless wounded and jobless. However, the Anglo-Americans, particularly the Americans, were not ready to stop there. They regarded it as their responsibility to initiate legal, moral and political steps that would forever destroy the fascist nightmare and define all later people who might take up that glorious cause as monsters. The Nuremberg trials and other steps we describe in this chapter may have facilitated some of this erosion of German glory, helping to turn Germany and all Europe toward a rejection not just of fascism but hyper-nationalism of any form and a shift from war toward social reconstruction and social democracy.

Ironically, though, the criminalization of fascists through Anglo-American war trials and other persecutions of fascists was as much the consequence of the rise of US glory after WWII as it was an effort to repudiate glory as a cause. Indeed, we show here that war crime trials and the broader assault on German fascism reflected simply the ability of victors in war and powerful glorious causes to impose their own views of morality and legality on the losers. While Germany was destroyed, the World Wars catapulted the US into an unprecedented position of global power and helped launch the glorious cause of American world hegemony that has been the dominant force in the world since World War II. The denazification process may have contributed to the discrediting of German fascism but it also simply reflected the ability of a victorious emerging glorious cause to impose its will on its defeated rivals. We show here that the effort to purge glory through denazification was profoundly contradictory, on the one hand helping discredit glorious wars in Europe but, on the other hand, a manifestation and consequence of the rise of a new American glorious cause that would move from the defeat of fascism to the building of the new American glorious cause that would take shape most clearly in the Reagan revolution and ultimately the triumph of Donald Trump. The end of German fascism did not destroy all fascism or glory; it simply reflected a transition from the threat of German fascist glorious causes to the rise of the American glorious cause, a transition that carries contradictory blends of morality and criminality – and ultimately of the end of fascist extinction of its enemies to the prospects of American extinction of any part of the world that rose to challenge the new glorious American century.

Despite the memory of veterans, much of it nostalgic, the world wars did not have anywhere near the impact upon the United States that they had upon Europe. Out of conservatively 20 million deaths (military and civilian) worldwide in the Great War, the US suffered only 116,708.[2] World War II cost at least 60 million lives (military and civilian) globally, but American losses were just 418,500.[3] We saw how the wars left Europe economically decimated, but established the United States as the world's dominant industrial power – by far. Although America may now have the planet's most aggressive military empire, it has not seen – on its own soil – the misery war can bring for 150 years. In the aftermath of the Civil War, the South experienced a trauma comparable to the Great War in Europe, but it only brought the North unprecedented prosperity. As we observed, World War I provoked two very different reactions in Europe, especially Germany: 1) a Left bohemian cosmopolitan response that such horror must never be repeated; and 2) a Right traditionalist insistence that glory must be restored, possibly by fighting and winning another war. This was very different than the American South after the Civil War, where the vast majority of politically active whites treated the cataclysm as a glorious cause that must be vindicated, even if that required waving the Yankee flag. Among post-bellum whites, there was only a rightwing traditionalist reaction; a leftwing bohemian cosmopolitan one hardly existed.

The victory of the traditionalist Far Right in the Weimar culture wars brought a disaster that dwarfed the Great War and the Great Depression. Despite Hitler's popularity until defeat was clearly inevitable, it is striking how few Germans acknowledged supporting the Third Reich when it was crushed. Germans interviewed after the war

> admitted to having been bored and irritated by the constant military drills and persistent indoctrination . . . They came to feel betrayed by the promises the Nazis held out . . . and guilty about the extent to which they had allowed themselves to be seduced by the Nazi vision of the future. But what really changed their perspective was the war. Despite being taught constantly that military prowess was the highest human achievement and heroism the noblest human quality, very few . . . framed their reminiscences as tales of derring-do rather than survival . . . they encountered brutality, violence, hardship, and death. The illusory belief in German victory that many shared in the early stages of the war vanished almost overnight after the Red Army's destruction of the Sixth German Army at Stalingrad. After this point, early in 1943, the majority realized the war was lost.[4]

When the Nazis seized power, they had the diehard support of about 30% of the population – a sufficient critical mass to overcome their enemies- but likely to leave a polarized population, some of whom would love the fascists, while others would despise them. Given the brutal suppression of civil liberties, Hitler's enemies could only survive through emigration or silence – acting as if they enthusiastically supported, or at least accepted, the regime. Typical Germans might engage in small acts of resistance, such as merely mumbling the required "Heil, Hitler!" greeting or hanging the smallest possible flag from their window on special days like Hitler's birthday ... many people were merely going through the motions of demonstrating the public support that the dictatorship required.[5]

With that attitude, the government could regard many as traitors, waiting to "stab Germany in the back." Although they did not dare publicly express their hostility to the Nazis while they were popular, they could secretly welcome the invading armies as liberators, and cooperate with them in creating a new anti-fascist Germany.

In the American South, reconstruction was doomed to fail for there was hardly any support – except for a few scalawags – among white Southerners, for the occupying army and the carpetbaggers. When the Yankees left, the Dixiecrats would strive to resurrect white supremacy through Jim Crow, since slavery was no longer viable. Post-World War II Germany was another matter. The victors would impose "Denazification," a policy similar to reconstruction but relatively successful. After World War I, the winners plundered Germany for booty through territorial grabs and reparations, but they left internal matters within German borders to their own fate. Germany was not occupied. After World War II, Germany was divided into four zones to be controlled by the United States, Great Britain, France and the Soviet Union. In 1949, the three capitalist zones merged into the country of West Germany or the Federal Republic of Germany, while the Russian zone became East Germany or the German Democratic Republic.[6] To prevent a resurgence of Nazism, the Western powers were willing to permit the moderately Left social democrats to be a major party within the West German government, but not the communists. The fact that even at height of the Third Reich, there was a moderate Left opposition, simmering underground, helped ensure the success of denazification. They could be installed as the leaders of the new Germany. Although official American and British policy was to purge all Nazi elements, there was debate between liberals who wanted to continue the détente with the Soviet Union and jointly police the world and conservatives who wanted to establish Anglo-American dominance but rebuild Germany as a buttress against potential Russian interests.

Over the objection of rightwingers like General George Patton, the decision was to create a demilitarized Germany, which rejected glory. It would become a capitalist democracy which could evolve into one of the world's leading economic, but not military, powers. Although the United States would discourage glory for Germany and other potential rivals, it would embrace glory for itself as it planned to become both the world's dominant economy and military. Patton, who led the Seventh Army in Sicily and the Third Army at the Battle of the Bulge, was convinced glory was in the essence of America's being. Just before D-Day when the United States and Britain landed in German occupied France, Patton hoped to inspire his troops with this exhortation.

> Americans love to fight. All real Americans love the sting and clash of battle.... Americans love a winner and will not tolerate a loser. Americans play to win all the time... The very thought of losing is hateful to Americans. Battle is the most significant competition in which a man can indulge. It brings out all that is best and it removes all that is base.... But the real man never lets his fear of death overpower his honor, his sense of duty to his country, and his innate manhood.... The brave men will breed more brave men. Kill off the goddamn cowards and we'll have a nation of brave men.[7]

Churchill wanted glory for Britain and hoped to resurrect as much as he could of the British Empire, although he unhappily recognized that it would be a junior partner to its former colony. However, the British people felt otherwise. They were tired of glory and war and wanted to focus on rebuilding their domestic economy. Despite Churchill's leading them to a huge victory, with Britain suffering less than half the deaths caused by World War I (449,700[8] vs. 994,138[9]), his Conservative Party was overwhelmingly defeated in the July 1945 parliamentary election and he was ousted as prime minister. The Conservatives fell from 386 seats to 197, while Labour rose from 154 to 393, with the popular vote being 8,716,211 for Conservatives and 11,967,746 for Labour.[10]

Not all Americans supported denazification. Patton became military commander of Bavaria during the American occupation. He systematically placed ex-Nazis in positions of authority and retained ex-SS officers as guards in former concentration camps, now being used to rehabilitate freed prisoners of the Nazis, including Jews. Until he was relieved of command, he planned to provoke a war with the Soviet Union on his own initiative and march across Poland. He intended to enlist ex-Nazis, whom he considered far more desirable than Jews, in his anticipated war with Russia.[11] Many of his attitudes were virtually indistinguishable from the Nazis.

> The noise against me is only the means by which the Jews and Communists are attempting and with good success to implement a further dismemberment of Germany. I think that if I resigned as I threatened to do yesterday, it would simply discredit me to no purpose ... I would like it much better than being a sort of executioner to the best race in Europe [Germans]. ... P.S. No one gives a damn how well Bavaria is run. All they are interested in now is how well it is ruined.[12] ... In the second place, Harrison and his ilk believe that the Displaced Person is a human being, which he is not, and this applies particularly to the Jews, who are lower than animals.[13] [Earl G. Harrison was the Dean of the University of Pennsylvania Law School. President Truman asked him to inspect the camps.[14]]

Patton was not alone in suggesting the United States was on the wrong side in World War II. Among the American Right, the idea persisted for decades. Phyllis Schafly gained fame as the founder of the Eagle Forum, a movement to "protect" women from cosmopolitan feminists and return them to traditional roles. In 1964, she wrote a book, *A Choice, Not an Echo*, in support of Barry Goldwater's presidential campaign. She charged that since World War II, Republicans had abandoned traditional values and she was outraged because:

> In 1940 the Republican candidate, Wendell Wilkie, did not campaign on the chief issue of that year, which was Roosevelt's

policy of consenting to Stalin's invasion of Poland, Finland, Latvia, Lithuania and Estonia while committing American boys to fight Hitler.[15]

The Soviet Union's campaign in those country evolved into the Eastern front in the war against Nazis, the front where Hitler overwhelmingly concentrated his troops.

The debate over the role Germany should play in anticipated hostility with Russia led to disputes among American and British policy makers about how to pursue denazification, if at all. The American military establishment was perfectly willing to use Nazis, especially ones with technical expertise, when it served their interests. Immediately after the war, over 1600 German scientists, engineers and technicians were secretly imported into the United States through Operation Paperclip to help in American weapons research. Perhaps the most prominent was Wernher von Braun who developed the V-2 rocket for Hitler and then designed intermediate-range ballistic missiles and the Explorer I Satellite for the United States, where he also served as the director of the Marshall Space Flight Center for the National and Space Administration (NASA).[16] The V-2 rockets were built with slave labor taken from concentration camps.

One inmate claimed:

> [T]he German scientists led by Prof. Wernher von Braun were aware of everything daily. As they went along the corridors, they saw the exhaustion of the inmates, their arduous work and their pain. Not one single time did Prof. Wernher von Braun protest against this cruelty during his frequent stays at Dora. Even the aspect of corpses did not touch him: On a small area near the ambulance shed, inmates tortured to death by slave labor and the terror of the overseers were piling up daily. But, Prof. Wernher von Braun passed them so close that he was almost touching the corpses.[17]

Who is a War Criminal?

The right of the victors to do whatever they wish to the vanquished – commit complete and total genocide, kill or torture them at random, or try them as war criminals, especially under the winner's laws – is simply a glorious prize of war. Although the Truman Administration privately assigned ex-Nazis sensitive positions in American military operations, publicly they professed wanting to guarantee the Nazis would play no role in the new Germany. To that end, with the support of British Prime Minister Clement Attlee, they decided to prosecute leading Nazis as war criminals at Nuremberg with the expectation that many would hang and others would suffer long prison terms. It appears the only difference between Nuremberg defendants, who faced severe sentences and the scientists rescued by Operation Paperclip, including Von Braun, who received high positions and honors, is the American military found the scientists of greater use.

Through war crime tribunals the Anglo-American victors could assert that they were inherently good and had the moral authority to impose whatever they wanted on the villains they had just conquered. The United States, in particular, now had the glorious duty of bringing its values, interests and way of life to the rest of the world. True, the Nazis were absolutely deplorable, perhaps the worst regime in the history of the world, but the Nuremberg War Trials were not simply an attempt to restore morality. It was a way for America to declare it had the inherent right to do whatever it wanted to the rest of the world and that anyone who stood in its way, be it fascist, communist or Islamic (labeled terrorist) must be destroyed for the greater American-defined good of humanity.

The truth is that the identification and prosecution of war criminals – whatever the moral arguments of the victors – is less a discrediting of glory than it is the expression of the moral arguments of the glorious victors. True, as we show later, there were strong and understandable moral horror at the Nazi crimes and an understandable desire to use all means necessary to discredit Nazi genocide. At the same time, the Nuremberg trials are far more than moral vindication; they were the consequence of a total devastation by the American victors. This leads to an interpretation of the denazification agenda that, on the one hand, recognizes how the world came to accept the definition of who was a war criminal, war crime trials, and denazification punishments as a victory for universal rights while, at the same time, they simply validated the ability of glorious winners to impose their own vision of glory and conquest in the guise of moral righteousness.

Some Americans and Britons opposed the Nuremberg tribunals because they thought the Nazis would be needed to fight the communists, while others deplored Nazi barbarism but worried that the trials were illegitimate and would set dangerous precedents. Had the Nazis themselves won, they might have simply claimed losers were weak and deserve their fate. The victors can do as they wished to vanquished as a glorious spoil of war. However, if – on losing – they appealed to universal values, something other defeated peoples might do, they might have claimed the winners had committed their own atrocities, such as the firebombing of Dresden, and were in no moral position to judge the conquered. The Japanese could have made an even stronger case and charged the atomic bombings of Hiroshima and Nagasaki were among the most vicious war crimes of all times. American bomber pilot John McCain was a war hero or a war criminal, depending upon your perspective. If the Nazis triumphed in the war, the defendants at Nuremberg would be glorified as heroes and saviors. Hitler would have been worshiped as a god until he was stuffed in his mausoleum, where he would continue to be venerated. As we said earlier, in a sense, the Nazis were right; the only real war crime is losing; the authority to hold war crime tribunals is a spoil of victory.

Although the Nazis atrocities may be particularly horrendous, many of them are not particularly different from what armies normally do in pursuit of glory and booty. Imagine if the Native Americans could have tried the United States army for genocide or if the Asian Indians could have tried the British for what they did in their country – acts for which, like the Nazis, the perpetrators felt proud and glorious but the victims might see very differently. In response to an Indian rebellion, British Lieutenant Kendal Coghill proclaimed: "We burnt every village and hanged all the villagers who had treated our fugitives badly until every tree was covered with scoundrels hanging from every branch. [One tree held 150 corps.]"[18] There was never any talk of putting King Leopold II of Belgium on trial for killing 10,000,000 in the Congo. The American army in Japan decided not to charge Emperor Hirohito as a war criminal because they believed he was a stabilizing force who could help the occupation go smoothly and they feared his trial could provoke riots.[19] Expect for a few outliers like Patton, most of the Anglo-American authorities in Germany did not expect ex-Nazis could help stabilize the country. The fact that there were no protests against Nuremberg tribunals shows how much popularity the Nazis had lost after defeat. The Nuremberg trials were intended to create a sense that it might be dangerous to express pro-Nazi sentiments and to eliminate any residue of Nazi influence. We do not know if public displays of Nazi sympathy would have reemerged earlier without the Nuremberg proceedings.

While the trials were in progress, federal judge Charles Wyzanski questioned their legitimacy. He was unambiguous in his moral condemnation of the Nazis: "[L]et me make it abundantly clear that as a human being I regard these murders, tortures, and persecutions as being morally . . . repugnant and loathsome."[20]

However, he feared that trying citizens for offenses that were legal, even obligatory, under the laws of their country when the acts were committed would set a dangerous precedent and raises the question: who has the right to try whom?

> [N]o crime and no penalty without an antecedent law . . . It rests on the political truth that if a law can be created after an offense, then power is to that extent absolute and arbitrary. To allow retroactive legislation is to disparage the principle of constitutional limitation . . . A question may be raised whether the United Nations [then meaning the nations united against Germany and Japan] are prepared to submit to scrutiny the attack of Russia on Poland, or on Finland or the American encouragement to the Russians to break their treaty with Japan . . . To some the count may appear as nothing more than the ancient rule that the vanquished are at the mercy of the victor.[21]

Under Nazi rule, refusing to commit the very acts which the Nuremberg Tribunal labeled war crimes would be considered treason, with potential dire consequences – imprisonment in a concentration camp or death. Submitting to the will of superiors and doing their bidding, even if it required committing atrocities, may be something only the bravest would reject. According to the Nazis and other militarists like General Patton and Confederate Generals, marching with them brings glorious valor.

However, it may require more courage to refuse to blend into the crowd like a sheep and defy their authority. Sometimes, you have to be very brave to be a coward. Many of the Nuremberg defendants insisted that they were merely following orders, obeying a chain of command with legal authority at the time. They were acting out of loyalty to their country and their leaders. If we refuse to acknowledge the plausibility of that defense than every soldier who kills when ordered is a murderer – a criminal. All military personnel, even non-combatants, are participating in a bureaucracy whose purpose is to kill. There is a very fine line between obeying orders to kill and committing atrocities. Whom do we prosecute as war criminals? Whom do we not? What is glorious? What is atrocious?

Although it would appear that defying Nazi authority was very dangerous, Hannah Arendt claimed otherwise. She was convinced it was relatively easy for an SS officer to avoid participating in the exterminations.

> We know how surprisingly easy it was for members of the extermination squads to quit their jobs without serious consequences for themselves . . . Not a single case could be traced in which an S.S. member had suffered the death penalty because of a refusal to take part in an execution . . . It was possible to evade a commission by an application for transfer. To be sure, in individual cases, one had to be prepared for a certain disciplinary punishment. A danger to one's life, however, was not at all involved.[22]

If Arendt was right, then it may have been almost impossible for a German Gentile to avoid serving in the "normal" Nazi war machine, without serious personal consequences. However, few Gentiles would have been forced to participate in the most brutal Nazi atrocities against their will. Who is the glorious hero? The one who obeys or the one who refuses, either silently or openly?

Of course, one of the goals of the war crimes tribunals was retribution, what some people call justice. However, as part of the denazification program, its other purpose was to prevent a Nazi resurgence, which required publicly exposing their barbarism. There may have been more effective ways of doing that. After apartheid was abolished in South Africa, Nelson Mandela, who rose from serving a 27-year prison sentence to be president of the new South Africa, organized the Truth and Reconciliation Commission (TRC) with the intention of revealing oppressive policies under apartheid but with little concern for punishing the perpetrators. Victims appeared before the commission and described the rights violations they suffered. Leaders of the apartheid regime also testified and could apply for amnesty if they admitted responsibility, although amnesty was denied in a majority of cases. Despite his personal memories of brutal incarceration, Mandela asserted that whites, willing to live in a state committed to racial equality, were welcome to stay. When he formally received the commission's report, he responded:

> We are extricating ourselves from a system that insulted our common humanity by dividing us from one another on the basis of race and setting us against each other as oppressed and oppressor . . . In doing so that system committed a crime against humanity . . . In denying us these things the Apartheid State generated the violent political conflict in the course of which human rights were violated . . . Let us celebrate our rich diversity as a people, the knowledge that when the TRC in its wisdom apportions blame, it points at previous state structures; political organizations; at institutions and individuals, but never at any community . . . It is for those who have suffered losses of different kinds and magnitudes to be afforded reparation, proceeding from the premise that freedom and dignity are the real prize that our sacrifices were meant to attain.[23]

We can applaud Mandela and the TRC for avoiding vindictiveness, and TRC has been praised as a more effective way for addressing human rights violations than the Nuremberg Tribunals. However, TRC did not resolve fundamental problems within South Africa. Apartheid was abolished and blacks gained political rights, but white elites continued to help shape economic policy. According to the World Bank, South Africa is the most unequal country in the world with 1% of the population owning 71% of the country's wealth, the bottom 60% owning only 7%, and the gap between white and black wealth actually expanding since apartheid ended. The World Bank assigns each country a "Gini index," a measure of inequality. As of 2018, South Africa is the highest in the world at 63.4. Germany is ranked 132 with an index of 31.4.[24] Whether or not the Nuremberg Tribunal was overly vindictive, this does imply the long-term impact of denazification was more successful 70 years later.

Civil Liberties For Nazis?
Despite Mandela's ambiguous legacy, he taught valuable lessons. We should confront ugly and oppressive history, and demonstrate how the pursuit of glory often leads to misery. Denying or hiding from it may make it only more likely that it will be repeated and more difficult to recognize the danger it poses. As part of denazification immediately after Nazi fell, the conquering armies banned displaying swastikas, "Heil Hitler" salutes and the publication of Hitler's *Mein Kampf*. The laws remained in effect when West Germany was formed. In Germany today, denying the Holocaust or participating in acts, speeches or publications that "approves of, glorifies or justifies the violent and despotic rule of the National Socialists"[25] theoretically carries a five-year sentence. Contemporary Germany has museums devoted to the Third Reich and it is permitted to use Nazi memorabilia for anti-fascist education, but it is illegal to display them without making it clear that they are unambiguously evil. Germany does not encourage tourists or students to see Nazi sights. The beer hall in Munich where Hitler and Ludendorff attempted to overthrow the Bavarian government in 1923 was torn down in 1979. A plaque marked an attempt to assassinate Hitler, but does not refer to

Hitler's earlier attempted coup. Other Munich beer halls have ceilings painted white but if you slightly squint, you will see underneath the whitewash (literal) a quilt-like pattern made of swastikas. To hide such artifacts may be self-defeating; it may make it easier to claim the Holocaust and related atrocities were exaggerated or never occurred at all.

These bans may be seen as violations of free speech, at least as American civil libertarians understand it, but Germans have argued that Americans have no real memory of fascism in power and if they did, they would be extremely reluctant to give fascists legitimacy and allow them free speech. They fear if they grant fascists a forum, they may gain a following or even come back. Slavery and World War I were remembered as glorious causes. There is a risk the Third Reich may also be. This suggests that denying free speech, even to Nazis, may backfire and empower them to resurrect their glorious cause. Black Americans who experienced – or whose ancestors experienced – slavery or apartheid in the South can make a similar case that Confederate monuments and symbols pose a comparable danger, but denying whites free speech may fuel their new Confederate or white supremacist glorious cause.

Even liberal states restrict free speech to guarantee it does not threaten the government or the elite. To assemble in protest, you usually need a permit from the very government you are protesting against. You can speak as long as your speech is ineffective and not translated into action.

> In the firmly established liberal society of England and the United States, freedom of speech and assembly was granted even to the radical enemies of society, provided they did not make the transition from word to deed, from speech to action.[26]

The American Supreme Court has ruled free speech can be suppressed when it poses "a clear and present danger." Danger of what? To whom? The metaphor most commonly used is "you can't shout 'fire' in a crowded theater," but that analogy was first used to justify imprisoning Eugene Debs observing a fire [World War I sacrificing citizens' life for the sake of the capitalist class] in a theater [the American people]. The Nazis abolished free speech to guarantee no one could challenge them. The ban against Nazi symbols has a "clear and present danger" of mirroring Nazi policies and could easily be used as a precedent should the ultra-Right regain power. While living in the United States, Herbert Marcuse argued against tolerating fascist-like speech. As a Jewish Marxist refugee from Nazi Germany, he experienced, first hand, the danger of allowing fascist speech to translate into action and allowing them to assume power, but he should have worried about the consequences of replicating Nazi suppression of speech. He said tolerance should be tolerated only when it is "liberating."

> Liberating tolerance, then, would mean intolerance against movements from the Right and toleration of movements from the Left . . . the speeches of the Fascist and Nazi leaders were the immediate prologue to the massacre. The distance between the propaganda and the action, between the organization and its release on the people had become too short. But the spreading of the word could have been stopped before it was too late: if democratic tolerance had been withdrawn when the future leaders started their campaign, mankind would have had a chance of avoiding Auschwitz and a World War.[27]

To justify silencing rightwing speech is to give the Right a weapon to use against the Left when it is in power and Marcuse knew how much more power the Right had than the Left in so-called capitalist democracies. He observed the repression of the Left not only in Germany, but also in the United States during the McCarthy Era of 1950s and the reaction against the student New Left of the 1960/70s for whom he was a mentor. Rather than squelching rightwing speech, a better response for the Left may be to let them speak and then expose their contradictions and lies. Allow Nazi monuments in Germany and Confederate monuments in the American South, but place plaques near them revealing their true meaning.

Germany Denazified?

Despite these problems, for the most part, denazification was successful – more successful than reconstruction in the American South. It created a liberal democracy in Germany with the moderately Leftist Social Democrats as a major party and its rival – the Christian Democrats – considered conservative by European standards, but possibly to the left of the American Democratic Party. Although for decades the xenophobic far right was hardly a noticeable force in European, especially German, political life, they did not vanish but rather simmered underground waiting for the moment to reemerge.

> a feeling of gloom and insecurity as the old demons of chauvinism and ethnic division are again spreading across the Continent. And as memory turns into history, one question looms large: Can we learn from history without having lived it ourselves? . . . But today, its younger generations have no memory of industrialized slaughter. Instead, their consciousness has been shaped by a decade-long financial crisis, an influx of migrants from Africa and the Middle East, and a sense that the promise of a united Europe is not delivering. To some it feels that Europe's bloody last century might as well be the Stone Age . . . Now as then, Europe's political center is weak and the fringes are radicalizing. Nationalism, laced with ethnic hatred, has been gaining momentum. Populists sit in several European governments.[28]

Immigration of foreigners, especially from the Middle East, into Germany and the fear that they may complete for jobs and other resources has restimulated xenophobia. In 2017 "Alternative für Deutschland" (AFD), which believes Germany should not be ashamed of its Nazi past, won 94 seats in the Bundestag, one of the houses of the German parliament. One AFD Member of Parliament advised:

> When the state can no longer protect its citizens, people will go into the streets and protect themselves. Very simple! Today it is the obligation of the citizen to stop the death – bringing "knife migration." It could have been your father, son, or brother![29]

In August 2018, members of AFD participated in riots in Chemnitz, a city of about 250,000, along with the "National Socialists of Chemnitz."

Since October 2014, the "Patriotic Europeans against the Islamisation of the West" (PEGIDA) routinely organizes anti-immigration marches in Dresden. Another neo-Nazi organization, "The National Socialist Union," has been accused of committing ten murders, two bombings and a number of bank robberies.[30] For now, it appears unlikely that any of these groups pose a serious threat to German democracy, but the same assessment would have been given to the Nazis in the 1920s.

There were Germans who were nostalgic for the Nazis and the world wars and passed that memory onto some within their children's and grandchildren's generation, especially those who felt entitled to more than they received. However, for decades that yearning was seldom expressed in mainstream German political discourse. After the fall of the Third Reich, hardly anyone would publicly profess believing the traumas of fascism and total war should ever be repeated. To Europe, especially Germany, the world wars and fascism brought nothing but death, misery and devastation. But the only time the United States experienced anything comparable was the Civil War and its aftermath, and even that was only experienced in the South, where the dominant sentiment was that glory must be restored, even if that meant marching with the Yankees. For the United States, the effect of total wars was unprecedented prosperity. To Europeans, especially Germans, one shock in the pursuit of greatness might produce a longing for vindication, but two shocks would convince them that being great is not so great. Rather than seeking glory and trying to establish themselves as destined to be masters of the earth, it is better to focus on their domestic economy and build the quality of life for their people. We would not want the United States to endure anything comparable to what Europe suffered, but we would hope that America would learn from Europe's example, cease to seek exceptionalism, glory and greatness, and transfer resources away from the military apparatus to programs that would enhance the quality of life for the American people.

Although striving for military glory resulted in disaster, concentrating on German's domestic economy brought prosperity. As of 2017, Germany has the highest GDP in Europe and the fourth highest in the world.[31] Social services are much more extensive than the United States.

Most students pay no tuition for bachelor and master degree programs in public universities.[32] Everyone is guaranteed health insurance, with a choice between private or public insurance.[33] German mothers or fathers can receive their full salary for six weeks before and eight weeks after giving birth and can earn 65%, up to 1800 Euros a month, for the remainder of the year after the child's birth.[34]

> Approximately 90% of the population participates in the social security system in Germany. The German version of the welfare state includes a national pension plan, public healthcare and nursing care, unemployment benefits, work-related accident insurance, and welfare aid.[35]

Let us hope that the cosmopolitan German social democracy and welfare state will prevail over the resurgence of hyper-nationalist traditionalists seeking to revive the Nazi glorious cause.

American Exceptionalism

Glory and military posturing are short-term solutions to induce popular support for state and corporate polices. In the long run, they must be matched with shared booty. Guns alone are not sufficient; butter is also necessary. Hitler was popular when his military spending brought prosperity and his wars brought victory, but when defeat was imminent, accompanied by civilian deaths and misery, his support collapsed. In the immediate decades after World War II, the United States declared itself "exceptional" with "God shedding His grace on thee," and its military strength and economic prosperity unparalleled by anyone else in the history of the world. America was glorious but that glory gave its people a domestic standard of living the world had not seen before. Americans would be proud and patriotic, ready to fight any adversary – real or imagined. If there were a crisis, they would rally behind their flag, but should glory fail to deliver the goods for an extended period time, their faith in their country might wane. If guns bring wealth and domination, they will be embraced; if they fail, attitudes might change.

While Germany and most of the rest of Europe abandoned militarism and dreams of glory and valor in the post-World War II years, the United States embraced them. World War II erupted at the end of the Great Depression. In fact, without the Great Depression, Hitler probably would have never come to power and there would not have been a second world war. However, by almost any measure it was World War II which ended the Great Depression, at least for the United States. In 1939, US GDP reached $92.2 billion, well above its 1933 nadir, $56.4 billion, but still below 1929, $103.6 billion. By 1945, US GDP rose to $223 billion (about $3.3 trillion in 2018 money)[36] and unemployment was near zero.

War is a gift to the corporate elite – the ultimate corporate welfare. Despite everything we hear from the bourgeoisie about the need to cut government fat, the capitalist class seldom complains when the state spends on guns, not butter. War can be presented as a national emergency for which parochial concerns would have to be forgotten. Everyone has a stake in defense. Government contracts for tanks, ships and bombs are an economic stimulus. Money from military contracts may "trickle down," through increased employment, but they first go to the corporations.

During World War II, the United States expanded its industrial apparatus, far more than in World War I. Immediately after WWII, when the United States temporarily considered military reductions, GDP fell 12.7%.[37] The Great Depression was showing signs of a relapse. Some economists argue the depression never ended; the American economy has been propped up by armaments spending ever since, with the glory of the post-war American empire boosting domestic welfare.

Soon after World War I, the American armed forces were dismantled from about 5,000,000 troops to about 280,000.[38] The rest of the world was so indebted to the United States that the wealth from European empires would fall into the hands of the American corporate elite. The British and French empires could be rebuilt to police the world and the economic benefits would accrue to the United States. Newly discovered oil in the Middle East, patrolled by Britain and France, would flow into the coffers of Esso and Mobil. World War II left the United States even more clearly the world's dominant economic power.

> The destruction of the war had left an extraordinary imbalance in the world's industrial power structure. Three quarters of the world's invested capital and two thirds of its industrial capital were concentrated inside one country, the United States; the rest was shared over 95 per cent of the earth's inhabited surface.[39]

Britain and France were now too weak to serve as the world police force. That responsibility or privilege would fall on the United States, whose corporations could gain from perpetual military contracts, as well as the army protecting foreign investments and markets and securing access to third world resources and cheap labor. Rather than reducing its military, America would now become a permanent garrison state. This was symbolized by renaming the Department of War as the Department of Defense. Defense may sound softer, but war is sporadic, while the need for defense never ends. The United States declared itself guardian of the "free world," including its former adversaries – Germany and Japan. America's clients were assured they need not maintain larger arsenals for the United States would defend them. As of 2018, the United States still has military bases in 80 countries[40] and spends more on weapons than the next seven countries combined.[41] Some under America's umbrella wondered how severe really was the menace from which they were allegedly being protected. They felt like Mae West: "Every man I meet wants to protect me. I can't figure out what from."[42]

The Soviet Union, the ally who had borne the overwhelming cost of defeating Hitler, was now declared an eternal enemy as brutal as Nazi Germany. According to Winston Churchill, the Germans sent 185 divisions against Russia in 1943, but only used six divisions in the Western Front.[43] No one knows how many Russian lives were sacrificed in what the Soviet Union called "The Great Patriotic War" but estimates range from 20 to 25 million.[44] Labeling the Soviet Union a perpetual irreconcilable enemy would result in an arms race, which would require building a nuclear arsenal capable of killing every person on this planet, many times over. It would enshrine the glorious cause of American world power, making the cold war against the Soviet Union the ticket to American glory.

The United States and the Soviet Union never actually engaged in outright war but the tension between them was so great and the risk of nuclear Holocaust was so threatening that the decades from the collapse of Nazi Germany to the collapse of Soviet Union were labeled the Cold War. Americans were warned to be unwavering in their dread of communist evil. J. Edgar Hoover, head of the FBI from 1924 to his death in 1972, admonished

> Until the American citizen learns for himself the nature of the present menace, communism will continue to be a deadly danger . . . Yet the individual is handicapped by coming face to face with a conspiracy so monstrous he cannot believe it exists. The American mind simply has not come to a realization of the evil which has been introduced into our midst. It rejects even the assumption that human creatures could espouse a philosophy which must ultimately destroy all that is good and decent.[45]

Although there never was an open war between the United States and the Soviet Union, containing communism led America to fight major wars in Korea and Indo-China and to intervene through the military or the CIA in Cuba, Chile, El Salvador, Grenada, Iran and the Congo among many other countries. During the Cold War, membership in the military was, of course, presented as a glorious patriotic adventure. General Douglas MacArthur exhorted cadets at West Point

> I have witnessed that enduring fortitude, that patriotic self-abnegation, and that invincible determination which have carved his statue in the hearts of his people. From one end of the world to the other, he has drained deep the chalice of courage. . . . I do not know the dignity of their birth, but I do know the glory of their death. They died unquestioning, uncomplaining, with faith

in their hearts, and on their lips the hope that we would go on to victory. . . . Always for them: Duty, Honor, Country. Always their blood, and sweat, and tears, as we sought the way and the light and the truth. . . . Yours is the profession of arms, the will to win, the sure knowledge that in war there is no substitute for victory.[46]

To prepare the public for a potential nuclear confrontation between the United States and the Soviet Union, an American Civil Defense Agency was created. It attempted to make the costs of such a cataclysm acceptable. These costs diverted resources that could have been used to improve the quality of civilian life. Civil Defense curtailed civil liberties, and tried to persuade the public that they could survive nuclear obliteration. As part of the civil defense campaign, homeowners were advised to build fall-out shelters, essentially cement mini-fortresses, in their backyards. Children were taught to go under desks or tables, bend down and place their arms over their necks. They were to follow the model of cartoon character Bert the Turtle, who hides in his shell and wears an army helmet.

> Bert the Turtle was very alert
> When danger threatened him he never got hurt
> He knew just what to do
> He'd duck and cover, duck and cover.[47]

The corporate and military elite would benefit from a country locked in cold war but the general population had to be enticed to believe they had a stake in post-World War II prosperity, that the wealth sparked by the armament industries and American global dominance was "trickling down" to them, they were attaining middle class status, achieving the American Dream. The federal government stimulated not only corporate investment through weapons purchases; it also encouraged consumptions by the 99%, including home purchase through federally subsidized mortgages. Returning World War II veterans particularly benefited. Through the GI Bill, they were able to buy houses, with the federal government underwriting their mortgages, in newly built suburbs, have babies and buy, buy, buy! The GI Bill set aside billions of dollars to help returning veterans readapt to civilian life. It effectively subsidized not only veterans, but also banks and the construction industry.[48] "Homeowners" might be heavily in debt but they would identify themselves as part of the propertied class.

To get the veterans to buy into the newly formed suburbs with their newly formed families, infrastructure was intentionally dismantled. Viable inner-city neighborhoods and downtowns were reduced to enclaves of poverty and bordered up buildings, as downtown department stores were replaced by monotonous strip-malls, which ringed the metropolitan areas. Neighborhood movie theaters closed down as suburbanites bought newly invented television. Central city public transportation was destroyed. The streetcar became a relic of the past.[49] Standard Oil and General Motors jointly bought the Los Angeles Transit system, then one of the finest in the world, and closed it down. They then pressured the California legislature to build freeways. Life in LA became almost impossible without a car.[50] Homes, stores, business, even schools and recreations centers, were now so far from each other that they could only be reached by automobile. People were encouraged to use cars instead of railroads. President Eisenhower undertook a public works project to build a network of multi-lane interstate highways, which crisscrossed the nation.[51] This was a kind of domestic corporate glory project, creating a sense of national American exceptionalism built on illusions of mass wealth that largely went to the rich.

World War II left America's competitors in Europe and Japan decimated, so American industry had little incentive to innovate. As early as the 1920s, automobile companies started changing the appearance of car regularly, even annually, but the actual technology remained essentially the same. Cars were marketed by making people's sense of status depend upon having this year's look. If people drive last year's car, their neighbor will think they are poor or "not with it." They may have to become poor to look rich, but that increased profit for the auto companies. By the 1950s, Ford and GM adopted "planned obsolescence."[52] They decided it was self-defeating to make well-built cars and focused on appearance, not quality. The sooner cars fell apart, the sooner people would replace them. From a corporate point of view, cars with life spans of three to five years was not a bad idea. Technological innovation was actually squelched. American auto companies held patents for engines, more efficient and less ecologically destructive than the internal combustion. However, these alternatives would compete with existing technology and developing them would require paying to retool plants that were yielding adequate profit, at least for the time being. The patents were locked in vaults to prevent other people, companies and countries from using them. Oil companies gave patents for solar and other green energy technologies a similar treatment. The corporate glory project would begin to unravel, but it took time for ordinary Americans to see how it undermined them in the name of "making America great" (decades before Donald Trump's presidency).

With little competition from abroad, American auto, oil and steel companies could afford to pay their employees enough to buy houses, cars and televisions and perhaps send their kids to college. In the 1950s and 1960s, workers typically identified themselves as middle class and often felt they had attained the American dream. Industrial corporations signed an armistice with unions and together, they worked to preserve industrial peace. By 1955, the average autoworker made $90 a week (about $850 in 2018 money). Wages were set to maintain consumption and social stability, not necessarily on the value of what the worker produced.[53]

One reason why industrial corporations could afford to pay their workers well and employ so many was that they were subsidized by the government, largely through weapons contracts. Armaments became America's staple product, the foundation of the rest of the economy. It supported aerospace, chemicals, energy, mining, communications and transportation. For many corporations, the Department of Defense was their largest customer, even outweighing the private consumer. After World War II, when the United States was the world's economic engine, military research sparked most innovation including transistors, computer circuits and plastics. However, American industry so dominated the world that American corporations felt little motive to apply these innovations to civilian consumer goods.

On the other hand, Europe and Japan took the discoveries from American military research to improve their televisions, tape players and cameras. Forced to rebuild their industries, which had been destroyed in World War II, from scratch, they adopted the latest technologies. With their people too poor to afford American cars, which were big, ostentatious, inefficient and short-lived, they built small, durable, more ecological ones. While foreigners didn't purchase American cars, by the late 1960s Americans regularly bought foreign goods.

By the early 1970s, Europe and Japan had recovered from WWII. Its people no longer felt poor, desperate and in awe of the United States. They had stronger unions, better social services and public transportation than America. Rather than destroy their inner-cities, they rebuilt them. By sacrificing civilian infrastructure to military domination, the United States had squandered its advantage. While American corporations hardly used weapons technology to improve the quality of civilian consumer goods, Toyota, Sony, Fuji, Volkswagen and LG most certainly did. America's borrowing to buy guns may have bought several decades of prosperity, but by the 1970s, it became self-defeating. Until then, United States domination stemmed from one specific historical fact: the world wars left America's infrastructure intact, but decimated its rivals. There is no inherent reason why the United States should rule; American exceptionalism is a myth. The pursuit of American global glory undermines the nation and the well-being of ordinary Americans.

It was Otto von Bismarck, the first prime minister of the Kaiser's Second Reich, who coined the phrase "guns and butter." Glory brings prosperity. When Europe followed that philosophy, it only brought them disaster. The world wars taught them to abandon guns and concentrate on butter. Especially in Germany, the advocates of guns were expunged from power and their people experienced decades of prosperity, social security and services including guaranteed healthcare and education. On the other hand, glory did bring the United States unprecedented wealth and power, at least temporarily. Focusing on guns can provide civilians with butter for a while, but it can also lead to allowing infrastructure to lie fallow and consequently causing the standard of living to deteriorate in the long run. In the next chapter, we shall consider how the pursuit of glory intensified the division between cosmopolitans and traditionalists in the United States, although the rift did not reach the level of Weimar Germany.

5
Weimar America

Vietnam, The Left, The Right & Reagan

America – Love It or Leave It

> STRIKE FOR THE EIGHT DEMANDS
> STRIKE BECAUSE YOU HATE COPS
> STRIKE BECAUSE YOUR ROOMMATE WAS CLUBBED
> STRIKE TO STOP EXPANSION
> STRIKE TO SEIZE CONTROL OF YOUR LIFE
> STRIKE TO BECOME MORE HUMAN
> STRIKE BECAUSE THERE'S NO POETRY IN YOUR LECTURES
> STRIKE BECAUSE CLASSES ARE A BORE
> STRIKE FOR POWER
> STRIKE TO MAKE YOURSELF FREE
> STRKE TO ABOLISH ROTC
> STRIKE BECAUSE THEY ARE TRYING TO SQUEEZE THE LIFE OUT OF YOU
> STRIKE[1]

The American dream offers the promise that each generation will live better than the one before, although ironically that can be a source of conflict between parent and child. By the early 1970s, that promise was beginning to break down. From 1948 to 1968, real gross family income rose 88.6%, but in the next decade family income in dollars rose only 9%, with real net income falling 3.1%.[2] Although post-World War II USA was the richest and most powerful military empire in the history of the world, it squandered its advantage as it produced weapons and allowed its domestic infrastructure to deteriorate while Europe and Japan rebuilt theirs. The US remained the world's largest economy but its share of the world's GDP fell from about 50% in 1945 to about 25% in 1980.[3] In that period, as the self-appointed world police force, the United States intervened either militarily or through the CIA in a long list of countries including Korea, Syria, Iran, Cuba, Guatemala, the Dominican Republic, Indonesia, Lebanon, the Congo, Guyana, Chile, Iraq and Afghanistan.[4] The assumption was the US was free – in fact, morally obligated – to go anywhere it wanted with impunity. After all, it was bringing democracy and saving the world from the evil clutches of communism. The US empire became the greatest in the world and was the pre-eminent glorious cause on the planet.

Destroying Vietnam to Save It

However, maintaining empires has costs and interventions can lead to quagmires, with the most draining of all being Indochina. Before World War II, Indochina was a French colony facing a revolution led by Ho Chi Minh, who initially admired the United States and expected to be granted independence when WWII was over and the invading Japanese were expelled. Instead, the United States returned Indochina to France, but Ho Chi Minh and his followers fought on for over a period of ten years until they defeated France at the battle of Dien Bien Phu in 1954. During the battle, American Secretary of State John Foster Dulles offered the French two atom bombs.[5] Knowing "possibly 80 per cent of the population would have voted for the Communist Ho Chi Minh as their leader,"[6] President Eisenhower installed Ngo Dinh Diem, a Catholic as the ruler of South Vietnam – an American puppet state with virtually no legitimacy among its own people. Although he hoped the French would leave, in the 1930s Diem worked with the French to squelch peasant uprisings supported by the communists.[7] To prevent its puppet from falling, the United States sent 2,000,000 soldiers over a period of 10 years, with up to 500,000 stationed there at a time and 58,000, including Magrass' brother, never returning. The

United States dropped about three times as many tons on Indochina as all the bomb tonnage that was dropped in World War II – 7,662,000 tons vs. 2,150,000 tons.[8] America used chemical weapons like Napalm and defoliates like Agent Orange, and brought so many weapons to Indochina that when the United States was defeated, the Vietnamese found themselves with one of the world's best equipped army with all the material they captured from the American intruder.

The American military, government and media claimed they were protecting South Vietnam from the invading army of North Vietnam. But America's primary target was the National Liberation Front (NLF) – South Vietnamese guerillas disparagingly called Vietcong, gooks or Charlie, although North Vietnam certainly did support the NFL. South Vietnam was invaded – by the United States, not North Vietnam. To quote Daniel Ellsberg, former analyst for the US Department of Defense and the Rand Corporation who released the *Pentagon Papers*, the Defense Department's classified analysis of the Vietnam War to the *New York Times*:

> We weren't on the wrong side, we were the wrong side. . . .[9] A war in which one side was entirely equipped and paid by a foreign power – which dictated the nature of the local regime in its own interest – was not a civil war. To say that we had "interfered" in what is "really a civil war," as most American academic writers and even liberal critics of the war do to this day, simply screened a more painful reality and was as much a myth as the earlier official one of "aggression from the North." In terms of UN Charter and of our own avowed ideals, it was a war of foreign aggression, American aggression.[10]

The NLF was popular among the country's villages. To rout out the NLF, American patrols would routinely go on "search and destroy missions" where they would enter villages, round up the men of military age, often killing them as potential Vietcong, then force the old, women and children to go to "relocation camps." As one Major remarked after an attack on Bến Tre: "It became necessary to destroy the town to save it."[11]

Villagers would supply the NLF with soldiers, food and assistance in the planting of land mines. What many U.S. soldiers feared most were land mines and then ambushes. Soldiers would become demoralized by weeks of mundane patrolling and then they would be hit unexpectedly by the explosion of land mines or an ambush. Enraged soldiers would go back to the nearest area they had just been through and brutalize the villagers in a racist fury. The effect of fighting a total war on an entire population was to create a situation where all Vietnamese people were seen as fair game to kill.[12]

Whether or not there was a civil war in Vietnam, it produced something approaching one in the United States, except one side had virtually all the weapons. One side – on the right with a large following among traditionalists – made a charge similar to what the Nazis claimed in Germany after World War I. The United States should have won, but it was "stabbed in the back." As the most glorious nation in the history of the world, the only power that could defeat America was Americans, certainly not bands of third world peasant guerillas. America lost its will for victory, so valiantly displayed in World War II and cowardly, unwilling to commit all it had, only fought half-heartedly. Like German troops in World War I, American boys in Vietnam were denied the victory that would have made their sacrifices meaningful. As the other side pointed out, this idea can only be called absurd; the United States fought with every resource at its disposal, but even the most powerful empire ever could not bring impoverished peasants to submit when they were prepared to struggle forever for their freedom – indeed their survival. What Vietnam proved is there is a limit to what unrestrained brutality can achieve. Even the greatest army can over-extend itself and find its power implode upon itself. True, the United States had the technical capacity to kill each and every Vietnamese but it could never win their "hearts and minds" through military might. Assuming Russia or China did not intervene or its own anti-war movement did not force withdrawal, the United States could have stayed in Vietnam as long as it wished – even a century or longer – but its puppet regime would be overthrown the minute it left. Unlike Germany in both world wars, the United States was rich and powerful enough to afford to lose a war, but while remaining the world's dominant empire, it would be weakened with its people less confident of their country's greatness and other nations – both capitalist clients and rivals as well as third world quasi-colonies – more emboldened to challenge it. Against the traditionalists' patriotism, there emerged another – more cosmopolitan – side, especially among the young, who were horrified at the atrocities their country would commit to assure domination, came to believe America's claim to be world's glorious beacon of freedom and democracy was a lie, and questioned if they wanted to inherit the society their parents were bequeathing to them.

Dad & Mom: I Don't Want Your Sacrifice

In the immediate years after World War II, more and more Americans could identify themselves as "middle class" because the economic pie appeared to be expanding indefinitely and they could feel relatively comfortable as long as they could anticipate their piece. Around the time of the defeat in Vietnam, the pie seemed to begin to contract, although it was still the world's largest. The problem was then who should bear the burden for a diminishing pie. With a shrinking pie, the elite would be less generous and willing to share, but they had to find a way to bring the public to accept deterioration or at least not blame the corporations and the state. As we have seen repeatedly, when people's rational needs are not being met, when they are not being delivered the goods, elites try to rally support by offering them a glorious cause, the idea that they are serving a great nation or some other higher purpose. However, defeat meant less glory.

To prevent hostility turning against the militaristic capitalist empire itself, somebody else had to be held responsible. At least two scapegoats were available. The Vietnam Era overlapped with the Civil Rights Era, and blacks and other racial minorities could now be presented either as parasites whose welfare was being paid for with the taxes of hard-working traditionalists or uppity upstarts threatening to take the jobs traditionalists struggled so vehemently to attain. We saw the hostility integrated schools provoke even in the Northern U.S. The other enemy held responsible for America's relative decline were also presented as parasites – privileged cosmopolitans who did not appreciate the gifts that the country they maligned gave them and often attacked traditionalists and sided with welfare parasites, although they themselves made little sacrifice.

The Vietnam Era cultural and political clash in the United States approached that of Weimar Germany, but it never quite reached that level of intensity, primarily because the country did not collapse. Nonetheless, the war exacerbated a conflict between cosmopolitan Leftists and bohemians – then called hippies or freaks – and traditionalists, which probably existed long before, although many children of traditionalists joined the cosmopolitans. Cosmopolitan Leftists insisted the blame for the Vietnam debacle did indeed rest with the American militaristic capitalist empire itself. Among the generation which grew up after the Great Depression and World War II, many cosmopolitans questioned if they wanted to inherit that empire and its bounty. For those who never knew relative poverty, affluence did not bring gratitude. The media spoke of a "generation gap." The generation gap was the theme of one the most popular television programs of the time, *All in the Family*. There was constant bickering between traditionalist Queens N.Y. shop foreman Archie Bunker (Carroll O'Connor) and his cosmopolitan son-in-law Mike Stivic (Robert Reiner) – the meathead, who is in the early episodes was a college student, supported by his resentful father-in-law, and later a professor of sociology.

Mike: You see, there's your difference between your generations right there, Archie. You've been spending the last 30 years checking under every bed for a Communist and going around thinking you're better and holier than they are with your stinkin' Puritan ethic, and what have you got to show for it?

Archie: A wife who's home at ten o'clock.

Mike: Sure, and the fear and the mistrust of the whole rest of the world! Well, you can live with that fear, Archie, and you can live with that mistrust. I don't want to have any part of it, do you hear what I'm saying? I don't want any part of it! ...

Archie: You are SICK, you know that? YOU NEED HELP. I've listened to this guy around here for ten months. All this pinko stuff, that's all right, that's what they're fillin' em up with in the schools nowadays, huh? ... YOU MIGHT AS WELL SHUT THE DOORS OF THIS COUNTRY AND HANG UP A SIGN, 'CLOSED. OWNER GONE NUTS.'[13]

Although Archie Bunker hardly embodied affluence, young cosmopolitans, often the children of traditionalists, wondered if they wanted to follow their parents dream: pursue a technical or professional career, go to work every day to compete in a rat race for wealth and status, get married, have 2.3 children, buy a house in the suburbs with a mortgage – work and buy for the sake of working and buying. Although folk singer Pete Seeger was of their parents' generation, they shared his sentiment as he offered this critique:

And the people in the houses all went to the university
And they all get put in boxes, little boxes all the same.[14]

Every morning, leave the little box to drive the tiny box to the big box, then get back in the tiny box to go to the little box, where you stare at the eensy box. Rather than living in little boxes which all look just the same, hippies – like the cosmopolitans of Weimar Germany – envisioned a society where everyone had the means to "do your own thing."

What had been special privileges to the depression-World War II generation became expected entitlements for their children. College education went from an exception to almost a norm with 13% having attended in 1940, 30% in 1970 and 48% in 1980.[15] However, students – even at elite universities, perhaps especially at elite universities – questioned where they were going and why they were doing it. At the University of Chicago and Columbia, students chanted: "Work, study, get ahead, kill!"[16] Part of the reason why such sentiments might be more prevalent at elite universities is their students had the luxury of knowing a secure professional job was waiting for them if ever they decided they wanted it. If they dropped out of the mainstream "straight" world, they could always drop back in. This gave them the time to question and reflect, with many choosing the liberal arts over more vocational majors, including a preference for pure science over engineering. With that luxury they could start to wonder what was their role within their society and their country's legitimate role within the world? Was it really necessary to destroy villages to save them? This would be less true for students more anxious about employment or living in less affluent times. Students, being nonchalant about a career and desiring to protest and challenge rather than earn money, might intensify the generation gap and breed resentment among parents who felt they sacrificed to provide their children with what they never had, as they insisted "We want the best for you." Magrass' father bitterly lamented:

> I think a college education is highly over-rated. All it does is give them wild ideas. If they had to work like we did, they wouldn't have the time to worry about what's wrong with the world.

The New Left: They Weren't Liberals

Like Magrass' father, many traditionalists had misgivings about the Vietnam War, but they were more anti-anti-war than anti-war. Even Mayor Richard Daley Sr., who encouraged the Chicago police to riot and bash the heads in of anti-war protesters during the 1968 Democratic convention, was privately against the war.[17] In 1972, when support for the war had really declined, President Richard Nixon carried 49 states against anti-war Democrat George McGovern. But there is survey data which suggests there actually was greater opposition to the war among the working class than the affluent and educated.[18] Just as most Germans supported Hitler's war until defeat was imminent, many traditionalists initially supported the Vietnam War but then turned against it when it was clear America would lose. However, these traditionalists felt their identity as patriotic Americans was threatened by cosmopolitans who suggested the war was more than a misguided decision by a generous nation who willingly sacrifices to assure the freedom and security of weaker peoples. Liberal opponents of the war considered it a well-intended mistake- a position, which eventually was shared by many conservatives and traditionalists.

In the 2000s, the real Left has been so marginalized that the media has led much of the population to believe "liberal" and "left" are synonyms, but we should speak of at least two Vietnam anti-war movements – a liberal and a Leftist one. In actuality, liberals have more in common with conservatives than Leftists on foreign policy because they accept the legitimacy of the American militaristic capitalist empire which Leftists do not. The liberal mainstream establishment included many of the very people who orchestrated the Vietnam War, but they changed their mind when they decided it was not winnable, too costly and no longer in American interests. These include Robert Kennedy, Vice President and Democratic presidential nominee Hubert Humphrey, billionaire Governor of New York and Vice President Nelson Rockefeller, President of American Motors and Governor of Michigan George Romney, Senator and Vice Presidential nominee Edmund Muskie, Generals James Gavin, David Shoup and Mathew Ridgway, Attorney General Ramsey Clark, Kennedy's court historian Arthur Schlesinger, and even President of Ford, President of the World Bank and Secretary of Defense Robert McNamara. The real Left peace movement insisted the war was not a mistake, stemming from a fundamentally sound policy carried out too zealously, but one of many examples of the brutal measures that the American militaristic capitalist empire would undertake to assure domination and guarantee that no one dare defy it. Leading voices within this movement include Noam Chomsky, Howard Zinn, Angela Davis, Dick Gregory, Tom Hayden, Joan Baez, Carl Oglesby and David Dellinger, who went to jail for refusing induction in World War II. About World War II, Dellinger explained: "I wasn't even tempted to pick up a gun to fight for General Motors, U.S. Steel, or the Chase Manhattan Bank, even if Hitler was running the other side."[19]

During Vietnam, he was, if anything, more adamant in his rejection of American patriotism and glory.

The way of life that destroyed Hiroshima and Nagasaki and is reported to have roasted alive a million people in Tokyo overnight is international and dominates every nation of the world, but we live in the United States, so our struggle is here. With this way of life, death would be more appropriate. There could be no truce or quarter. **The prejudices of patriotism, the pressures of our friends and fear of unpopularity and death should not hold us back any longer. It should be total war against the economic and political and social system which is dominant in this country.** The American system has been destroying human life in peace and in war, at home and abroad for decades. Now it has produced the growing infamy of atom bombing. Besides these brutal facts, the tidbits of democracy mean nothing. **Henceforth, no decent citizen owes one scrap of allegiance (if he ever did) to American law, American custom or American institutions.**[20]

To the real Left, the American invasion of Vietnam was a manifestation of a society controlled by a small corporate elite who orchestrated foreign and domestic policy to insure their continued wealth and power. Poverty, racial discrimination, militarism and imperialism were all symptoms of the same core cause. From the Left point of view, liberals were members, or at least allies, of that corporate elite, attempting to contain protest in ways which do not threaten the rich and powerful. Martin Luther King used the language of the Left when he turned against the war and called the United States' government "the greatest purveyor of violence in the world today." He charged:

> [it] again fell victim to the deadly Western arrogance that has poisoned the international atmosphere for so long. With that tragic decision we rejected a revolutionary government seeking self-determination and a government that had been established not by China – for whom the Vietnamese have no great love – but by clearly indigenous forces that included some communists . . . .
>
> The war in Vietnam is but a symptom of a far deeper malady within the American spirit . . .

> When machines and computers, profit motives and property rights, are considered more important than people, the giant triplets of racism, extreme materialism, and militarism are incapable of being conquered.[21]

King was clear that the capitalist system itself was designed to serve the corporate elite at the expense of everyone else – black and white – and it was at the root cause of almost of the problems with which he was concerned.

> Capitalism does not permit an even flow of economic resources. With this system, a small privileged few are rich beyond conscience, and almost all others are doomed to be poor at some level. That's the way the system works. And since we know that the system will not change the rules, we are going to have to change the system.[22]

King's Left assessment of the United States was very different from that of liberal critics like CBS News anchorman Walter Cronkite, once called "the most trusted man in America," but despised as a traitor by many traditionalists for what he said about Vietnam. Observing Cronkite and his traditionalist detractors, John Marciano pointed out:

> Cronkite did not come to "protest" the war, however, because it was a moral outrage and a violation of international law – an act of mind-numbing and staggering horror. It was simply not working out as planned; honor and pledges to defend democracy had nothing to do with it... In Cronkite's view, the war was a Noble Cause, fought by an "honorable" U.S. that, according to his editorial, had "[pledged] to defend democracy [in Vietnam]."[23]

Marciano quoted Cronkite:

> "[T]he only rational way out, then, will be to negotiate, not as victors, but as an honorable people who... did the best they could."[24]

The voice of the real Left was then loud enough that some leaders of the liberal establishment adopted its language. Among them was Cronkite's competitor, NBC news co-anchor David Brinkley. As the war progressed, he became more sympathetic with the younger side of the generation gap.

> It must be because this generation has grown up in a different world, is more skeptical, more doubting, fully aware it has often been lied to . . . And less than willing to fight when there is no need to fight, and die when there is no need to die, simply because some political figure says so . . . in this and other advanced countries young men can no longer be ordered to march into battle unless they are given some reasons, and the reasons are good ones . . . government itself . . . has become increasingly self-centered and arrogant. Hassling young people with the draft and an absurd war, hassling working people with an unfair tax system, and hassling the old with a pension system inadequate and unfair . . . No wonder one of the issues is the government itself . . . [N]ew American weapons cost more than what they are meant to destroy, which certainly is a breakthrough in weapons technology . . . [A]ll the working people in the United States, from the highest to the lowest income levels, for ten years, have paid all their income taxes to support the Pentagon. That is what we work for.[25]

Distrusting liberals like Cronkite and older Leftists like Communist Party USA, which had been crushed during the McCarthy purges, the young referred to themselves as the "New Left." Although they rejected American capitalism and considered American foreign policy fundamentally hypocritical and flawed, they felt the old American Left had been too apologetic for Stalin and the Soviet Union. Disavowing communism as authoritarian, manipulative, secretive and undemocratic, they shared a critique similar to Emma Goldman and Rosa Luxemburg. Embracing rather than shunning the generation gap, they proclaimed "Don't trust anyone over 30." Fifty years later, as most of the rebellious youth are about 70, that slogan does not seem to offer the most effective long-term strategy. Actually, many bonded with their professors as substitutes for their parents and considered old Left folk singers like Pete Seeger and Woody Guthrie, and Marxist refugees from Nazi Germany like Herbert Marcuse, mentors.

The dominant student organization within the New Left was Students for a Democratic Society (SDS). Originally, it was a loose federation, with few requirements for sharing ideology or activities as conditions for membership. To rally opposition to the war and galvanize that opposition into a mass movement demanding a radical transformation of American society, SDS organized teach-ins on college campuses around the country, supported draft resistance and sponsored anti-war marches which attracted tens of thousands of participants in cities like New York, Chicago, Boston, San Francisco and Los Angeles, and nation-wide gatherings converging on Washington, D.C.

A consensus emerged within SDS that universities do not produce objective value neutral knowledge, but train professionals and conduct research in service to the ruling corporate elite. Students demonstrated against the university itself, opposing the Reserve Officer Training Corp (ROTC), war-related research, and the welcoming on campus of recruiters for the military and for corporations producing weapons, like Dow Chemical. In April 1968, the Columbia chapter of SDS took over several buildings, effectively shutting the university down. When the university administration called the police, activity did not return to normal but instead erupted into a campus-wide student strike. The Columbia demonstration was followed by similar strikes and building take-overs on hundreds of campuses over the next several years.

By 1968, SDS had at least 350 chapters totaling at least 40,000 members, while the number who identified themselves with the New Left was much larger. Despite its success, SDS was becoming an organization reeking with internal problems. Its commitment to openness and tolerance and loose organizational structure made it possible for a small minority to speak indefinitely at meetings and seize control of the agenda. Supporters of Progressive Labor (PL), whom most of SDS regarded as authoritarian, dogmatic, manipulative and anti-democratic, used this opportunity and became so persistent, and some would say disruptive, that by 1969, it was almost impossible for SDS to function as a viable coalition. SDS dissolved into small fractions and ceased to lead the New Left as a unified organization. However, the New Left continued to grow for several years, including a 1970 national student strike which simultaneously shut down hundreds of campuses.

The mainstream media presented the national student strike as a protest against the killing of four students by national guard at Kent State University in Ohio, but the way it really started illustrates how the New Left actually functioned as spontaneous actions by inexperienced young students with little formal leadership and showed how effective they can be. Students were congregating in New Haven, Connecticut, and on the Yale campus for a demonstration as they learned President Nixon had further escalated the war and invaded Cambodia, with Princeton going out on strike in response. A few students from Brandeis with little movement leadership experience were bored and depressed. Somebody sighed, "Wouldn't it be nice if all the campuses in the country went out on strike." Most laughed and sighed, except somebody who said: "We have about two hours to kill before the rally. Why don't get a hold of a Yale chapel, print a leaflet to discuss a national student strike. Maybe a few people will show up. It will keep us busy." Half an hour later, they approached the chapel which they were going to use, but walked out. They thought they had come to wrong room; it was packed. Somebody said, "This is our meeting." Somebody else crawled to the center of the room and starting chairing. There was a vote for a national student strike with these demands:

1) The United States withdraw from Indo-China.
2) The United States release Bobby Seale [Chairman of the Black Panther Party, indicted for murder and earlier indicted for conspiracy to incite a riot when Mayor Daley released the Chicago police to attack demonstrators] and all other political prisoners and end political repression.
3) The universities end their complacency with the war machine.

By then, the rally had started. Rennie Davis (a former co-defendant of Seale's during the Chicago conspiracy trial; Seale, Davis and the six other defendants were referred to as the Chicago Eight) was speaking on national television. Someone from the meeting got to the podium and handed Davis its statement, which he then read to the crowd and effectively to the nation. Thousands of people raised their fists into the air and shouted STRIKE! STRIKE! STRIKE!

Dig the Vibe! Man

As in Weimar Germany, the New Left's rejection of the American militaristic capitalist empire's wars, economics, politics and environmental negligence was joined by hippies, cosmopolitan bohemians who saw themselves creating a counter-culture. Like Weimar artists who saw World War I as stemming from capitalist irrational rationality (CIR) run amuck, they ascribed the same root cause to Vietnam. While they usually rejected mainstream religions, most identified themselves as "spiritual" and believed individuals must look inside their own psyche and purge CIR from their beings.

While hippies and religious traditionalists were often enemies, they shared an embrace of the irrational as a source of truth and good. Many cosmopolitan counter-culturalists were skeptical of Western science for dismissing intuition and feeling, attempting to quantify reality, and regarding nature as an object rather than a living being. They saw science as acting as a handmaiden for militaristic capitalism, with partial responsibility for providing the weapons and mindset that justified adventures like Vietnam. Alienated from Western culture and its separation of mind from body, many pursued astrology or the occult, or turned to popularized versions of Buddhism and Hinduism, although few had knowledge of how they were actually practiced in the East. Some strove to attain what they called "cosmic oneness" where they attempted to transcend their individual identity and merge with what they considered to be a higher consciousness which unified the universe. In the words of Alan Watts, who helped popularize the concept, destruction comes "in the hands of people who do not realize that they are one and the same process as the universe."[26]

For all the hostility between hippies and traditionalists, Kurt Anderson – who regularly publishes in *The Atlantic* – has proposed the counter-culture laid the seeds for Donald Trump and others on the Right claiming there are "alternative truths" which make global climate change denial, Holocaust denial and rejecting evolution legitimate. By calling for intellectual anarchy, embracing the irrational and saying everyone is free to believe whatever they want, they undermined criteria to separate fact from falsehood and truth; consequently, truth rests not with whomever can offer logical or empirical validity but with whomever has the power to impose their version of reality.

> The first was a profound shift in thinking that swelled up in the '60s; since then, Americans have had a new rule written into their mental operating systems: Do your own thing, find your own reality, it's all relative . . . Mix epic individualism with extreme religion; mix show business with everything else; let all that ferment for a few centuries; then run it through the anything-goes '60s and the internet age. The result is the America we inhabit today, with reality and fantasy weirdly and dangerously blurred and commingled . . . The idea was to be radically tolerant of therapeutic approaches and understandings of reality, especially if they came from Asian traditions or from American Indian or other shamanistic traditions. Invisible energies, past lives, astral projection, whatever – the more exotic and wondrous and unfalsifiable, the better . . . the younger generation's "brave" rejection of expertise and "all that our culture values as 'reason' and 'reality.'" . . . During the '60s, large swaths of academia made a turn away from reason and rationalism as they'd been understood. Many of the pioneers were thoughtful, their work fine antidotes to postwar complacency. The problem was the nature and extent of their influence at that particular time, when all premises and paradigms seemed up for grabs. That is, they inspired half-baked and perverse followers in the academy, whose arguments filtered out into the world at large . . . Believe whatever you want, because pretty much everything is equally true and false.[27]

Religious traditionalist and cosmopolitan counter-culturalist may have shared skepticism over scientific and academic expertise, but they had very different lifestyles and visions of the good society. For some hippies, drugs – including marijuana, cocaine or LSD – became an integral part of their lifestyle, for reasons ranging from sociability, recreational pleasure and a belief that they led to deeper consciousness. Denouncing capitalist consumerism, they wore long hair, beards and casual clothes, which allowed mainstream media to stereotype them as dirty. The counter-culture was part of what was called the "sexual revolution" which made premarital sex socially acceptable and monogamy an option rather than morally obligatory, although in actual practice, jealousy was still common. Identifying traditional families as part of the "straight" world, they would say they lived in communes, but these were often little more than apartments with multiple roommates or off-campus dormitories. Wanting to return to nature, many urban cosmopolitans hippies moved to rural areas, but they seldom knew much about rural life and did not easily blend with their neighbors.

Hippies and the New Left overlapped, with some hippies engaged in political debates and activities, and others seeing politics of any sort as over-intellectualizing and participating in the very destructive culture they were trying to overcome. Idolized by many hippies, John Lennon (of the Beatles) saw himself as an anti-war activist, who spent his honeymoon with Japanese artist Yoko Ono naked in bed as a "peace-in" with the press invited to attend.[28] However, he shared a critique that many hippies had of the New Left: before you try to change the larger society, you must change your individual consciousness.

> You tell me it's the institution . . .
> You better free you mind instead . . .[29]

While some cosmopolitan counter-culturalists tried to completely withdraw from anything that could be construed as political, others saw the transformation of consciousness as a path to the transformation of society. Rather than avoiding politics, meditating and looking inward was their way of pursuing politics. Beat poet Allen Ginsberg, a mentor for hippies and a self-proclaimed Buddhist (actually a New York Jew) helped the Chicago Eight organize their demonstration. When subpoenaed to testify at their trial, he said:

> [W]hat we can do to solve the Vietnam war, to present different ideas for making the society more sacred and less commercial, less materialistic . . . as the population grew and as politics became more and more violent and chaotic . . . A gathering-together of younger people aware of the planetary fate that we are all sitting in the middle of, imbued with a new consciousness, a new kind of society involving prayer, music, and spiritual life together rather than competition, acquisition and war . . . There was what was called a "gathering of the tribes" of all the different affinity groups, spiritual groups, political group, yoga groups, music groups and poetry groups that all felt the same crisis of identity crisis of the planet and political crisis in America, who all came together in the largest assemblage of such younger people that had taken place since the war . . . people were involved in a life style that was intolerable to young folks, which involved brutality and police violence as well as a larger violence in Vietnam; . . . the planet Earth at the present moment was endangered by violence, overpopulation, pollution, ecological destruction brought about by our own greed.[30]

Ginsberg melded hippiedom and the New Left, as did many musicians. The most famous hippie gathering, where over 400,000 came to Woodstock, NY for "3 days of peace and music," merged music and politics, including Country Joe's Vietnam song

> [W]hat are we fightin for? Don't ask me, I don't give a damn, the next stop is Vietnam . . .
> [O]pen up the pearly gates. Well there ain't no time to wonder why . . . we're all gunna die.[31]

Violence: As American As Cherry Pie[32]
While the Beatles sang "All you need is love," the Rolling Stones sang "[T]he time is right for violent revolution."[33] At first most New Leftists leaned toward pacifism, but by the late 1960s, many endorsed violence.

There was a parallel debate within the black liberation movement which overflowed onto the young white Left, with Martin Luther King – a Marxist, a pacifist, but not a communist – the leading voice of one side, and Malcolm X and later the Black Panther Party, the dominant spokespeople for the other. King was convinced that violence was the tool of the racist capitalistic militaristic state and turning to violence would put the revolutionaries on the turf of the other side, where they were likely to lose. He shared a concern with Mahatma Gandhi, Rosa Luxemburg and Emma Goldman: a violent revolution, if successful, would create a violent society, little different from the one it was trying to overthrow.

> Violence as a way of achieving racial justice is both impractical and immoral. I am not unmindful of the fact that violence often brings about momentary results. Nations have frequently won their independence in battle. But in spite of temporary victories, violence never brings permanent peace.[34] . . . The limitation of riots, moral questions aside, is that they cannot win and their participants know it. Hence, rioting is not revolutionary but reactionary because it invites defeat. It involves an emotional catharsis, but it must be followed by a sense of futility.[35]

King was clear: pacifism did not mean passivity: "Freedom is never voluntarily given by the oppressor; it must be demanded by the oppressed."[36] With his commitment to non-violence, he was jailed, beaten, continually harassed by the FBI and other state security agencies, and finally assassinated. Despite this, many on the Left – both black and white – attacked King, just before his assassination, as an "Uncle Tom" – a weak counterrevolutionary patsy for whites. Malcolm X charged: "The White man pays Reverend Martin Luther King so that Martin Luther King can keep the Negro defenseless."[37]

For Malcolm X, violence was a sign of manhood, an intrinsic good, whether or not it served a utilitarian purpose, a glorious defense of honor similar to dueling among aristocrats, Southern planters or Aaron Burr and Alexander Hamilton. To be worthy of freedom and equality, you must be willing to fight for it, maybe kill and die for it. We can ask how different is this embracing of violence from traditionalists' craving for glory and war for war's sake.

> Nobody can give you freedom. Nobody can give you equality or justice or anything. If you're a man, you take it.[38] . . . If you're not ready to die for it, put the word "freedom" out of your vocabulary[39] . . . It's hard for anyone intelligent to be nonviolent. Everything in the universe does something when you start playing with his life, except the American Negro. He lays down and says, "Beat me, daddy."[40] . . . Be peaceful, be courteous, obey the law, respect everyone; but if someone puts his hand on you, send him to the cemetery.[41]

Soon after Malcolm X's assassination by fellow Black Muslims, the Black Panthers became the model of revolutionary sheik, for white students as well as ghetto blacks. Non-violence, embodied in Martin Luther King, had lost its hipness. It took too long and was too frustrating. There was a need for immediate action and results. The Weatherman – a violent splinter group formed after SDS dissipated – declared the Panthers the vanguard of the revolution and all white radicals were expected to follow their lead and accept their pronouncements as the "correct line." You had to show the Panthers you were revolutionaries. One Panther declared when he visited Brandeis: "When I come back here next year, I don't want to see a beautiful campus. I want to see rubble." At rallies, former pacifists cheered when they heard "You white students have shown you can march, but can you kill. I want to see if you can kill." "Go Left! Go Right! Go pick up the gun." Only a tiny number actually did pick up guns, but they were acclaimed as heroes by some former pacifists who were intimidated in accepting that pausing to think, consider consequences and sticking to non-violence showed a lack of revolutionary discipline and more important, a lack of machismo, honor and glory.

We [Magrass and Derber] knew Susan Saxe, one the few who actually picked up a gun. She participated in a bank robbery in which a policeman was killed. She was then placed on the FBI's "most wanted list." Like several of the Weatherman, she would say she had to do something to prove she was not simply playing a game. She had to do something irreversible to force her to commit her life to the revolution. What that act was, what purpose it would serve or consequence it would produce, was less important that it was something dramatic – violence for violence sake.

The fear of being labeled counterrevolutionary squelched debate and pressured Leftists into either sprouting slogans they felt uncomfortable with or leaving the movement altogether and becoming apolitical, some seeking mainstream careers or some taking a more hippiesque personal psychological approach to liberation through transforming yoga, meditation or drugs into a "touchy feely" lifestyle. Many sought jobs in the school system or in social services.

Violence is glorious and cathartic. It creates a sense that you are not out for fun; you are a committed revolutionary, even if it is self-destructive. Once you turn to violence, it is irreversible. There is no turning back. It is also a way separating those who blindly follow from those who will insist upon thinking for themselves. Violence requires discipline. It entails military-like hierarchies, even among tiny factions. It destroys visions of egalitarianism or open debate.

The whole Left and counter-culture became deeply divided as more splinter groups and parties, black and white, like Progressive Labor, the Weatherman, the Spartacus and the October League – each claiming to be the vanguard – emerged. Different parties accused each other of being wimpy or counter-revolutionary. Nixon, the FBI, the CIA, the military and Ronald Reagan could not has asked for better allies for discrediting, in fact destroying, the Left. Very likely, many who tried to provoke random violence were government agents. In a Santa Barbara (California) commune where Magrass lived, someone showed up and offered karate lessons so his students would be capable of fighting for the revolution. A year later, he led a police raid of the commune. Even if agents did ignite violence, putting the blame on them is too easy. It exempts the sincere Leftists from responsibility for following them and allowing themselves to succumb to their enticement. As we study "glory causes," we must consider why violence is so attractive even for people on the Left or in the counter-culture. Otherwise, this risks becoming a history that might repeat itself.

Support Our Troops; Bring Them Home
Whether they applauded violence or shunned it, most New Leftists – but not liberals – shared Martin Luther King's assessment that the Vietnam War was a symptom of the essence of the American militaristic empire. They did not believe any of America's objectives in Vietnam were legitimate. They wanted peace, but that could only be achieved through a revolution – violent or nonviolent – against a militaristic empire. While they knew complete American withdrawal from Vietnam would result in an NLF victory, they nonetheless demanded it. At marches and rallies, many chanted, "Ho! Ho! Ho Chi Minh! NLF is going to win" and "One side's right and one's side wrong. We're on the side of the Vietcong." Rather than seeing the Vietnam War as a glorious cause or an honorable mistake, they considered it an atrocity comparable to Nazi war crimes. To emphasize the similarity between the United States and Nazi Germany, they spelled AmeriKa with a K. The best thing that could happen for the world, including the American people, would be for the United States elite and military to lose their war in Vietnam. Like Germans who resisted Hitler, they could be seen as traitors from the point of view of the ruling oligarchs. They were maligned as cowards, with no sense of glory, unwilling to fight and die for their country. Just as Germans fled their country rather than serve Hitler, about 100,000 sought asylum in Canada or Sweden as they refused to be drafted in the American war machine.[42] The traditionalist right attacked them as cowards, not only betraying their country but also the troops who were sacrificing and dying instead of them. Many veterans of the New Left insist the "stab in the back" claim is similar to one the Nazis made about World War I and is an attempt by the security establishment to scapegoat the Left for a war which they lost. But either the anti-war movement was completely ineffective or else it was a factor in forcing the US to leave Vietnam. This would give a degree of legitimacy to the "stab in the back" thesis, but it should be something New Left veterans should be proud of, not quiver from. Again we must ask the same question we asked

when we discussed Nazi Germany: is treason against an immoral regime and an immoral war moral or immoral?

Many non-commissioned soldiers saw the anti-war movement not as traitors, but as comrades. Divisions among the troops was so profound that there was something approaching a civil war within the military itself with potential mutiny on the frontline, and that may have been a consideration in the decision to withdraw from Vietnam. Rifts on the frontline were comparable to German soldiers in World War I. There were many gung-ho patriotic troops who were committed to kill and die to preserve America's honor and show the world that no one dare challenge the greatest democracy in world history. They despised liberals and well as the New Left, who they were convinced were "stabbing them in the back." However, there were others who wondered why they were there, turned against the war effort and were grateful to the peace protestors for telling the world how meaningless what they were going through was.

> During the Vietnam era, there were approximately 10 million men in uniform. Among those in uniform, 563,000 received less-than-honorable discharges (including 34,000 who were imprisoned during court-martial). There were 1,500,000 AWOL and 550,000 desertion incidents . . . The rate of AWOL offenses incidents increased as the war dragged on, ranging from 38.2 per 1,000 men in 1968 to 84.0 in 1971. The desertion rate ranged from 8.4 per 1,000 in 1966 to 33.9 per 1,000 in 1971 . . . Added to this were escalating problems associated with substance abuse, petty and serious acts of sabotage, and assaults on officers and other cadre.[43]

Three soldiers who refused deployment to Vietnam were sentenced to two years in the stockade. At their trial, one declared:

> We have been in the army long enough to know that we are not the only GIs who feel as we do. Large numbers of men in the service either do not understand this war or are against it . . . We have made our decision. We will not be part of this unjust, immoral

and illegal war. We want no part of this war of extermination. We oppose the criminal waste of American lives and resources. We refuse to go to Vietnam.[44]

Returning veterans organized Vietnam Veterans Against the War. Its spokesperson, John Kerry, testified before the US Senate:

[O]ver 150 honorably discharged, and many very highly decorated, veterans testified to war crimes committed in Southeast Asia. These were not isolated incidents but crimes committed on a day-to-day basis with the full awareness of officers at all levels of command . . . They relived the absolute horror of what this country, in a sense, made them do. They told stories that at times they had personally raped, cut off ears, cut off heads, taped wires from portable telephones to human genitals and turned up the power, cut off limbs, blown up bodies, randomly shot at civilians, razed villages in fashion reminiscent of Ghengis Khan, shot cattle and dogs for fun, poisoned food stocks, and generally ravaged the countryside of South Vietnam . . . How do you ask a man to be the last man to die for a ***mistake***?[45] [our emphasis]

Later, as a senator himself, Kerry voted for the American invasion of Iraq and ran for president as a war hero, while his opponent, George W. Bush Jr., reminded the American people of his anti-war treachery. Kerry began his acceptance speech at the Democratic Convention with a military salute as he announced: "I'm John Kerry, and I'm reporting for duty." Sitting behind him was a row of Vietnam veterans, whom he referred to as "brothers" as he declared, in very different language from his testimony before the Senate 34 years earlier:

Our band of brothers doesn't march together because of who we are as veterans, but because of what we learned as soldiers . . . We fought for this nation because we loved it . . . We may be a little older, we may be a little grayer, but we still know how to fight for our country. . . . [W]e're here tonight united in one purpose to make America stronger at home and respected in the world... Tonight, I am home... where our nation's history was written in blood.[46]

Many peace protesters harbored hostility toward soldiers, with some holding contradictory feelings, torn between seeing them as murderers or victims. During his draft physical, Arlo Guthrie told the psychiatrist, hoping it would get him labeled crazy and thus exempt, "Shrink, I want to kill. I want to kill! I want to see blood and gore and guts and veins in my teeth!" But instead he heard, "You're our boy."[47] One popular chant while Lyndon Johnson was still president was "Hey! Hey! LBJ! How many kids did you kill today?" with "kids" referring to both Vietnam children killed in bombings and young American soldiers sacrificed in the rice paddies.

> Protestors massed outside the White House at all hours. They circled alongside the fence, carrying signs reading "Stop the War," "Bring the GIs Home Now," and "We Mourn Our Soldiers, They Are Dying in Vain.[48]"

Whatever frontline soldiers felt about war protestors, New Leftists saw themselves as struggling to rescue the troops. In solidarity with conscripted soldiers, peace activists built coffee houses near military bases.

> They were places soldiers could go for support and to get organized and were part of the huge groundswell of anti-war resistance in the military that saw mutinies, fragging of officers and a mass campaign against the draft.[49]

For some Vietnam era soldiers, the coffee houses were more welcoming than the larger society. Many felt they had sacrificed for their country's glorious cause and expected to be cheered as heroes like veterans of the world wars and the Civil War, but there were fewer pubic celebrations honoring them. Often, they suffered from post-traumatic stress syndrome, felt isolated, faced unemployment or homelessness, but many did not feel they were getting the services they believed they should be entitled to. Again, we do not want to understate the antagonism between soldiers and anti-war protesters. There are stories of deep hatred with demonstrators spitting on returning Vietnam veterans, but sociologist Jerry Lembcke investigated and could not find a single documented case. Contrary to the commonly accepted image, he discovered Vietnam veterans actually faced more hostility from rightwing traditionalists who could not forgive them for losing. World War veterans were especially unwelcoming with the reaction: We won our war; Why couldn't you prove yourself and win yours?

> [T]he spit almost always flew from pro-war right-wingers onto anti-war activists . . . these reports could have gotten invented and turned into stories of the opposite having occurred. There were also actual incidents of Vietnam veterans being treated abusively, but in all the documentable cases it was pro-war people who were the abusers[50] . . . some veterans of previous wars not only did not embrace Vietnam veterans . . . for having lost the first war in American history. The behavior of these superpatriotic veterans actually provided grist for the myth that Vietnam veterans were spat upon.[51]

If Vietnam War troops were "stabbed in the back," it was not by anti-war leftwingers alone. Richard Nixon, one of the original architects of the Vietnam War, advocated US intervention as early as the battle of Dien Bien Phu. However, in 1968 he was in danger of losing his second attempt to become president and the opportunity to end the war "honorably" if it was settled before the election. He had his representatives approach America's puppet, South Vietnam, and, with a promise that he would not concede as much to the communists as Johnson, urged them to stymie the peace negotiations until he was in the White House, where he dragged the war on for another five years with 21,000 more American deaths during his reign.[52] For all the outrage over Trump's possibly receiving foreign help – Russian – in seeking the Presidency, what Nixon did was at least comparable, if not worse. Lyndon Johnson reacted in a private conversation "This is treason."[53]

In 1968, Nixon ran for the White House with a "secret plan" to end the war, one that he could not share with the American people whose trust and vote he was asking for. Some analysts – many of them of the Left – interpret this to mean that voters considered Nixon a peace candidate and his vote represented opposition to the war, but it was clear to anyone who listened, he was running as a victory candidate, with a promise of an "honorable" peace. He did not challenge Johnson's goals in Vietnam, only his tactics, and possibly his commitment. If anything, he thought Johnson was being "squishy soft" and he would be more aggressive in beating the Vietnamese in submission.

As president, Nixon justified continuing the war by insisting he needed to assure the release of the Prisoners of War (POW). The traditionalist Right – some of them, his supports and some of them thinking even he was being too squishy and too willing to sell the troops out for peace – orchestrated a campaign to honor the POW- MIA (Missing in Acton) through victory. They designed a flag which, as of now, still flies in virtually every public building in the United States. It represents essentially the same "stabbed in the back" thesis as Hitler's swastika. Since Vietnam, the cry has been "support the troops," a discourse that liberals and even many Leftists dare not challenge. Support the troops does not mean bring them home, rescue them from the horrors of war. If you support the troops, you must embrace the cause for which they are fighting and possibly dying. You must be committed to victory, the only outcome that will vindicate their sacrifice. Perhaps tactics can be debated, but the ultimate objective cannot be.

Saving America From Americans

Nixon was clear: just as Hitler was convinced that Germans as the master race could only be defeated by Germans, America was the greatest nation in the history of the world and it could only be vanquished if it lost its will and failed to purge itself of cosmopolitans who were sapping its greatness.

> Let us understand: North Vietnam cannot defeat or humiliate the United States. Only Americans can do that.[54]

Like in World War I, what Nixon rationally hoped to achieve in Vietnam was less important than that withdrawal would convey an image of a nation without honor. Once it has committed itself, whether that commitment be wise or not, it must pursue victory for victory's sake. America must show the world and itself that no one can dare mess with it.

> A nation cannot remain great if it betrays its allies and lets down its friends . . . Our defeat and humiliation in South Vietnam without question would promote recklessness in the councils of those great powers . . . Far more dangerous, we would lose confidence in ourselves. . . . inevitable remorse and divisive recrimination would scar our spirit as a people . . . I know it may not be fashionable to speak of patriotism or national destiny these days. But I feel it is appropriate to do so on this occasion . . . Today we have become the strongest and richest nation in the world. And the wheel of destiny has turned so that any hope the world has for the survival of peace and freedom will be determined by whether the American people have the moral stamina and the courage to meet the challenge of free world leadership[55] . . . I'm not going to be the first American president to lose a war.[56]

Nixon knew the American people were behind him because he heard the "silent majority," the traditionalists:

In his acceptance speech at the 1968 Republican convention, Nixon offered this rallying call:

> We see Americans hating each other; fighting each other; killing each other at home . . .
>
> Did American boys die in Normandy, and Korea, and in Valley Forge for this? . . .
>
> It is another voice. It is the quiet voice in the tumult and the shouting.
>
> It is the voice of the great majority of Americans, the forgotten Americans – the non-shouters; the non-demonstrators . . .

> They provide most of the soldiers who died to keep us free.
> They give drive to the spirit of America.
> They give lift to the American Dream.[57]

Nixon's vice president, Spiro Agnew, was even more vehement in dividing the traditionalists from the cosmopolitans. He belittled the cosmopolitans.

> A spirit of national masochism prevails, encouraged by an effete corps of impudent snobs who characterize themselves as intellectuals. In the United States today, we have more than our share of the nattering nabobs of negativism.[58]

When Nixon prophesized that defeat in Vietnam would free other countries to challenge American dominance, he had a point. The war exposed the United States as the paper tiger Mao Tse Tung, founder of the People's Republic of China, said it was. Vietnam had been selected largely as a test case to show third countries what would happen if they risk defying America and what it showed was that if they have enough will, they can win. America's loss in Vietnam coincided with the beginning of its relative economic decline. With politicians fearful of raising taxes in the midst of an unpopular war, the conflict produced rampant inflation. European and Japanese industries were now in a position to outcompete American. Middle Eastern oil sheikdoms formed OPEC (Organization of Petroleum Exporting Countries). From the 1920s through the 1960s, Western oil companies like Esso, Mobil and Shell could treat Middle Eastern oil almost like their private property. Around the time of the American defeat in Vietnam, OPEC began to demand much higher payments. The result was a direct assault on the lifestyle dependent upon cheap oil to which Americans had been accustomed. By the late 1970s, there were mile-long lines to get gas, if you could get gas at all.

There was a malaise throughout the country, largely stemming from a sense that the government and the 1% did not really care about the 99%. On the factory floor, this resulted in "Monday morning cars," made by workers who came in drunk from the weekend. With American workmanship deteriorating, even the American people preferred foreign goods.

With their profits declining, American industrial corporations became less willing to offer the high wages and secure employment to which their workers had become accustomed. They broke their accommodation with the unions and deemed American workers lazy and greedy. Third World dictators opened their country for factories with low wages, few regulations, low environmental standards and minimal worker protections. American corporations could say to their employees, "If you won't work on our terms, we can just close the factory and move to other countries. You'll be out on the street and we'll keep making money." Real wages fell to the point that it was no longer possible to keep a middleclass lifestyle on one income. The American dream seemed to be turning into a nightmare.

The question then was: who was to blame? Although it was the corporate elite who were closing the factory, white working-class traditionalists were told that uppity blacks were lazy and wanted their jobs, which they were stealing through government policies like affirmative action. Their taxes were going not to pay for genocidal wars like Vietnam, but to support lazy parasites through welfare. Their enemy was not the military branch of the state or the corporate rich, but the social service branch of the government, the very poor receiving state benefits – especially blacks, hippies and overeducated cosmopolitan elitists. It is important to emphasis that for traditionalists, the word "elite" referred to cosmopolitans: academics, the media, especially Hollywood and professionals in state social services, not the corporate rich.

As we already pointed out, reactions to the war in Vietnam among the working class were multi-layered, with opposition growing as defeat seemed imminent, like in Germany in World War II. Lower class people were less likely to appear at demonstrations or join the anti-war movement than wealthy cosmopolitans, whose children were less likely to be drafted because college students were exempt. Unlike affluent highly educated activists, working class traditionalists did not view the war as a moral failing, but rather a waste of lives, money and resources. Whatever they thought of the war, working people resented affluent youth who protested from the comfortable luxury of the college campus or the countercultural commune, who were seen as unpatriotic "dirty hippies," contemptuous of American values and typical American lifestyles. They felt unappreciated as they struggled to provide for their families while their sons – not the children of the affluent – faced hardship, maybe even death in Vietnam, much like many of them sacrificed in the world wars. The rulers, especially the Nixon regime, presented their militaristic capitalist leaders as allies against treacherous but privileged hippies and radicals, who were undermining the fiber of American life and the morale of the troops, who chanted "Ho! Ho! Ho-Chi-Minh!" and were denying the troops the victory their sacrifice had earned.

Lacking the knowledge and resources to evade the draft which their affluent counterparts had, poorer youth often felt they had to patriotically support a war when they had no choice but to fight in it. Many lower class frontline soldiers and veterans bitterly resented privileged people who protested against a war they were able to evade fighting, whom they perceived as ungrateful, turning against the nation that gave them freedom, opportunity and security – benefits denied the very working class people who were forced to endure hardships, continents away, to win these rights for people who did not appreciate them and, in fact, held them in contempt.

Occasionally working-class hostility toward protesters turned violent. In 1970,

> New York City construction workers turned out in the streets in a frenzy of "jingoistic joy" aimed against war protestors ... The protests began when brightly helmeted construction workers, many wielding their heavy tools, pushed through a weak line of police and violently descended on an anti-war demonstration ... The workers' goal, besides venting their rage, was to raise a flag lowered to half mast ... They then proceeded to storm the steps of City Hall, chasing student protestors through the streets of the financial district, and bloodying about seventy people in the process.[59]

Seeing both the civil rights movement and the Vietnam anti-war movement as intertwined and orchestrated by cosmopolitan enemies, if not communists, Alabama Governor George Wallace spread his appeal to traditionalists to all 50 states. In 1968, he ran for president promising "these college professors who are making speeches advocating victory for the Viet Cong Communists – I would deal with these people as they ought to be dealt with, as traitors."[60]

As he moved his campaign up north, he spoke before a crowd of 16,000 in Madison Square Garden, New York. He addressed one long-haired male protester: "'Hey there, sweetie . . . Oh, excuse me, . . . I thought you were a girl.' . . . If you'll just sit down, I'll drown 'em out . . . all he needs is a good haircut." He continued before his more sympathetic traditionalist audience.

> Our system is under attack: the property system, the free enterprise system, and local government. Anarchy prevails today in the streets of the large cities of our country, making it unsafe for you to even go to a political rally here in Madison Square Garden, and that is a sad commentary. Both national parties in the last number of years have kowtowed to every anarchist that has roamed the streets . . . Mr. Nixon and Mr. Humphrey, [vice president and Democratic nominee for president] both three or four weeks ago, called for the passage of a bill on the federal level that would require you to sell or lease your own property to whomsoever they thought you ought to lease it to. [Blacks, reference to civil rights equal housing legislation] I say that when Mr. Nixon and Mr. Humphrey succumb to the blackmail of a few anarchists in the streets who said we're going to destroy this country . . . Yes, the pseudo-intellectuals and the theoreticians . . . have looked down their nose long enough at the average man on the street: the pipe-fitter, the communications worker, the fireman, the policeman, the barber, the white collar worker.[61]

Some on the far right charge the New Left, the sexual revolution and the counter-culture were orchestrated by German Jewish Marxist refugees from Nazi Germany who, after being defeated when the Weimar Republic fell, came to America. Prominent among them were members of the Frankfort School, especially Herbert Marcuse, who inspired the New Left and manipulated American youth to undermine the United States and help them impose their communist vision upon the country.

> Germany can be seen as a trial run or dress rehearsal for the Sexual Revolution of the 1960s, a revolution in attitudes and behavior that was to convulse America and then spread like a moral virus to Europe and the rest of the world . . . These cultural Marxists . . . were revolutionaries intent on complete social control by the imposition of their Marxist worldview on the rest of society . . . With Jewish intellectuals like this at the helm, doing their utmost to promote moral anarchy . . . is it any wonder that the Germans went helter-skelter? . . . They would turn race against race (engineered ethnic conflict), parent against child (attack on authority), and man against woman (radical feminism).[62]

Just as the extreme polarization of Weimar Germany brought the German bourgeoisie and Junkers to reluctantly turn to the Nazis, the American corporate elite feared a situation they could not control. Someone Wallace-like from the right could gain enough popular support to become America's Hitler or the Left protest movements could successfully prevent the American militaristic capitalist elite from ruling as they chose. David Rockefeller, CEO of Chase Manhattan Bank, was convinced that America was no longer capable of being the sole world police force and it should share the burden with the Western European and Japanese upper class. In the name of "realism," he formed the Trilateral Commission, composed of state and corporate leaders from the three centers. Among the Trilateral Commission's concerns were that "excessive democracy" and "democratic distemper" was impeding capital accumulation and therefore could no longer be afforded. They solicited Harvard professor Samuel Huntington to write a report who found

> There are potentially desirable limits to the extension of political democracy ... the governability of democracy is dependent upon the sustained expansion of the economy. ... A program is necessary to lower the job expectations of those who receive a college education.[63]

Overly entitled citizens were demanding that state and corporate policies reflect their needs and were becoming less willing to entrust decision making authority to an elite core. They were expecting higher wages and better social services at a time when the overall rate of economic growth was declining and the international bourgeoisie felt it needed more capital for retooling. No longer was there a sufficiently supportive consensus to allow foreign policy experts to coordinate the protection and expansion of the American empire without public scrutiny. To combat the public taking too seriously its sense of entitlement, autonomy and political potency, the Trilateral Commission recommended lowering expectations and reducing education levels.

America's Savior: Ronald Reagan

Jimmy Carter, his vice president, Walter Mondale, and George H.W. Bush Sr. were members of the Trilateral Commission, but not California Governor and former Hollywood actor Ronald Reagan. In previous chapters, we noted that a sector of capitalists could be considered cosmopolitans; some could be called liberals but they would want to restrain the Leftists and hippies. Since before the Civil War up to the Civil Rights era, Southern traditionalists had been deeply suspicious of monopoly capitalists, especially if based in Wall Street, seeing them as profiting from Southern depression and wanting to undermine the natural order along with Southern values and traditions. However, traditionalism breeds patriotism and respect for authority. Just as Hitler was brought in to crush the Weimar Left and bohemia, perhaps someone who could effectively appeal to traditionalists might offer an anecdote to democratic distemper, ideally someone less abrasive than George Wallace who could attract a larger base and have more respectability in the North. That role fell on Ronald Reagan.

If you listed to Reagan's rhetoric, he would sound pretty harsh, but he was perceived, especially by the media, as having a smooth reassuring charismatic style. Some corporate capitalists worried that Reagan could accelerate the unraveling of the social consensus that adhered since Roosevelt's New Deal and World War II, but it was collapsing anyway and perhaps Reagan could create a new accord. German capitalists thought they could let Hitler come to power, but then control him. The results were disastrous. They made similar assumptions about Reagan, but appear to have been correct. People who nostalgically insist Reagan was more conciliatory than Trump seem to have forgotten who Reagan was. Reagan defeated California Governor Edmund Brown Sr., the very governor who trounced Nixon, by promising to destroy the campus radical Left. He pledged "to clean up the mess at Berkeley" and eliminate "a small minority of hippies, radicals and filthy speech advocates." They will "be taken by the scruff of the neck and thrown off campus – permanently.[64]" Comparing them to Vietnamese communists, he declared: "If it takes a bloodbath, let's get it over with. No more appeasement."[65] During a strike at San Francisco State College, he wrote the chancellor of the campus,

> How far do we go in tolerating these people & this trash under the excuse of academic freedom & freedom of expression? ... Hasn't the time come to take on those neurotics in our faculty group and lay down some rules of conduct for the students comparable to what we'd expect in our own families?[66]

Hitler promised that never again would Germany lose a war; Reagan made the same commitment to America. Implying Nixon had not brutal enough in Vietnam, he would cure the "Vietnam syndrome," a disease that saps America of its will.

> For too long, we have lived with the Vietnam syndrome. This is a lesson for all of us in Vietnam. If we are forced to fight, we must have the means and determination to prevail, or we will not have what it takes to secure peace. And . . . we will never again ask young men to fight and possibly die in a war our government is afraid to let them win.[67]

When he ran for president, Reagan insisted it was no time for "doom and gloom" and he would combat the sense that America's best days were behind it. It would be "morning in America" and he would "make America great again,"[68] the exact same slogan Trump borrowed as the theme for his campaign. As we already pointed out, Reagan accomplished something very unlikely, building an alliance between traditionalists and corporate capitalists. He would adopt the neoclassical-neoliberal economics of Ayn Rand and Alan Greenspan but make it attractive to white traditionalists by reminding them it punishes parasites and "those people" and promising to restore individual initiative – the sense that you're on your own – and morality. As he planned to nearly double the military budget, he harangued against "big government" which virtually everyone understood to mean state social services.

> In this present crisis, government is not the solution to our problem, government IS the problem. It isn't so much that liberals are ignorant, it's just that they know so much that isn't so.[69]

In thinly disguised racist language, he promised to reign in "welfare queens" who would no longer be permitted to mooch, lie around, watch television and have babies. Decoded, the fundamental equation of Reaganism is:

> Government = Welfare = the N word.

When Reagan was governor of California, his superintendent of public schools, Max Rafferty, was convinced that the education system must combat "secular humanists" who were undermining the moral fiber of the young. They were cosmopolitan atheists who believed individuals should be free to choose their own ethical values and lifestyles rather than submit to Divinely dictated principles. He sponsored a report that recommended

> Our schools should have no hesitancy in teaching about religion. We urge our teachers to make clear the contributions of religion . . .

> We want the children of California to be aware of the spiritual principles and the faith which undergird our way of life . . . [We] express our profound concern for the lack of self-discipline being displayed by the motion picture industry, television, and the public media – in general, on matters of decency and morals. . . . This moral crisis is reflected in the increased use of drugs at colleges as well as increased sexual promiscuity and illegitimate births and incredible increases crimes of violence, especially among teenagers. It was the consensus of the committee that such a moral crisis is at root a spiritual crises . . . the moral laws which govern mankind remain constant.[70]

While Nixon heard the "silent majority," Reagan won the support of the "Moral Majority." Organized by Jerry Falwell, it was intended to combat a "vocal minority of ungodly men and women [plotting] to bring America to the brink of death." He was convinced

> [t]he decay in our public school system suffered an enormous acceleration when prayer and Bible readings were taken out of the classroom by the U.S. Supreme Court. Our public school system is now permeated with humanism. . . . In the Christian schools, education begins with God. The objectives are based upon biblical principles, with God as the center of every subject. The philosophies taught stand as witness to society, as the ultimate goal, not as a reflection of man's sinful nature. In science, the student learns God's plan for the universe. In history, God's plan for the ages; and in civics, God's requirement of loyalty and support for the government He has ordained.[71]

Falwell's associate Tim LaHaye, California Chairman of the Moral Majority, co-authored the *Left Behind* series that sold over 65 million copies. According to LaHaye

> surveys reveal that the higher a person has advanced in education, the more likely he is to be atheistic . . . No humanist is qualified to hold any governmental office in America . . . If you received Jesus

Christ as your saviour and Lord, it is clear who you are: You are a child of God and a servant of God. The why has likewise been revealed: Your purpose on earth is to serve Him.[72]

If the Moral Majority's agenda had been fully implemented, the United States would have transformed into an Evangelical Protestant's image of a Christian commonwealth, where even liberal Protestants and Catholics, to say nothing of Jews, Moslems, Buddhist and atheists, would not feel they comfortably belonged. Obviously, this has not happened but Reagan's appeal to the Christian Right allowed him to form a ruling coalition. Although Reagan was elected by two landslides, the worldview of the Christian Right is extremely polarizing. Like fascism, it could rule by galvanizing a critical mass without attracting the broad majority, in fact, repelling much of the population. It is meaningless, perhaps even absurd, to people who do not have faith in the Jesus of fundamentalist Protestantism as an active God who governs the universe and intervenes routinely in human affairs. It is based in the irrational, a truth that is not grounded in science, observation and reason, but will be revealed to a select few who intuit it in their gut. Only they are fit to rule and only those who accept their authority are fit to be true Americans.

The New Deal is Dead; Long Live the New Beginning

Reaganism united traditionalists within the middle and working class with the corporate elite but it actually offered few rational material benefits to members of the 99%. As of 2019, it has been the ruling paradigm for nearly 40 years, with the Democratic regimes of Bill Clinton and Obama temporarily softening it but not fundamentally changing it. With a promise of a "New Beginning," Reaganism offered traditionalists within the 99% a sense that they could be part of a glorious great and moral nation, that would be admired and feared by the rest of the world. Reagan would stand up against treacherous parasites within America's midst, both poor and cosmopolitan, who were "dissing" them and undermining the nation's will and moral fiber. Reagan succeeded in moving the political spectrum way to the right with liberalism, formerly the mainstream, recast as the "L" word and the real Left pushed off the edge, at least until the Bernie Sanders campaign. Few would now dare speak of the militaristic capitalist empire itself as the integrated root cause of almost all political-economic problems. Almost everyone would cower from appearing unpatriotic or a hint that they did not "support the troops." Supporting the troops permitted questioning if specific military interventions were misguided and not in American interests, but it did not allow suggesting the American militaristic capitalist empire is the most destructive force in the world today and must be fought on every level. Although the invasions of Iraq and Afghanistan provoked opposition, they did not inspire an anti-war movement comparable to Vietnam. The Left – if we now can even use that word – shifted its emphasis from resisting the militaristic capitalist system itself to identity politics, which rather than challenging the empire, worked to bring women, racial and sexual minority onto corporate boards and the frontline of war – a demand for equal opportunity body bags.

One victory of the New Left and the counter-culture was "child-centered" education which emphasized critical thinking and questioning authority rather than rote memorizing and indoctrination in the inherent superiority of American-Christian civilization. It was introduced largely by cosmopolitan former New Leftists and hippies who entered the school system when they decided to pursue professional careers. The Reaganesque response was to bring schools "back to basics," following prescribed curricula with routine standardized testing of students and penalizing teachers who did not conform. One strong advocate of this was Lynne Cheney, wife of Secretary of Defense and Vice President Richard Cheney, and herself Chair of the National Endowment for the Humanities during the Reagan and Bush Sr. presidencies. Alarmed that multi-cultural child-centered education was undermining patriotism and support for military adventurism, she wrote sarcastically:

> As American students learn more about the faults of this country and about the virtues of other nations, . . . they will be less and less likely to think this country deserves their special support. They will not respond to calls to use American force, and thus

we will be delivered from the dark days of the early 1990s, when President George Bush was able to unify the nation in support of war against Iraq, and be able to return to the golden days of the late 1960s and early 1970s, when no president was able to build support for Vietnam.[73]

Within two weeks of Bush Sr. initiating his Iraqi war, there was a march of 500,000 protestors.

Despite Reagan's pledge to honor Vietnam veterans

> [h]is first act in office was to freeze hiring in the veterans "Readjustment Counseling Program." He soon moved to eliminate all Vietnam veteran outreach programs, including an employment-training program for disabled veterans.[74]

After Reagan, veterans routinely faced poverty, lack of services, unemployment and homelessness. Until then, homelessness was rare but then it became commonplace along with hunger and malnutrition. Programs to foster the health of poor school children, like school lunches, were routed. The Reagan regime declared ketchup to be a nutritionally adequate vegetable. As the welfare roles contracted, prisons expanded. Prisons became the new welfare. Under Reagan, the prison population went from 329,000 in 1980 to 627,00 in 1988;[75] by 2018, it was about 2.3 million, the highest in the world.[76] Most were jailed as victims in a "war on drugs." The motive for replacing welfare with prisons was not to save money. In 1985, it cost about $16,000[77] annually to keep someone in jail, but AFDC provided a family about $4,200 a year.[78] The reason was to change a palatable system to a punitive one and make dependency so distasteful that almost anyone would try to avoid it.

Despite Reaganism galvanizing support among the traditionalist 99%, they rationally received few economic benefits. Almost all accrued to the top 1%. Average income for the highest 10% is 40 times greater than the other 90%. For the top 0.1%, income increased 7.5 times since 1973.[79] Reagan claimed that cutting taxes for corporations would stimulate investment and cause the economic pie to grow and wealth to "trickle down." There were no conditions on Reagan's corporate tax cuts and deregulations and thus no real incentive to invest the windfalls in the American domestic economy. Rather than using them to rebuild industry in the United States, corporations used them to close down factories, displace workers and build plants in Mexico, Singapore and the Philippines. Infrastructure was dismantled, not updated. Unions were threatened to choose between lower wages, benefits and security or bordered up plants. Often even when the unions acquiesced, the factories still closed. Former thriving metropolises like Detroit became depressed shells of abandoned buildings with rampart poverty, crime and drug addiction. Reagan, who had once been head of the Screen Actors' Guild, was intent upon undermining unions, both private and governmental. One of his first acts as president was to respond to a strike among federal air traffic controllers by firing them all. Eliminating jobs, both private and public, in the name of efficiency, was presented as a good thing; "down-sizing" became the mantra. The 1% were virtually given a license to do whatever they wanted.

If anything, militarization, destruction of infrastructure and the widening gap between the ultra-rich and the ordinary citizen since Reagan's presidency intensified in the years that followed and reached a new extreme under Trump, whom the media presented as maligning Reagan's legacy but as we said before – and flesh out with more detail and nuance in the next chapter – Trump is actually Reagan's heir.

The United States continues to seek glory and play the world's sheriff despite the Vietnam fiasco. When it was the world's unqualified dominant economy, it could afford glory and in fact, use it as an economic stimulant. But when Europe and Japan recovered from the world wars and become economic rivals, while third world countries like Vietnam and Middle Eastern nations like Iran felt empowered to challenge its authority, American elites chose glory over the quality of life for its citizens. They tried to convince traditionalists that the blame for American relative decline rested with unappreciative treacherous cosmopolitan hippies and Leftists along with parasitic blacks and other poor minorities – all of whom had to be put in their place. Just as German elites turned to Hitler to crush the Weimar Left, American elites embraced Reagan in the hope that he would bring traditionalists to accept their diminished standard of living and make cosmopolitan Leftists and hippies irrelevant. For decades America has been living under Reagan's legacy, with Trump being its latest manifestation, and in the next chapter, we consider how to assess Trumpism as a crusade for glory.

6

Making America Great Again

The Reagan in Trump and the Failures of Anti-Trumpism

We're going to win. We're going to win so much. We're going to win at trade, we're going to win at the border. We're going to win so much, you're going to be so sick and tired of winning, you're going to come to me and go "Please, please, we can't win anymore." You've heard this one. You'll say "Please, Mr. President, we beg you sir, we don't want to win anymore. It's too much. It's not fair to everybody else . . ." I'm going to say "I'm sorry, but we're going to keep winning, winning, winning, We're going to make America great again."[1] (President Donald J. Trump)

Be polite, be professional, but have a plan to kill everyone you meet . . . there are some assholes in the world who just need to be shot. There are hunters and there are victims. By your discipline, you will decide if you are a hunter or a victim . . . If you fuck with me, I'll kill you all.[2] (Former four-star Marine General James Mattis, an "adult," who resigned as President Trump's Defense Secretary)

The day after Donald Trump was elected president, millions of angry and grieving protesters, led by women, marched through hundreds of US cities wearing pink "pussy-hats." Meanwhile, Trump supporters in his boisterous huge campaign rallies and endless presidential pep talks wore their own red "Make America Great Again" (MAGA) hats. Both sides seemed to agree on one thing: that Trump was a new force who might take down both the Republican and Democratic establishments in the name of MAGA, creating a new America of Trump glory.

Just the words – "Make America Great Again" – seemed to scream that Trump was championing a new glorious cause. His "forgotten people" supporters believed he would solve their problems and deliver America from the corrupt "swamp" of both the GOP and the Democrats. Fox News, Ann Coulter and Rush Limbaugh saw in Trump a new American savior who would destroy the scourge of "radical Islamic" terrorism, end the invasion of aliens crossing the Southern border from Mexico with a big "beautiful wall," and purge the nation of the secular liberal "big government" traitors who refused to stand during the Pledge of Allegiance and made it impossible to say "Merry Christmas." They believed Trump would restore glory to the traditional culture of America, the world of hard-working, self-reliant Americans who believed in God, family and patriotic nationalism.

Meanwhile, anti-Trumpists also saw the traditionalist Trump militaristic nationalism as a new corrupt crusade for glory, but, in the case of liberal and Democratic anti-Trumpists, one that would destroy the cosmopolitan diversity and American exceptionalism that had always made America great. Democrats and liberals, including the liberal media such as MSNBC and CNN, seemed to almost pine for the days not just of LBJ and Clinton but of Reagan and Bush. The Republican presidents may have been too conservative for the liberal anti-Trumpists but at least they accepted core American values of democracy and protected American power and respect in the world. And conservative anti-Trumpists, including many in the FBI and CIA who became commentators on MSNBC and CNN, also saw Trump as dangerous, threatening the Reagan revolution and the core principles of American glory that it enshrined. Former Republican President George W. Bush Jr. feared Trump could undermine fundamental American values and American security.

> We've seen nationalism distorted into nativism . . . public confidence in our institutions has declined . . . Our governing class has often been paralyzed in the face of obvious and pressing needs . . . Discontent deepened and sharpened partisan conflicts. Bigotry seems emboldened . . . Foreign aggressions – including cyberattacks, disinformation and financial influence – should not be downplayed or tolerated . . . This is a clear case where the strength of our democracy begins at home. We must secure our electoral infrastructure and protect our electoral system from subversion.[3]

Mitt Romney, the 2012 Republican nominee, challenged Trump's business credentials and feared his foreign policy would prove reckless rather than help preserve the American empire:

> What he said on "60 Minutes" about Syria and ISIS has to go down as the most ridiculous and dangerous idea of the campaign season: Let ISIS take out Assad, he said, and then we can pick up the remnants. Think about that: Let the most dangerous terror organization the world has ever known take over a country? This is recklessness in the extreme.[4]

To these anti-Trumpist conservatives, Trumpism was deranged populism, upending Reagan's genuine glorious cause, which had ended Vietnam era doubts about American exceptionalism, wiped out the 1960s radicals and hippies, and enshrined America once again as the beacon of freedom and "leader of the free world."

Certainly, Trump's claim that "I alone can save you" created rhetoric hinting at a new glorious cause. Trump branded himself as the first new leader who would enshrine American national greatness in the twenty-first century, when America appeared to be in danger of both economic and military decline. Trump presented himself as the new leader who would not just destroy the liberal threats to hard working, mainly white Christian people in the heartland but also create a new national glory – which his early chief advisor, Breitbart editor Steven Bannon, introduced to his followers as a populist white nationalist crusader that would save the nation from its foreign enemies invading its borders and the traitors already inside them. Bannon does not believe the mainstream Republican party is sufficiently vigilant in defending the country against a political class which is undermining it.

> We don't believe there is a functional conservative party in this country and we certainly don't think the Republican Party is that . . . It's going to be an insurgent, center-right populist movement that is virulently anti-establishment, and it's going to continue to hammer this city, both the progressive left and the institutional Republican Party . . . We think of ourselves as virulently anti-establishment, particularly "anti-" the permanent political class.[5]

But while there were all the rhetorical trappings of a new glorious cause, both Trump's supporters and opponents got it wrong. Reagan needed a glorious cause because the nation faced a continuing crisis of national faith in its glory, arising from the bruising defeat in Vietnam and the persistence of doubts about American wars and social justice that were the legacy of the 1960s civil rights and social justice movements. But while many problems persisted when Trump threw his MAGA hat in the ring in 2015, there were no new imminent or catastrophic threats to American power of the kind that Reagan had to confront in the aftermath of Vietnam and the 1960s and 1970s Left. The Reagan revolution failed to meet the needs of many hard-working Americans, but it built renewed faith in American militarized capitalism – and its brand of American power and glory endured. It had wiped out any mass American Left opposing the system. The '60s revolutionaries fragmented into siloed identity groups who didn't talk much about capitalism or American empire. And the empire, wrapped around and sustaining the growth of billionaire global capitalists like Donald Trump himself, could still be presented as glorious.

This does not suggest that Trump did not promote American glory or present himself as essential to sustaining it. But we show in this chapter that while Trump presented himself as the bearer of a glorious cause, he was championing more or less the American glory that the Reagan revolution had embraced almost 40 years earlier. True, there were changes in rhetoric and in some policy, with Trump rhetorically opposing "silly wars" and "globalism," and also proposing some changes in trade and industrial policy that departed from Reagan. Moreover, Trump personalized American glory in a new way that made him look a bit more like Louis XIV than Reagan. But the idea of a new glorious cause was largely a Trump "reality show," a pretense that disguised Trump's embrace of the corporate and militarized system, appealing to cultural and religious traditionalists, enshrined and glorified in the Reagan revolution. Trump was recycled Reaganism, dressed up in the narcissistic pomp and illusion of a tv candidate with no new and coherent cause to glorify, other than the personal brand of a world-class entertainer and real estate con man.

Why Trump is Reagan's True Successor

Trump's glorious cause has been, in reality (rather than reality show) a perpetuation of the Reagan revolution, with some important nuances in rhetoric and policy. The Reagan glorious cause can be summarized in four broad forms of American glory (civilizational, super-power, capitalist and great leader), and all are integral to Trumpism.

1) Civilizational Glory

All glorious causes are manifestos for what political scientist Samuel Huntington called civilizations – nations or groups of nations sharing common religions, family values and other cultural beliefs which bind the civilization together.

> In the post-Cold War world flags count and so do other symbols of cultural identity, including crosses, crescents, and even head coverings, because culture counts, and cultural identity is what is most meaningful to most people. People are discovering new but often old identities and marching under new but often old flags which lead to wars with new but often old enemies . . . One grim Weltanschauung for this new era was well expressed by the Venetian

nationalist demagogue in Michael Oibdin's novel, *Dead Lagoon*: "There can be no true friends without true enemies. Unless we hate what we are not, we cannot love what we are. These are the old truths we are painfully rediscovering after a century and more of sentimental cant. Those who deny them deny their family, their heritage, their culture, their birthright, their very selves!"[6]

Glorious causes involve political elites weaponizing civilizational values to bind followers with them against their shared civilizational enemies. Promoting civilizational glory – typically by demonizing civilizational enemies as they threaten the very existence of the nation's core traditions – is rightwing identity politics.

The Reagan revolution linked white Christian evangelicals with corporate elites, odd bedfellows who came together around fear of 1960s leftwing cosmopolitanism and anti-capitalist values. The New Right emerging in the early 1970s was a corporate project that exploited Nixon's idea of a "silent majority" of God-fearing Christians, most white and concentrated in the South but spread throughout the heartland. The Southerners identified with Confederate civilizational values, and were horrified by the 1960s' anti-war, anti-capitalist and civil rights agenda. Nixon won election and re-election by appealing to the "silent majority" of white traditionalists while also championing the big corporate interests. Reagan consolidated this civilizational politics, turning it into a glorious cause that would end the liberal New Deal and cement a great American empire governed by a coalition of big corporations and working class white Christian evangelicals and other traditionalists. He assured them he would make God America's guide.

> We can't have it both ways. We can't expect God to protect us in a crisis and just leave Him over there on the shelf in our day-to-day living ... Without God there is no virtue because there is no prompting of the conscience ... without God there is a coarsening of the society; without God democracy will not and cannot long endure ... America needs God more than God needs America. If we ever forget that we are One Nation Under God, then we will be a Nation gone under.[7]

Trump rode to power by promising to restore the glory of an earlier America which this Reagan coalition felt was being trampled by minorities and liberals. His base was Reagan's base, the strange marriage of traditionalist evangelicals and conservative workers with big capitalist corporations ironically empowered by the Reagan revolution to screw the American worker more than ever. The question of why workers voted for a billionaire corporate promoter like Trump is the same question one could ask about why workers voted for Reagan (Reagan Democrats). The answer: the Christian white working class base fell for the civilizational glorious cause embodied by Reagan and recharged by Trump.

2) Super-power Glory

Reagan's glorious cause was all about making America the uncontested ruling Super-power of the world. He promised to build a military that was so big that no nation – or group of nations – could even imagine challenging US control. And he promised that he would lead a glorious crusade that would destroy the "evil empire" of the Soviet Union. And he would wipe out any other rival Super-power challenging US hegemony. Maintaining America's military strength was a mission assigned to him by God. He will not permit him to consider a proposed freeze on American nuclear arsenal.

> There is sin and evil in the world, and we're enjoined by Scripture and the Lord Jesus to oppose it with all our might ... I pointed out that, as good Marxist–Leninists, the Soviet leaders have openly and publicly declared that the only morality they recognize is that which will further their cause, which is world revolution ... they must be made to understand: we will never compromise our principles and standards. We will never give away our freedom. We will never abandon our belief in God. ... A freeze would reward the Soviet Union for its enormous and unparalleled military buildup. It would prevent the essential and long overdue modernization of United States and allied defenses and would leave our aging forces increasingly vulnerable. ... Let us pray for the salvation of all of those who live in that totalitarian darkness – pray they will discover the joy of knowing God.[8]

Reagan's glorious cause resonated with many Americans because the Vietnam disaster and the rise of anti-American Leftist groups globally, from Central America (think the Nicaraguan Sandinistas) to the Middle East (think the Iranian Ayatollah), put the supremacy of American hegemonic power in question. Moreover, the Soviet Union still existed with many thousands of nuclear weapons and occupation of Eastern Europe. Americans had long felt that it was, as George Washington had said at the founding, "providentially destined" to be the world's great empire. As early as 1778, he envisioned the United States as "[h]aving pleased the Almighty Ruler of the universe to defend the cause of the United American States, and finally to raise a powerful friend among the princes of the earth."[9]

The defeat in Vietnam, followed by Leftist anti-American nationalist revolutions around the world, created a fertile environment for a new glorious cause, in which Reagan would turn the tide and bring America back to its "providential destiny."

By attacking American "silly wars" and cozying up to Putin, it might appear that Trump was abandoning Reagan's crusade for global Superpower glory. But as we show later, Making America Great Again, a slogan which he borrowed from Reagan, was a Trumpist commitment to rebuild both a nuclear force and a conventional military that had been grievously depleted. Democrats like Obama were weak, and integrating themselves into multilateral alliances that held America back from bulking up militarily and acting unilaterally to protect its own interests. Trump's glorious cause was to restore the Reagan vision of America on top, the righteous Empire that would rule the world. Trump poured hundreds of billions into a Reagan-style military build-up and intensified air and drone strikes in the Mideast and other areas, ensuring US global dominance. Nothing could have made Reagan prouder!

3) Capitalist Glory

As noted in earlier chapters, Ayn Rand, best-selling author of *The Fountainhead*[10] and *Atlas Shrugged*,[11] saw the businessman as the authentic American hero. Rand believed business was central to US and Western civilization and that the business classes were the source of American creativity and even spirituality. The business man's innovation, genius and drive were the ingredients of American prosperity and freedom. Rand wrote:

> America's abundance was not created by public sacrifice to "the common good," but by the productive genius of the men who pursed their own personal interests and the making of their own private fortune. . . . They gave the people better jobs, higher wages and cheaper goods with every new machine they invented, with every scientific discovery or technological advance.[12]

Capitalist glory was the foundation of everything glorious about the United States. Rand was thus horrified by what she saw as the demonization of businessmen by the anti-capitalist radicals of the 1960s and their fellow travelers of liberal Democratic Party architects of President Johnson's Great Society. In the early 1970s, she was writing up a storm of angry books against the 1960s societal turn against business. Rand raged:

> The American businessmen, as a class, have demonstrated the greatest productive genius and the most spectacular achievements ever recorded in the economic history of mankind. What reward did they receive from our culture and its intellectuals? The position of a hated, persecuted minority. The position of a scapegoat for the evil of the bureaucrats.[13]

She traced this horror back to the liberal bureaucrats behind FDR's New Deal, the progressive social welfare state that President Johnson's Great Society in the 1960s tried to complete. Her horror was shared by businessmen themselves and by the New Right of the early 1970s that laid the foundation for the Reagan revolution.

Reagan's glorious cause owes a huge debt to Rand and her band of outraged fellow conservative thinkers who gave business elites a philosophical basis for their grievances against the 1960s revolt and a moral sense of their own greatness as the source of American exceptionalism. The New Right brought together organizations of the biggest American businesses and global corporations with leaders of the Republican Party and traditional white Christian working people to restore a politics of capitalist glory. In Reagan, they found the leader who would bring this new crusading politics of business glory to power, creating a domestic regime change from a New Deal America to a Gilded corporate America restoring businessmen as the heroes and architects of an America made great again.

Reagan had far more charisma than Nixon, but he recognized Nixon's appeal to the "silent majority" was essential to his own success. Business elites were the heroes but they were too small a fraction of the population to win elections on their own. So Reagan's glorious cause brought together business heroes with traditionalist workers and Christian evangelicals in the silent majority who hated the cosmopolitan secular and Leftist values of the 1960s. Not only were the student anti-war radicals allegedly spitting on their kids returning from fighting in Vietnam but also promoting unfair government handouts to blacks and other minorities at the expense of the hard-working, self-reliant white American worker. Reagan's glorious cause – which united aggrieved business elites with the aggrieved traditionalist workers – created a new majority that found respect and, yes, glory in the Reagan assault on not just the 1960s revolution but on the liberal New Deal and Great Society that had turned the taxes of the hard working white majority over to what Rand called the parasitical class of welfare bums and the liberal policy elites enabling their anti-capitalist and self-indulgent way of life.

Despite the anti-Trumpists who saw Trump as upending the Republican establishment of the Reagan era, it is hard not to see how deeply Trump drew on the Reagan revolution's glorious cause of restoring business to its rightful heroic position. Trump himself was a billionaire business man who claimed that his genius was the "art of the deal" that made him fabulously rich. Trump's main agenda was to cut the crippling corporate taxes, to get rid of stifling regulations over business, and break the unions unfairly fighting them, thereby unleashing the business class to carry out its heroic mission. At the same time, Trump would dismantle the social programs of the Great Society, refusing to coddle the minority welfare-gobbling parasites or pad the wallets of their liberal social service patrons. He would remember the "forgotten" working Reagan Democrats and bring them once again into a Republican Party that united heroic business with heroic workers against the welfare queens and the government bureaucrats and Democratic Party liberals who serviced them. Despite nuanced differences around trade, anti- globalist rhetoric, and government jawboning of industry bordering sometimes on Keynsian rather than neo-liberal Reaganism – all matters that we discuss later – Trump's glorious cause of business was so thoroughly Reaganesque that one can only guess Reagan would applaud his fellow entertainer-turned-president as his true twenty-first century successor.

4) Great Leader Glory

A glorious cause almost always requires a glorious leader, and this was certainly the case in the Reagan revolution. Since FDR and JFK, there had been no American president seen as a stirring, charismatic leader, whether Nixon, Ford, Carter or even Johnson. But Reagan captured the imagination of the country and became known as "the great communicator." With his years of experience as a movie and television actor, and his congenial personality, Reagan became one of the country's beloved leaders, and one of the few capable of mobilizing a majority around a new glorious cause.

Reagan embodied a distinctive feature of the American glorious leader, a claim to greatness combined with a folksy style that allowed ordinary people to identify with him. The American style is to embed great power leadership in the image of the "aw shucks" ordinary guy. Such leaders, including Reagan, stress their roots in small-town or small-business America, often coming from a hard scrabble existence like that of much of the working population. Such a man's rise to greatness symbolizes the greatness of the American people, since he speaks their language and embodies the heroism, patriotism and love of freedom of the hard-working masses. He tried to project the persona of his friend's – Jimmy Stewart – character in the 1939 movie *Mr. Smith Goes to Washington*, the story of a young innocent senator from a rural state who does not understand the corruption of urban cosmopolitan political machines and calls for a return to traditional American values. In a filibuster, he pleads:

> I wouldn't give you two cents for all your fancy rules if, behind them, they didn't have a little bit of plain, ordinary, everyday kindness and a – a little lookin' out for the other fella, too . . . That's pretty important, all that. It's just the blood and bone and sinew of this democracy that some great men handed down to the human race . . . Fighting for something better than just jungle law, fighting so's he can stand on his own two feet, free and decent, like he was created.[14]

Reagan's "aw shuck" Jimmy Stewart leadership would become glorious, elevating the ordinary traditionalist Americans who identified with and loved Mr. Smith and Reagan. Recall that the glorious cause works because its leader's glory and power enhance the glory and power of his followers. His power can become so great that it might appear to threaten democracy. But since the American great leader is a man of the people, his power and greatness become not a threat but a booster of self-respect and even glory for his followers. The more they can identify with him, the more his greatness becomes a deeply felt sense of their own greatness, even if his policies may not serve their own economic interests.

Like Reagan, Trump emerged as a "Great Leader" who became, personally, an even more dominating figure than Reagan. In the Trump era, it was hard to turn on a cable television station and not see Trump's picture or hear his name within seconds. There may be no president in American history who dominated the American landscape quite like Trump. More even than Reagan, Trump championed a cult of his own greatness to his base, telling them that he would be an iconic president sculpted on Mount Rushmore with Washington, Jefferson and Lincoln. There is a petition to add Trump's face:

> Donald J. Trump is the personification of the American dream. He is a true patriot and successful businessman. Every day, he

offers ordinary Americans hope to make America greater than ever before. In the political field, he has been doing things that have never been done before. He has single handedly reshaped American politics forever and political analysts will be studying Trump's campaign and presidency many years from now. It is our wish that Mr. Trump's face be put on Mount Rushmore.[15]

The sheer force of his personality and dominance of his political era seems to suggest a Trumpist glorious cause, superseding Reagan's. But this is another illusion, cultivated by both liberal and conservative anti-Trumpists who focus heavily on Trump's autocratic or authoritarian tendencies. Yes, as we show shortly, Trump personalized his glorious cause in himself, appearing to create an entirely new Trumpist America. But this was another form of reality show rather than reality, with Trump's personalistic glory ultimately in the service of Reagan's agenda and glorious cause.

But Trump Did It His Own Way

I've lived a life that's full . . .
I did what I had to do. . . .
I did it my way.[16]

While Trump advanced the Reagan glorious cause, he did it in his own way, and sometimes deviated from the Reagan script. The differences are modest but are sometimes significant, deserving new consideration about whether Trump was advancing at least a show of his own glorious cause. Since both liberal and conservative anti-Trumpists have tended to see Trump as anti-Reagan rather than his true successor, it is important to assess where Trump set his own compass and whether it truly altered Reagan's enduring glorious cause.

In the previous section, we looked at four pillars of Reagan's glorious cause, all of which Trump advanced. We now return to these four pillars of glory, showing that Trump built on all of them but sometimes in ways that pointed toward a new path of glory, uniquely Trumpist but one still building on Reagan glory.

1) Civilizational Glory

Trump pursued and advanced Reagan's civilizational warfare at the heart of their shared glorious cause. While Samuel Huntington focused on mainly clashes of civilization as between nations, he recognized that they emerge as intra-civilizational conflicts as well, pitting one group or set of racial, religious or ethnic groups in a nation against another. Glorious causes involve elites pursuing power by rallying their followers against civilizational enemies – the "others" – both inside and outside the country. Both Reagan and Trump pursued this strategy, championing nationalist US exceptionalism and broader traditionalist Western civilization against both foreign and domestic enemies or others. Trump's framing of civilizational warfare differs mainly in his updating of the civilizational enemies list, weaponizing civilizational differences with some distinct new arsenals and divide-and-conquer strategies against some newly horrifyingly dangerous "others."

Reagan and Trump both branded themselves as carriers of the glorious cause of white European civilization. Their voting base – corporate elites, white Christian evangelicals and white workers – united around the glory of being white and Christian in a free and prosperous capitalist America. For Reagan, that glory had been threatened by communists abroad and the '60s-style revolution at home waged by uppity blacks and anti-war and anti-capitalist white student radicals and secular intellectuals who helped create defeat in Vietnam as well as undermine white power and Southern evangelicism. The Reagan revolution mobilized the white "moral majority" against these traitorous "others" to destroy them or keep them in their place.

Trump led a similar campaign, with a similar focus on the danger of uppity and parasitical blacks, who in the name of civil rights and affirmative action would suck from a bloated government as much welfare as they could, all squeezed from the taxes of hard-working white workers and America's great capitalists, such as Trump himself. It is hardly surprising that the South became Trump's fervent base, as he mobilized his Southern, economically hard-pressed base with non-stop dog-whistle racism tied to promises of reviving a Christian America. He touted the glory of an earlier white America now being subverted by a new generation of welfare queens and Black-Lives-Matter types, threatening the law and order enforced by the civilizational heroism of white police and the white-dominated justice system. Hispanics and Muslims bring crime and disrupt the harmony of white American Christian civilization.

> When Mexico sends its people, they're not sending their best. . . . They're sending people that have lots of problems, and they're bringing those problems with us. They're bringing drugs. They're bringing crime. They're rapists. . . . It's coming from more than Mexico. It's coming from all over South and Latin America, and it's coming probably – probably – from the Middle East.[17]

Trump's racism was credible to the South and racist conservatives because his New York City real estate career had been built on racial discrimination against tenants and young blacks like the "Central Park 5," the black kids who allegedly raped a white female jogger in the Park; Trump had taken out numerous ads in New York papers calling for their execution, which he never retracted even after they were proved innocent. Trump wrote in the *New York Times*:

> I want to hate these muggers and murderers. They should be forced to suffer and, when they kill, should be executed for their crimes. They must serve as examples so that others will think long and hard before committing a crime or an act of violence. . . . I am not looking to psychoanalyze them or understand them, I am looking to punish them.[18]

This was a New York capitalist that Southerners could believe in!

Civilizational glory almost always festers on racial resentments, and Trump disparaged and disenfranchised blacks not just by dog whistle rhetoric but by policies directed against affirmative action, voter enfranchisement and virtually all social welfare. But Trump also generalized the "other" beyond Reagan's focus on uppity blacks at home and "commies" abroad. Muslim terrorists became the primary civilizational enemy in the world after the Soviet Communist "evil empire" collapsed. Trump would save Western civilization from an Islamic civilization seeking to terrorize the world into submission and wipe out Western civilization. And Trump's racial "other" expanded from US blacks, who were bad enough, but a new invading army of brown invaders, surging across the Southern border (sometimes Trump alleged infiltrated by Muslim terrorists), and vastly expanding the number of Hispanics multiplying like rabbits as illegal aliens and taking jobs and bringing degraded values undermining Western civilization.

Huntington himself anticipated the rise of the new civilizational enemy, with his last book, *Who Are We?*,[19] focusing on the clash between Latin civilizations and the growing threat to the US posed by Hispanic immigrants flooding into the US. Trump named them "rapists" and "criminals" while also attacking a judge with Mexican heritage, Gonzalo Curiel, as incapable of being a true and "impartial" American judge because of his Mexican ancestry. He should "recuse" himself, recognizing his in-bred Mexican bias:

> I've been treated very unfairly by this judge. Now, this judge is of Mexican heritage. I'm building a wall, OK? I'm building a wall. I am going to do very well with the Hispanics, the Mexicans . . . Well, he's a member of a society, where – you know, very pro-Mexico, and that's fine. It's all fine, but . . . I think he should recuse himself.[20]

And, then, came Trump's most important promise in his 2016 presidential campaign: the Wall! He shut down the government when the Democrats refused to fund it. Building a "big, beautiful Wall" became the centerpiece of the Trump presidency – and there was no more iconic symbol of how Trump would weaponize civilizational glory than his great Wall that would keep American civilization safe from the invading brown hordes who brought only crime, drugs and human trafficking as well as, like Muslims, a heritage diluting the purity of white traditional American culture.

Immigration is weaponized in the politics of civilizational glory, because immigrants typically come from other civilizations and can threaten to overrun a nation's traditional civilizational values. In the Trump era, this threat became existential for conservatives rallying to the Trumpist cause because of demographic shifts that were on track to make the US a "majority minority" nation by 2050. The surge of invading Mexican and Central American "invaders" that Trump promised to halt was really less about stopping a diminishing group of border-crossers than preserving a dominantly white America that Trump's followers feared would soon look more like Mexico or Guatemala.

Trumpist glory thus generalized Reagan dog-whistle racist glory to a new dual civilizational focus beyond US blacks themselves. He aimed to stop in their tracks the Muslim and the Hispanic existential threats to American Western civilization. Immigration had created a demographic turning-point in US civilizational identity, and Trump was the one man who could save it. This is what he meant when he said repeatedly "I alone can save you." His wall and his anti-immigrant policies – as well as his defense of the traditional American way of life – was the last and best hope of defending the glory of both the Old South and twenty-first century Western civilization.

Ironically, the thrice-married Trump who never went to church mobilized Southern evangelicals arguably even more than Reagan in a promise to restore the religious glory of traditionalist America. The New Right and Reagan built their base on appeals to white Christian evangelicals who saw the 1960s as trashing religious liberty and Christian morality about family values, abortion and homosexuality, Christian values at the very heart of Western civilizational glory. But while white evangelicals stuck with Reagan all the way, they became somewhat disenchanted with his failure to end abortion or reverse the terrifying trend toward secularism. Evangelical leaders such as Pat Robertson noted in a 2018 CNN documentary that Reagan had not truly delivered on his promises to the evangelicals. Pat Buchanan or George W. Bush, who called himself a "vessel of God's will" did better but did not halt the secular tide. Bush did claim his wars were divinely inspired.

> I am driven with a mission from God. God would tell me, "George go and fight these terrorists in Afghanistan". And I did. And then God would tell me "George, go and end the tyranny in Iraq". And I did.[21]

Trump stepped into this breach. His then press secretary Sarah Huckabee Sanders was confident: "I think God calls all of us to fill different roles at different times and I think that he wanted Donald Trump to become president . . . And that's why he's there."[22] At the time of this writing, Trump has won the hearts of Southern evangelicals arguably even more than Reagan. Evangelical leaders such as Jerry Falwell Jr., Tony Perkins and Pat Robertson all bet the ranch on Trump, even as Trump began to fail after his Congressional defeat in the 2018 midterms and his failures around the Wall. Falwell reflected the pragmatism of many Evangelical leaders as they explain their support for divorced adulators like Reagan and Trump.

> The government should be led by somebody who is going to do what's in the best interest of the government and its people . . . What earns him my support is his business acumen. . . . I don't think you can choose a president based on their personal behavior . . . There's the earthly kingdom and the heavenly kingdom. In the heavenly kingdom the responsibility is to treat others as you'd like to be treated. In the earthly kingdom, the responsibility is to choose leaders who will do what's best for your country.[23]

White evangelicals were Trump's most loyal civilizational warriors, staying with him at more than 75% in approval polls.[24] This may be because Trump delivered even more than Reagan on religion. Trump's judicial picks were more fiercely supportive of "religious liberty," which includes the liberty to deny liberty to LGBT people, and his Supreme Court selections created a majority, with appointments of Judge Neil Goresuch and Brett Kavanaugh, who would protect religious liberty in cases such as Hobby Lobby, who would defend the right of Christian bakers not to make wedding cakes for gay marriages, and might overthrow Roe vs. Wade and finally eliminate abortion as a constitutional right. Trump kept inviting evangelical leaders such as Falwell Jr. into White House meetings and promised a revolution in appointing federal judges who would finally restore religion to its rightful place. This points both to the importance of religion in civilizational glory and to Trump's savvy understanding of the existential threat that traditionalist Americans were experiencing from the cosmopolitan secularism of bi-coastal liberal elites who saw the evangelical South and religious American heartland as a civilizational "backwater."

2) Super-power Glory

Reagan built a glorious crusade to destroy the "evil empire" of the Soviet Union and make the US so overwhelmingly dominant militarily that no country or group of countries could even imagine challenging it. President W. Bush pursued the same path after 9/11, building up the US military in the name of crushing terrorism and taking down Osama Bin Laden and the Taliban in the invasion of Afghanistan. Bush and his neo-conservative policy advisors led by Vice President Cheney, then doubled down militarily by overthrowing Saddam Hussein in the 2003 Iraq invasion, a war designed to restore American power and economic interests throughout the Middle East and the world.

But the bloody failures in Afghanistan and Iraq, and the rise of ISIS in their wake, threatened the glory Reagan had promised and temporarily delivered as the Soviet empire collapsed. Trump was the strong-man who would step up to ensure that US military power would remain dominant. He would crush "radical Islamic terrorism," and all the regimes, such as Iran, that were rising US rivals, often linked to Shiite Muslim movements that represented threats to critical regional US power in the Middle East – and ultimately its global hegemony. Trump would be the bully of the world, armed with a new arsenal of overwhelming conventional and nuclear weapons that would ensure in the twenty-first century the Super-power glory that Reagan had promised as American's destiny. Trump asked: "If we have nuclear weapons why can't we use them?"[25]

This view of Trump as Reagan's heir of military glory has been heavily contested, especially by anti-Trumpists on both the Right and Left. Both conservative and liberal anti-Trumpists have denounced him for his wild or "crazy" talk about withdrawing from NATO, cozying up to Putin's Russia, and ending America's "silly wars" in Iraq and Afghanistan. Attacking Trump as withdrawing from America's sacred commitments to fight for liberty and US security all over the world, anti-Trumpists called him an "isolationist" who was sabotaging not only the US global military posture but the entire US foreign policy and security establishment. Douglas H. Wise, a career CIA official and former top deputy at the Defense Intelligence Agency, suggested that Trump's personality and ideology are undermining intelligence professionals:

> This is a consequence of narcissism but it is a strong and inappropriate public political pressure to get the intelligence community leadership aligned with his political goals . . . The existential danger to the nation is when the policymaker corrupts the role of the intelligence agencies, which is to provide unbiased and apolitical intelligence to inform policy.[26] [As if intelligence could ever be apolitical – our observation.]

Democrats on congressional intelligence committee criticized Trump for rejecting the experts.

> "People risk their lives for the intelligence he just tosses aside on Twitter," Sen. Mark Warner of Virginia, the top Democrat on the Senate Intelligence Committee, said of Trump . . . Rep. Adam B. Schiff, D-Calif., chairman of the House Intelligence Committee, said "If you're going to ignore that information, then you're going to make poor decisions . . . It means the country is fundamentally less safe."[27]

Trump responded:

> The Intelligence people seem to be extremely passive and naive when it comes to the dangers of Iran. They are wrong! When I became President Iran was making trouble all over the Middle East, and beyond. Since ending the terrible Iran Nuclear Deal, they are MUCH different, but . . . a source of potential danger and conflict. They are testing Rockets (last week) and more, and are coming very close to the edge. Their economy is now crashing, which is the only thing holding them back. Be careful of Iran. Perhaps Intelligence should go back to school![28]

Anti-Trumpists of all persuasions went after him for destroying the CIA, the FBI and key US military commitments. So did the "adults" in the Pentagon, such as Defense Secretary James Mattis, who resigned from the Trump administration because it was pledging to pull troops out of Syria and perhaps Afghanistan. Most of both conservative and liberal anti-Trumpists were pleading with him to stay in Syria, Afghanistan and Iraq, or at least stay until "responsible withdraw" was feasible, not to mention get tough on Russia and promise to build up NATO rather than pull out of it. John Brennan, Director of the CIA under Obama, said to liberal MSNBC commentator Rachel Maddow that Trump, by ignoring the intel community and Pentagon, was weakening the nation and being "treasonous:"

> I think this is an egregious act that it flies in the face of traditional practice, as well as common sense, as well as national security.... He did not live up to I think what Americans expect of the president of the United States, to speak with great forcefulness but to do it with integrity and honesty. What Mr. Trump is doing, basically trashing the reputation of his country worldwide and the way he has treated Americans, fellow Americans, how he refers to them, the divisiveness, the incitement, the fueling of hatred and polarization. This is not what this country is about. . . . I said it was nothing short of treasonous . . . I know what the Russians did in interfering in the election. I have – you know, I'm 100 percent confidence in what they did . . . [Trump has given] Mr. Putin, the Russians, a pass time after time after time, and he keeps referring to this whole investigation as a witch-hunt, as, you know, bogus, as you know – and, to me, this was an attack against the foundational principle of our great republic, which is the right of all Americans to choose their elected leaders . . . I did say that it rises to and exceeds the level of high crimes and misdemeanors and nothing short of treasonous.[29]

With even the liberal anti-Trumpists at MSNBC and CNN helping lead the charge against Trump – that he was undermining US global power and the American security establishment – a narrative developed of Trump as undermining the glory of US leadership of the "free world." Reagan had been the architect for that glory and Trump was now threatening to kill it, through irrational military withdrawals weakening US hard power around the world. The American security establishment has been the greatest threat to world peace since World War II. So if Trump really were dismantling it – something completely untrue – he would deserve the Nobel Prize. While MSNBC and CNN were promoting this narrative couched in a liberal view of the need for US alliances against Russia and other global "hostile powers," the neoconservative architects of Reagan's military glory savaged Trump's dangerous "isolationist" tendencies. Ironically, joining the anti-Trumpist analysts on MSNBC and CNN were neo-conservative intellectual hawks who were architects of the Iraq war with Bush and Cheney, such as super-hawkish neo-conservative journalist and editor Bill Kristol, and top CIA and National Intelligence Directors such as John Brennon. They claimed that Trump was creating the horrifying prospects of an endangered world in which US troops were not leading the charge for freedom, creating chaos from the Middle East and the Gulf to Ukraine and Crimea to China and the South China Sea.

But the anti-Trumpist narrative was profoundly wrong. It did accurately reflect some of Trump's rhetoric about the need to withdraw from "silly wars" such as Iraq and Afghanistan and his desire to establish good relations with Russia while considering pulling out of NATO (long aims, ironically of the anti-war Left). But the anti-Trumpists and others charging that Trump was undermining US military power and global hegemony were confusing rhetoric with reality.

In the real world, Trump ran and governed as a super-militarist. Trump's Make-America-Great-Again started in his budget, with Trump pouring hundreds of billions of dollars to make up for what he called Obama's weak-kneed military policy, evoking Reagan's program to spend so much money on the military that it would bankrupt the Soviet Union or any other rival. Beyond following Reagan's footsteps by spending billions of more dollars for the Pentagon, Trump promised a global war on terrorism that would wipe out not only terrorists and their families but any nations that were sympathetic to terrorism.

> We are also working with allies and partners to destroy jihadist terrorist organizations such as ISIS. The United States is leading a broad coalition to deny terrorists control of their territory and populations, to cut off their funding, and to discredit their wicked ideology. I am pleased to report that the Coalition to Defeat ISIS has retaken almost 100 percent of the territory once held by these killers in Iraq and Syria. There is still more fighting and work to be done to consolidate our gains. And we are committed to ensuring that Afghanistan never again becomes a safe haven for terrorists who want to commit mass murder of our citizens. I want to thank those nations represented here today that have joined in these crucial efforts. You are not just securing your own citizens, but saving lives and restoring hope for millions. When it comes to terrorism, we will do what is necessary to protect our nation – we will defend our citizens, and our borders.[30]

This would be the basis of a foreign policy aimed at potentially catastrophic war with Iran, long supported by his National Security Advisor, John Bolton, arguably the most hawkish policy maker ever in the US government who for decades has argued for US military build-up and intervention in every corner of the world. The essence of Bolton's policy seems to be: bomb first, ask later.

> To Stop Iran's Bomb, Bomb Iran . . . Time is terribly short, but a strike can still succeed. . . . We have a very limited amount of time left before North Korea gains deliverable nuclear weapons. We've got to look at the very unattractive choice of using military force to deny them that capability . . . Tell me you have begun total denuclearisation, because we're not going to have protracted negotiations. You can tell me right now or we'll start thinking of something else . . . America has to defend its own interests in the United Nations, because you can be sure no one else will.[31]

The anti-Trumpist view of Trump as going soft militarily on Russia is contradicted by most of his actual European-related military policies. In February 2019, he withdrew from the treaty banning intermediate range nuclear missiles in Europe, opening the door to putting a nuclear strike force right on the Soviet borders. Trump also pushed successfully for trillion-dollar modernization and expansion of America's nuclear arsenal, much of it funded through the Department of Energy, that would include billions of dollars for tactical nuclear weapons to be stationed in Europe, as well as hundreds of billions more for antimissile defenses in Eastern Europe that would threaten Russian and other nation's abilities to respond to an American attack or first strike.

> Mr Trump has previously said he would expand the Army to 540,000 active-duty troops from its current 480,000, increase the Marine Corps from 23 to 36 battalions – or as many as 10,000 more Marines – boost the Navy from 276 to 350 ships and submarines, and raise the number of Air Force tactical aircraft from 1,100 to 1,200.[32]

In Trump's own words:

> We have to start winning wars again – when I was young, in high school and college, people used to say we never lost a war. We need to win or don't fight it all. It's a mess like you have never seen before . . . This budget follows through on my promise on keeping Americans safe . . . It will include a historic increase in defense spending.[33]

Nobody would likely have more applauded Trump's gargantuan increase in military spending and build-up on Russian borders than Reagan, who would see his old Cold War reinforced by a New Cold War against Russia, interwoven with Trump's sometimes paradoxical calls for better relations with Putin.

Meanwhile, the narrative of Trump pulling out of wars in Syria, Iraq and Afghanistan was equally wrong. Yes, Trump talked about pulling out combat forces on the ground. But that was very different from withdrawing America from the wars. Before and after his announcement of ground troop pull-outs, Trump actually intensified the US air and drone strikes at the center of these wars, permitting killing of the families of alleged terrorists and of other civilians, which he declared was absolutely essential to winning the war on terrorism, even though deliberate killing of civilians violated international law and US policy. In the name of anti-terrorism, Trump supported Saudi Arabian vicious attack on Yemen which killed tens of thousands of innocent civilians. It was hard to disagree with the claim that Trump was out-Bushing Bush Jr. in his brutal militaristic "anti-terrorist" policies in the Middle East.

US engagement with forces in early 2019 to overthrow Venezuelan president Nicolas Maduro suggest a perpetuation of Reagan-style Cold War interventionism for regime change against hostile or Leftist nations. Trump acknowledged that "all options are on the table," following the lead of Bolton who had long advocated not only a war against Iran but overthrow of Venezuelan president Cesar Chavez, Maduro's predecessor, and then Maduro himself after being elected Venezuelan president in 2013. US policy has long sought to discredit Maduro and support oppositionist forces gaining strength in the light of Maduro's economic failures, declining oil prices and US sanctions, and weakening the Venezuelan economy and destabilizing the Maduro regime. Trump likewise supported Brazilian forces leading to the election of Far-Right president Jair Bolsonaro after the imprisonment of Leftist former president and popular worker leader, Luiz Inácio Lula da Silva, known simply as Lula. The US helped lead a "soft coup" against Lula, and the Trump administration, led by Bolton, promoted the ascension of Bolsonaro, as Noam Chomsky notes:

> Well, it's entirely natural for Bolton to welcome Bolsonaro. Bolsonaro is definitely his kind of guy. He's vicious, brutal, a strong supporter, enthusiastic supporter of torture. He was a little bit critical of the military dictatorship – because it didn't kill enough people. He thought it should have killed 30,000 people, like the Argentine dictatorship, which was the worst of the U.S.-backed dictatorships in Latin America. He wants to throw the country open to investors, turn Brazil into a kind of a caricature of a country. This includes opening up the Amazon to his agribusiness supporters. It's a serious blow, if not even a death knell to the species. It means virtual genocide for the indigenous population.

According to Bolsonaro, they don't deserve a square centimeter. But, by and large, just the kind of guy that Bolton would greatly admire.[34]

Both the Venezuelan and Brazilian cases are strong evidence of Reagan-style intervention for "freedom" by the Trump administration that leads to regime change and installation of rightwing governments sympathetic to and dependent on US support. Once again, Reagan would see his legacy honored in Trumpist regime change interventions in Latin America, which Reagan himself repeatedly championed as integral to his glorious cause.

3) Capitalist Glory

One of Reagan's first and most important acts was slashing the taxes on millionaires and billionaires. Reagan reduced top tax rates on the rich from a peak of 91% to a maximum marginal rate of 37%. In his assault on government, encouragement of global expansion and celebration of deregulated business in a neoliberal world dismantling the New Deal, Reagan turned the state over to the 1%, seeing the successful business and corporate chiefs very much in Ayn Rand terms: the creative class whose genius and hard work created the prosperity enjoyed by the great American working population and enshrining a glorious American capitalism.

As in the case of military glory, much media and intellectual commentary argued that Trump broke with Reagan's legacy by promising to "drain the swamp" and take down the Wall Street elites in a new populist war that Trump would wage to attack the globalist financial elites and bring back jobs and honor to the forgotten American worker. Trump's populist rhetoric was real, but once again the pundits have confused rhetoric and reality. Trump's policies would coddle the wealthy and make them even wealthier, while increasing the economic insecurity and insecurity of the forgotten working people who helped elect him. Despite some real differences in trade and industrial policy, Trump was a champion of Reagan's revolution to liberate and enrich big business leaders like himself at the expense of the vast majority of workers and farmers scraping by from paycheck to paycheck. But they could find glory in the glorious cause of unfettered American capitalism that created the greatest prosperity and freedom of any nation in history. Trump's personal fortune was not just his glory but brought glory to all Americans. Trump touched a raw nerve by speaking to the "forgotten" worker of the Rust Belt, the South and the small rural towns. He was right that they had gotten a raw deal for decades, though he didn't blame Reagan for it but rather the "big government" that had been created by the liberal New Dealers pandering to blacks and immigrants. The ties to Reagan here are clear. Reagan created a base of "Reagan Democrats," conservative white workers who voted Republican because they believed Reagan would honor them rather than disrespect them the way the Democratic Party had when it was captured by blacks, and liberal Hollywood elites. These Reagan Democrats were the same traditionalists as Trump's "forgotten" culturally conservative white workers, who would become as glued to Trump as they were to Reagan, lured by the same glory of a gilded capitalism uniting corporations and their workers in an American capitalism honoring all true hard-working Americans against the parasites feeding off of government welfare programs and writing fat paychecks to the bureaucrats doling out the goodies.

Nonetheless, Trump initiated a few highly publicized rhetorical and real policy distinctions from Reagan, even while broadly perpetuating Reagan's glorious causes of big business and capitalism. One big difference is symbolized by Trump's own moniker of himself as "TARIFF MAN." Trump won over the hard-pressed Rust Belt workers in Ohio, Michigan and Pennsylvania, who delivered his electoral college victory, by going after trade policies that gave away the store to China, Europe and Canada and Mexico. He promised to rewrite NAFTA to stop GM and US steel from relocating production in Mexico or China and to stop unfair Canadian subsidies hurting Wisconsin dairy products; he went after Chinese trade surpluses by imposing 25% tariffs on steel and other Chinese manufacturing and agricultural goods; he went after Europe with tariffs on manufacturing and agricultural subsidies of EU imports, and he attacked rhetorically the entire World Trade Organization (WTO) architecture of free trade as stacked against the US.

Despite his pro-business policies, much of the corporate elite became as alarmed as the security elite.

> Corporate America loves Trump's business tax cuts and deregulation, both of which have helped accelerate economic growth and send the bull market into overdrive . . . But business can't stand Trump's populist instincts that have led to tariffs, a trade war with China and efforts to thwart immigration – despite a severe shortage of workers . . . Executives running America's biggest companies know that Trump could attack or demonize them at any time. The commander-in-chief has broken with precedent by attacking individual CEOs as well as some of America's largest employers. . . . Trump has gone after everyone from Amazon CEO Jeff Bezos to Merck (MRK) boss Ken Frazier, one of the nation's most prominent black corporate leaders. He attacked Harley-Davidson . . . Corporate America has quite the rocky relationship with what was supposed to be one of the most business-friendly administrations ever.[35]

There are important deviations from Reagan, who promoted all these "free trade" arrangements as triumphs of his own neo-liberal capitalist glory. Trump was savvy enough to see that this allegedly glorious neo-liberal trade system was hardly glorious for US workers, who feared their jobs might be outsourced and their wages devastated by competition from global traders. Trump's attack on unfair trade deeply resonated with a US workforce, especially in manufacturing, deeply in decline. It became part of Trump's crusade for a 2.0 capitalist glory post-Reagan that would ensure America would bully and economically devastate every nation now taking America for a ride through unfair trade.

The attack on trade was part of a second rhetorical break from Reagan around the glories of "globalism." Reagan had presided over a great new era of corporate globalization. It delivered new resources and profitable markets to giant American corporations, but it was part of a neo-liberal globalization that devastated many US workers. Reagan argued that globalization would lift US corporations and workers together.

Trump campaigned on the idea that the "forgotten" working people were victims of cosmopolitan elite "globalists," that might even include some big US global corporate elites hob-nobbing at places like Davos, where the global elites gather to coordinate and celebrate global capitalism.

Trump thus campaigned as a "nationalist" opposing predatory anti-American globalists. Making America Great Again meant attacking the globalists whose cosmopolitan values and trade policies were sabotaging traditional American economic greatness, especially the great era in which Mid-Western manufacturing was the engine of US and world economic growth. Trump's glorious causes involved restoring that traditional manufacturing base to its rightful place at the center of the US and world economy.

Trump was willing to employ a strategy of selective industrial policy to achieve his "nationalist" aims. He angrily called out particular companies such as Carrier, a manufacturer of air conditioners in Indiana, who was shutting down jobs to be relocated in Mexico; he assaulted GM for shutting down auto production of brands going to China; he went after US Steel for likewise shutting down Ohio and other mid-Western steel plants, and he went after Harley-Davidson for increasingly producing motorcycles abroad, a symbol of how globalism was undermining America, for what was more great about America than its motorcycles? Trump tweeted:

> Many @harleydavidson owners plan to boycott the company if manufacturing moves overseas. Great! Most other companies are coming in our direction, including Harley competitors. A really bad move! U.S. will soon have a level playing field, or better.[36]

While pundits concluded this nationalism of "tariff man" meant that Trump was abandoning Reagan's legacy of globalist capitalist glory, this is another misreading of Trump. Trump was actually what we call a "national globalist." He seamlessly melded his rhetoric of nationalism with a view of restoring US dominance in the global economy. Making America Great Again meant making America the most economically powerful and glorious nation in the great world of global capitalism.

Trump said he was not attacking "free trade" but simply making it fairer by preventing other countries who didn't play by free trade rules from exploiting a naïve or overly generous America. As a candidate, he promised:

> I'm not running to be President of the world. I'm running to be President of the United States – and as your President, I will fight for every last American job . . . Predatory trade practices, product dumping, currency manipulation and intellectual property theft have taken millions of jobs and trillions in wealth from our country. . . . The same so-called experts advising Hillary Clinton are the same people who gave us NAFTA, China's entry into the World Trade Organization, the job-killing trade deal with South Korea, and now the Trans-Pacific Partnership. I'm going to direct the Secretary of Commerce to identify every violation of trade agreements a foreign country is currently using to harm our workers. I will use every tool under American and international law to end these abuses . . . I am going to instruct my Treasury Secretary to label China a currency manipulator, and to apply tariffs to any country that devalues its currency to gain an unfair advantage over the United States. If China does not stop its illegal activities, including its theft of American trade secrets and intellectual property, I will apply countervailing duties until China ceases and desists . . . We are going to stop the outflow of jobs from our country, and open a new highway of jobs back into our country . . . We Will Make America Wealthy Again. We Will Make America Strong Again. And Will Make America Great Again.[37]

He would stand up for the interests of the United States but had no intention of withdrawing from the global economy. Rather, his nationalism would ensure that every global transaction favored the US and restored it to its rightful place as the most creative and powerful economy in the world.

Moreover, his initial tariffs and jawboning of particular companies didn't work out well, creating stock market jitters, howls from his corporate backers, and resistance from businesses such as Carrier and GM, which refused to go along with his interference. Trump backed off, with no passion or capacity to bring the government into a war with the biggest corporations and banks in America, who were also the funders of his own Republican Party. The outcome of his trade wars, whether with China or Europe, remain unclear, but Trump has no intention of withdrawing from the global economy or trading system. Moreover, his aim is to promote the profits and glory of US companies in the spirit of Reagan, not to help US workers. Trump has relentlessly attacked minimum wage laws, unions, social service programs for health care, education and technical training, housing or child care that workers desperately need. His major economic success was a massive tax cut for big business, without delivering any significant tax relief for working people. It is hardly surprising that extreme inequality spiking under Reagan continued to mushroom under Trump, with wages barely budging since the mid-1970s for the average workers while corporate profits and the wealth of billionaires skyrocketed. By 2019, 26 billionaires accumulated more wealth than 4.8 billion people in the world, about two-thirds of every person on the planet. In the US itself, inequality reached astonishing highs, with the compensation of CEO compared to worker wages exceeding 300 to 1,[38] three white men having as much as 160 million, and the top 0.1% of the US population owning as much wealth as the bottom 90%.[39]

But, in the spirit of Reagan, the new gold-plated glory of US billionaires like Trump, himself the founder of a global business empire, was viewed as something contributing to the pride and glory of the US worker. This has always been the way of glorious causes, that define the power, money and glory of the leaders as the blessing that showers their underlings with self-respect and a prized membership in a glorious nation. Trump's nationalism fits Reagan's globalism: our glorious team is winning the great global world series.

4) Great Man Glory
Whether it be Augustus, the long-lasting early Emperor of the Roman Empire, or Quarterback Tom Brady and New England Patriot Coach,

Bill Bellichek, the glory of the glorious cause is always embodied in a Great Leader. The Reagan revolution depended on the extraordinary success and popularity of Reagan himself who, after humble beginnings, rose from the California governorship to one of the most iconic US presidents. The "great communicator's" glory was the personalized brand of his glorious cause, the Great Leader on which all such causes depend and flourish.

But while Reagan was a congenial, likeable and positive person, who could credibly use the rhetoric of "Morning in America," Trump is a far darker personality, known as the bully in the bully pulpit. He was a chronic liar, narcissistic, exploitative of his Trump empire workers, his business clients and contracts whom he stiffed regularly, abusive of his presidential staff who would resign to tell horror stories about him, and a cheater on his wives. Widely seen as a "child" who had to be supervised by "adults" in the White House, it is hard to think of a less personally attractive or loveable figure. Even his loyal supporters grimaced and felt unfavorably about his lack of personal morality, immaturity and dark rage-filled personality, a man who could clearly use some anger-management. Indeed, a group of eminent psychiatrists published a book, *The Dangerous Case of Donald Trump*,[40] in 2017 on all the clinical pathologies Trump exhibited. Even some in his own Party considered using the 25th Amendment to remove Trump as "unfit" for his lofty office.

It is thus ironic that Trump personalized glory perhaps more than Reagan or any other US president. While Trump followed Reagan in pursuing Great Leader glory that would cement the cause, arguably Trump's greatest difference with Reagan was the extent to which he personalized the glorious cause and centered it around his own gigantic personality.

The personal dominance of Trump may have been his most unique quality, even if it ultimately sustained Reagan's glorious cause rather than a new one. Pundits tend to see Trump as an altogether different and new leader reconfiguring US politics. But while he personalized his politics to an extraordinary degree, and created an unprecedented Great Leader model, he did not fundamentally alter the Reagan or Republican cause. While seen by many as engineering a "hostile takeover" of the

GOP, he was actually created by the New Right and Reagan's Republican Party. Nonetheless, in understanding glorious causes, there is no more compelling president than Trump in analyzing the role of personalism, and the extent to which the power and glory of the Great Leader can become central to the cause itself.

Trump not only retained the fevered devotion of his base, but was a dominating figure on the American landscape. It was impossible to read a headline or watch a cable news channel without seeing his image. His giant personality even penetrated ordinary Americans' emotional subconscious, creating both unbreakable hope and loyalty from his base and loathing and hatred from much of the rest of the population. The Trump era was more than anything else about Trump himself.

Unlike Reagan, Trump was not a man of humble origins. While he tried to hide it, it became known that Trump inherited over $450 million from his wealthy father, and never had to pay it back. And he lived the life of the ostentatious business aristocracy, commanding a huge business empire, living in ostentatious urban towers and gold-plated country clubs, flying in private airplanes, employing an army of lawyers and in every way living a lifestyle at odds with the ordinary working American, a man "born on third base" as inequality analyst, Chuck Collins, has dubbed people like himself inheriting great wealth.

Perhaps because of his gilded upbringing, he grew up with enough money and power to expect huge personal power and glory, a capitalist aristocrat who doesn't have to worry about being reined in by institutions or laws or other people. In his world, he could make the rules. The Trump business empire was entirely under his personal control, and he learned he could circumvent the law and act like a mob boss because he could depend on an army of fixers like Roger Stone and lawyers like Michael Cohen, both indicted for crimes by Special Counsel Robert Mueller.

When he came down the gold-plated escalator in Trump tower to announce his presidential campaign in 2015, Trump was already looking a bit like Louis XIV in Versailles rather than Ronald Reagan. He had all the material and symbolic trappings of nobility. It is thus hardly surprising that his presidential campaign and then his style of ruling could be viewed as a kind of personal branding of America. Making America Great Again meant embracing the personal glory of a modern-day billionaire capitalist aristocrat.

Trump's personalistic focus was unusual only in the sense to which his cause was centered almost entirely around himself and his own glory. Reagan could help build his glorious cause with the power of his personality, but the cause was never as centered on "personalism" as Trump's style. There was no widespread concern that Reagan would dismantle the entire Constitutional political structure through arbitrary use of his personal authority.

Trump is a different story. His personalism was so central to the cause – even if that cause, as we have argued, was perpetuating a variant of Reagan's glorious revolution – that it bordered on the prospects of threatening the constitutional American system. When he said "Only I can save you," he was forecasting the actual way he saw ruling the country. He would pay little attention to institutional checks and balances, including even the Congress, and instead rule by increasing the loyalty of his base to himself. He ultimately had to pay attention to Congress and the courts, but he assumed he could and should personally control them through either his power of judicial appointment or his ability to issue executive orders that might override Congressional legislative and appropriations power. Such was his approach to the Wall, which he claimed that he would build by declaring an Emergency if Congress didn't surrender and give him the money.

> I have the absolute right to declare a national emergency. I'm not prepared to do that yet, but if I have to, I will.[41] (and in 2019, he actually did declare an emergency).

Trump's personalism became a source of fear that he could turn America from constitutional democracy to autocracy. If his personal glory is great enough, no other institution or person should be able to get in his way. His view of the world becomes truth and opposing him makes you a traitor.

Trump's personalism led more and more pundits and ordinary people to see him as an authoritarian who didn't like democracy. He cozied up to the world's autocrats like Putin, Kim and Bolsonaro while attacking democratic allies such as Trudeau in Canada or Merkle in Germany. His white nationalist associations – and his behavior in crises such as the neo-Nazi march in Charlottesville in 2017 – where neo-Nazis killed a liberal rival protester and Trump said there "were fine people on both sides" amplified the fear that Trump had elements of a Hitler figure. His racism, bullying and calling for "punching out" protestors at his rallies, emboldened Far Right groups like the Klan as well as unstable individuals who felt freer to use guns to shoot others, often those groups targeted by Trump, in rampages in schools, restaurants or just pedestrians on the street. It is hardly surprising that some began to see Trump turning into Mussolini or even Hitler, in an age where Far Right groups and mass violence were becoming common-place. Michael Moore warned:

> Hitler and Trump are not the same thing. But you are making a foolish mistake if you do not at least take a look at history and the patterns of history and how the manipulation of fear, the manipulation of the public works, . . . I'm not a sky-is-falling person. I don't believe in conspiracy theories. But I am conscious enough to see what's going on. And anyone who's still thinking "it's not that bad," "it's not going to get that bad," it's time to wake up.[42]

All this suggests that Trump's personalism potentially could lead to his own Far Right glorious cause, moving beyond Reaganism to outright authoritarianism and rule by presidential fiat. And if economic or military declines or defeat were to become more acute, it was reasonable to imagine that Trump's base might support his suspension of democratic rights in an "emergency" the president declared. Then, indeed, Trumpism could morph into his own glorious cause, with Trump rallying the public to save the nation by vesting him with long-term extra-constitutional powers.

But while this is not an idle fear, at this writing it is not reality. Trump may want to rule like Big Brother but he remains within the tradition of the Reagan capitalist aristocratic model of American democracy. His personalism has not yet expanded into formal authoritarianism but rather simply reinforced the kind of corporate rule that Reagan enshrined. It remains in serious tension with democracy but has not, at this writing, suspended or eliminated constitutional rule.

The parallels with Reagan, both personally and in the political glorious agenda, remain more persuasive for now. Like Reagan, Trump was seen by millions of ordinary working and small-town Americans as "one of us." Yes, he was rich and, by his own account, greater in almost every way than everyone else, greater in a way that concentrated huge power in himself. But his greatness was experienced in a similar way to Reagan's, as one that millions of ordinary working Americans could look at and feel that "this man is like me and I can trust him." His glory elevated the self-regard – and ultimately the glory – of everyone in his base, including the "forgotten Americans" hungry for a little respect and with real grievances about their wellbeing and status. And by 2019, half way through his first term, Trump had not shut down Congress or otherwise seized emergency power the way Hitler did after the Reichstag fire, when the Nazis ended the democracy of the Weimar republic. Rather, Trump perpetuates Reagan's 1% corporate agenda and Reagan's own veiled dog-whistle calls for a return to the glorious America traditional white Christianity.

Despite all the differences noted earlier in personality, some parallels with Reagan's "great leader" style are striking. Both presidents were successful professional entertainers. Both mastered a folksy style of communicating with their base of traditionalist working and religious Americans. Both seemed to transcend mundane politics, and to speak from the gut rather than consultant or speech-writer scripts. Both were famous guys you probably could enjoy having a drink with at the local bar. In other words, both enjoyed greatness and glory that infused their base with emotional gratification and a sense that his power and glory became their own power and glory.

Given their striking similarities as "Great Leaders," it is easier to understand why Trump would ultimately become a voice for the Reagan glorious cause. Both men appealed to the same kind of base with the same kind of emotional style and traditionalist cultural appeals.

Trump had a bigger-than-life personality but no coherent agenda other than one that would appeal to his corporate buddies along with rhetoric catering to his religious and traditionalist working class base. And the glorious cause that that base responded to in Reagan was exactly what it wanted from Trump. And that is what it got from him.

7

WE CAN'T AFFORD GLORY

TURNING TOWARD EQUALITY AND HUMAN SURVIVAL

I refuse to accept the cynical notion that nation after nation must spiral down a militaristic stairway into the hell of thermonuclear destruction. I believe that unarmed truth and unconditional love will have the final word in reality. This is why right temporarily defeated is stronger than evil triumphant. I believe that even amid today's mortar bursts and whining bullets, there is still hope for a brighter tomorrow . . . I have the audacity to believe that peoples everywhere can have three meals a day for their bodies, education and culture for their minds, and dignity, equality and freedom for their spirits . . .

This faith can give us courage to face the uncertainties of the future. It will give our tired feet new strength as we continue our forward stride toward the city of freedom. When our days become dreary with low-hovering clouds and our nights become darker than a thousand midnights, we will know that we are living in the creative turmoil of a genuine civilization struggling to be born. (Martin Luther King; Nobel Prize Acceptance Speech; Oslo, Norway; December 10, 1964)

> Yes, 'n' how many times must the cannon balls fly
> Before they're forever banned? (Bob Dylan, *Blowin' in the Wind*)

Do you know the game called "chicken?" Derber learned it in high school. Two people – often high school boys who love to play – get out on a country road in their cars. They face their cars toward each over about half a mile apart and roar their engines. Then they put the pedal to the medal. The driver who refuses to turn off the road, to avoid a head-on crash, is the winner. He gets all the glory, showing he's even willing to risk dying to win the game. When he goes back to school, the other kids look at the winner admiringly. They applaud him as he strolls down the hallways. The girls think about how they can snare him for a date.

The Chicken game is a little like international politics. Nations are all drivers and they rev up their cars as they approach each other. The winner is typically seen as the driver of the nation willing to crash into everyone else, making clear they better blink because the consequences for them are dire if they don't. The nation who never blinks – never backs down even at the cost of national suicide – gets the glory in this game too. The nation's great leader is adored by many of his people and feared by others around the world. Other nations feel ashamed when their leader blinks, and may begin to search for leaders who won't blink and bring glory to their own country.

Winning this glorious game has been the way powerful countries have long played international politics. It has sustained leaders who might otherwise have been in trouble politically because of economic decline or defeats in war. They have seduced many of their people to support them for the glorious cause of winning. The would-be glorious leaders are willing to sacrifice other major interests of the people and spends vast amounts of money to build the national car and mobilize the national will that can bring a restless population back in their camp. As Noam Chomsky observed, "When the state says, 'Whip up hysteria against the evil empire,' everybody starts yelling, jumping up and down, and screaming about the evil empire."[1]

The glory game is still seductive, and many national leaders are still mobilizing their people for glorious causes. But today is a new era. For one thing, if you choose a leader who won't blink, you may well be in a war that could destroy the country or blow up the world. Do you really want glory at the cost of total destruction?

Moreover, it takes a lot of money to play and win glory. It requires diverting resources from meeting the rational economic and social welfare interests of the people. In this book, we have shown that leaders mobilize the masses for glorious causes to divert them from real interests and urgent needs that are not being met. It may be irrational, but it has emotional appeal for desperate people whose economic needs or sense of self-worth are being battered by economic exploitation or military defeat. The glorious cause turns popular attention away from rational interests but it can all seem worth it to the victorious country, who gets the symbolic gratification of national victory and shares in the global power and pride of their glorious leader.

But in an age of extreme inequality, climate change and war with weapons of mass destruction, the consequences of diverting millions of people from their rational interests are far, far more dangerous. The real interests of all people now involve urgently creating an economy that serves the majority, a world without war, and a sustainable environment. To continue playing the glory game – which requires forsaking those rational interests – is to risk extinction of civilization and all life on the planet.

To put it simply, we can't afford glory today. Glorious causes, as we have shown, have always been dangerous and always had dire effects. But the effects now are existential, involving the potential end of the human experiment.

In the following pages, we explore briefly how we might move away from a world of glorious causes toward the only sane and rational course: preventing extinction, whether through climate change, nuclear war or mass impoverishment. This means learning to blink and, indeed, moving past the game of chicken that has consumed nations for centuries.

European nations spent centuries playing the game of chicken, in pursuit of glory that would divert ordinary people from the grinds of daily life and their lack of power, while also draping them with the trappings of world power. The European publics were willing to follow leaders who would pursue colonies and the glorious cause of empires from sea to shining sea.

But after two world wars of devastating violence and destruction of their own nations, the Europeans saw the world in a revolutionary new way. They abandoned glorious causes as inglorious, and set out to build a new course devoid of glory and in pursuit of real interests and social needs.

This deserves more attention because it shows that it is possible for nations long engaged in glorious games of chicken and empire to change. One hopes that it doesn't require the tens of millions killed in two of the biggest and most murderous wars ever fought to bring about this change. But looking at the European new path offers a few hints about moving beyond glory.

World War I was a disaster fought for pure glory, among colonial empires that wanted a bigger share of imperial spoils. Some 37 million people died in this "Great War" including the flu epidemic of 1919 that people were told would probably end in a few months. The prolonged bloody savagery of trench warfare between civilized French and German soldiers became a symbol for Europeans of the insanity of war. The scale of murder and destruction was so great that it began to chip away at the glory of glorious causes. Even in the US, a large peace movement, now mostly erased from the history books, rose in horror at the "Great War." Europeans began to believe in President Wilson's rhetoric that this should be "the war to end all wars." In *All Quiet on the Western Front*, Erich Maria Remarque reminded us how difficult it was to find a purpose in a Europe left in shambles.

> A man cannot realize that above such shattered bodies there are still human faces in which life goes its daily round. And this is only one hospital, a single station; there are hundreds of thousands in Germany, hundreds of thousands in France, hundreds of thousands in Russia. How senseless is everything that can ever be written, done, or thought, when such things are possible. It must be all lies and of no account when the culture of a thousand years could not prevent this stream of blood being poured out, these torture chambers in their hundreds of thousands. A hospital alone shows what war is.[2]

But even such marred glory can beget more glory. The Allied victors imposed such punitive terms on Germany that the German economy collapsed and the German people suffered extreme humiliation. The Allied harsh punishment of Germany set up the conditions for a new glorious cause in Germany led by Hitler, as discussed in Chapter 3. And this, in turn, led to World War II, in which about 60 million people died in the "Good War" against fascist Germany and Japan.

After World War II, the "Good War" was used by the big winner, the US, as a basis for a new American glorious cause of fighting the "evil empire" of the Soviet Union and endless war to prevent the spread of communism and project America's glory around the world. President Trump used it repeatedly in his 2019 State of the Union Address to justify his war on terrorism and continued US global dominance.

> In June, we mark 75 years since the start of what General Dwight D. Eisenhower called the Great Crusade – the Allied liberation of Europe in World War II. On D-Day, June 6, 1944, 15,000 young American men jumped from the sky, and 60,000 more stormed in from the sea, to save our civilization from tyranny . . . nearly 75 years ago, after 10 months in a concentration camp . . . Suddenly the train screeched to a halt. A soldier appeared. Judah's family braced for the worst. Then, his father cried out with joy: "It's the Americans." . . . Now, we must step boldly and bravely into the next chapter of this great American adventure . . . friend and foe alike must never doubt this Nation's power and will to defend our people . . . our triumph over communism, . . . our unrivaled progress toward equality and justice – all of it is possible thanks to the blood and tears and courage and vision of the Americans who came before . . . We must choose whether we will squander our inheritance – or whether we will proudly declare that we are Americans . . . we must always keep faith in America's destiny – that one Nation, under God, must be the hope and the promise and the light and the glory among all the nations of the world![3]

Europe took away a different lesson from the two apocalyptic world wars, which virtually destroyed the continent itself. The overwhelming European feeling was that this can't ever happen again. European nations began to develop the architecture of a post-glorious world, in which international law, the UN, and the formation of what is now the European Union would end centuries of glorious wars fought by Europeans against each other and against colonized peoples across the planet.

This has required a slow and painful revolution. Long-standing militaristic and capitalist economic, political and cultural systems have had to undergo major reforms. Europeans have had to rethink their glorious empires and way of life. These changes are still in process, and threatened by new waves of Far Right glorious movements triggered by Middle East immigration. But they have created a new European rational focus on resolving conflicts through international law and attending to the real social welfare needs of European populations.

The possibility of moving beyond glory is suggested also by the deep transformations in Germany after Hitler's disastrous glorious cause. Two generations of Germans wrestled agonizingly with the sins of their parents and grandparents. Younger Germans were forced to re-evaluate their identity, core values and ideas about the nation, patriotism and war. Germany became a leading architect of a post-glory European order and the German public has undergone a deep atonement. Michael Sontheimer, German historian and staff writer for *Spiegel*, the most popular news magazine in Germany, observed:

> For us Germans, whether we like it or not, the past is always present . . . the war lingers in almost every German home . . . Only in the 1960s, did rebellious teenagers like me start to question their parents and grandparents: What were you doing between 1933 and 1945? . . . We did not accept the collective amnesia regarding the Nazi crimes. We also refused to buy the popular legend of an evil demon called Hitler who single-handedly seduced and betrayed an innocent German people who knew nothing about

the atrocities . . . Wladimir Kaminer, a Jew from Moscow . . . now a German citizen . . . told me. "Your defeat in World War II has helped you build up a true democracy. The Germans are hopeless now when it comes to anything militaristic and totalitarian . . . unfortunately, on the fringes of German society – particularly in the impoverished former East Germany – anti-Semitism and neo-Nazism still exist and at the moment seem to be thriving.[4]

Repeated Gallup surveys of the level of "patriotism" in different nations have shown that Germany has become one of the least patriotic countries in the world, suggesting that most Germans renounce the nationalist glorious causes that Hitler led. The rise of the Far Right AFD (Alternative for Germany) shows this has not destroyed the German quest for glory but it has limited it to a small fraction of the population that, at this writing, is declining.

Between the two world wars, the 1929 Wall Street crash triggered a global Great Depression that helped fuel Hitler's glorious cause, but had different effects in the US. A depression is the kind of event that can easily fuel a glorious cause. But in the US, the rise of President Franklin Roosevelt's New Deal showed that it is not inevitable that economic crisis or collapse will trigger a new quest for glory. The New Deal represented a rational approach to dealing with the real interests and social emergencies created by the Depression. FDR threw his popular appeal behind a major public investment into jobs, social welfare and social security, without using a glorious war, as Hitler had done, to justify his program.

As Hitler gained power in Germany and prepared for war, pressure grew in the US to aid Great Britain and other European powers. FDR had responded to the aftermath of World War I, and then the Depression, in a quasi-isolationist fashion, resisting the impulse to get the US into war again. It could have been a glorious way of building the New Deal, but even though he did begin to aid anti-German European allies, and also sought to limit Japanese expansion in Asia by cutting off oil supplies, he did not rush to war or try to build support for a new glorious cause.

This suggests some hope that New Deal-type programs in the US can play a role in diminishing the rush to glory. New Deal programs were not an explicit rejection of glory, but in the height of the Depression, glory was seen as a luxury that was hardly affordable. At best, the New Deal mitigated the depression, not end it. The Depression did end as World War II approached and a new emphasis on glory stimulated military spending which ricocheted throughout the whole American economy. After World War II, the US took up its new global glorious anti-communist cause, so today we are confronted with the stubborn and deep attachment of the US to the pursuit of glory.

Nonetheless, the New Deal shows that when the country faces great challenges such as a depression, the US does not inevitably turn to glory. If glory was once seen as an unaffordable luxury, there remains the prospect that people will return to that view. When great challenges emerge, history suggests the possibility of a rational response to end the crisis rather than a diversion to glory. And a Green New Deal, to deal with the greatest challenge we have ever faced, remains one of the most hopeful possibilities in an age when the world now faces the possibility of extinction from both climate change and nuclear war.

In the mid-term elections of 2018, a blue wave swamped the Republicans and turned the House of Representatives back to the Democrats under Speaker Nancy Pelosi. Trump suffered a major setback, his poll numbers plummeting to under 40% approval afterward despite his fevered pursuit of glory to make American Great Again by keeping out the Brown hordes invading over the Southern border and banning the terrorists from Muslim nations. Trump declared:

> This is a moral issue. The lawless state of our southern border is a threat to the safety, security, and financial well-being of all Americans. We have a moral duty to create an immigration system that protects the lives and jobs of our citizens. . . . defend our very dangerous southern border out of love and devotion to our fellow citizens and to our country . . . Tolerance for illegal immigration is not compassionate – it is cruel. Tens of thousands of innocent Americans are killed by lethal drugs that cross our border and flood

into our cities – including meth, heroin, cocaine, and fentanyl . . . they almost all come through our southern border . . . . Year after year, countless Americans are murdered by criminal illegal aliens.[5]

Large majorities opposed his Wall, his racism, his tax cuts for billionaires and his promise to crush all "terrorists" or anyone challenging US power over the world. This might suggest America is dramatically moving, as Europe did after the world wars, away from glorious causes.

This is more wish fulfillment than sober analysis. Still concerned about border security and the power of America to lead the world against terrorists and other "bad guys," the public, Democrats and anti-Trumpist Republicans did not reject glorious causes. In fact, liberals on MSNBC and CNN opposed Trump, as noted earlier, by arguing he was going soft on Russia, pulling precipitously out of wars such as Syria and Afghanistan, and claiming victory over terrorism long before ISIS or al Qaeda had been defeated. Supporters of Trump still wore their MAGA hats and Republicans rallied around Trump's rebranding of Reagan's glorious cause for US global power, with the US the essential and exceptionalist nation leading the world against terrorism and for freedom, a view shared by millions of liberals.

Nonetheless, the blue wave of progressive Democrats in 2018 – headlined by the election of Democratic Socialists such as Alexandria Ocasio-Cortez – hint at a stirring in the grass roots for a turn toward dealing with issues of equality and human survival. The popular vote for the Democratic mid-term candidates was *twelve million* more than their GOP opponents received, the largest wallop of a reigning party in a mid-term ever seen. And the new class of Democrats was led by progressives such as Cortez, who made no bones about the need for a drastic change from the Reagan neo-liberal glorious revolution that Trump was pursuing in the name of destroying terrorism and building his huge Wall to keep out the brown Hispanic hordes.

Using the social media savvy and authenticity that millennials and many others crave, Cortez and her young progressive colleagues – many female and people of color – moved (literally danced on social media and in the halls of Congress) toward a Bernie-style transformation.

Bernie Sanders, who nearly captured the Democratic nomination in 2016 with an explicitly democratic-socialist program, became a role model for Oscaio-Cortez and others of her generation to propose a Green New New Deal. If carried out, it would create a regime change at home, where the country would finally challenge the extreme inequality of neoliberal global capitalism and focus on the needs of most people, not just the elite. This would be a new brand of politician, with one foot in electoral politics and the other in popular social movements. The Green New Dealers wanted not glory but a serious plan to address the real problems and interests of the people, none more important than the need to ward off the emergency threat of extinction from climate change and militarism in a nuclear age.

Like Bernie, Cortez and her new colleagues in the House did not lead with an open assault on the glorious cause of US empire and its endless wars. In the spirit of FDR at the beginning of his New Deal, they offered a Green New Deal which would represent the first serious US government response to poverty, the jobs crisis and the threat of extinction from climate change, fueled by major government investment in new green infrastructure and green jobs. As one of her first legislative big-time initiatives, in February 2019, Cortez collaborated with Massachusetts Senator Ed Markey to sponsor a comprehensive Green New Deal legislative framework. New wealth taxes on the rich, as proposed by leading Democrats such as Senator Elizabeth Warren as well as Cortez, along with big cuts in the military budget, might erode glory but it would fund real and urgent popular needs.

From the point of view of glorious causes, the Green New Deal played a role similar to FDR's New Deal. The new blue wave of Democrats, much like FDR, did not rail against US "security interests" and American global power. Rather, like FDR and Martin Luther King, they kept their eye on the prize of the real interests of people and survival, seeing glory as something that in the face of overwhelming economic, social and environmental challenges was self-indulgence. Not only was it way too expensive and morally problematic, but it diverted the public and national resources away from the emergencies of economic stagnation and human survival. Those were the real threats to the public interest, and the blue or "red-green" wavers were elected in 2018 to redirect the country to end poverty, provide free or affordable health care and education, and stop extinction with green jobs and infrastructure funded by taxing billionaires and the Pentagon. Cortez's Green New Deal proposed a genuine New Deal social transformation:

> Unabashedly progressive ideals anchor the resolution. A section outlining guidelines for future Green New Deal bills reads like a laundry list of populist policies, including everything from ramped-up antitrust enforcement – "ensuring a commercial environment where every businessperson is free from unfair competition and domination by" monopolies – to a vastly expanded social safety net, "providing all people of the United States high-quality health care, affordable, safe and adequate housing, economic security, and access to clean water, air and healthy and affordable food, and nature."[6]

Can this agenda work? Can it end the insane crusade for glory? Can it elect a new government repudiating the American glorious cause? Nobody can answer this question with any certainty. But there are indicators of hope, of possibility.

First, the demographic base of the country is moving toward a diverse minority–majority population. People of color are victims of war and glorious causes, and are the most likely group to reject them. Moreover, a high percentage are young. Both the millennial generation, as well as Generation Z, have the greatest interest in, and support for, a social justice agenda at home that will promote survival with equality. This goes so far as not just to overwhelmingly support strong green climate policy but to embrace the idea of socialism more strongly than capitalism: Frank Newport, director of Gallup Polling, writes that:

> Americans aged 18 to 29 are as positive about socialism (51%) as they are about capitalism (45%). This represents a 12-point decline in young adults' positive views of capitalism in just the past two years and a marked shift since 2010, when 68% viewed

it positively. Meanwhile, young people's views of socialism have fluctuated somewhat from year to year, but the 51% with a positive view today is the same as in 2010.[7]

Public opinion polling backs up the idea that the larger US public is becoming exhausted by long and endless wars, such as Afghanistan and Iraq, that were US defeats and brought little glory. Public attitudes show a population that seeks to pursue social reconstruction at home, deeply anxious about short-term jobs and long-term survival. A major poll in December 2018 showed overwhelming support for the many social welfare, job and climate elements of the broad Green New Deal program, noting that the new progressive Democrats were speaking to a very large supportive public in their green infrastructure and jobs agenda. When Cortez and other young Congressional Democrats led protests for change, national attention crystallized favorably, even among conservative Republicans:

> [T]he demonstrations thrust the Green New Deal into the national spotlight. It proved popular. In December, 81 percent of registered voters said they supported a plan to generate 100 percent of the nation's electricity from clean sources within the next 10 years, upgrade the U.S. power grid, invest in energy efficiency and renewable technology, and provide training for jobs in the new, green economy, according to a poll by the Yale Program on Climate Change Communication and George Mason University. That included 92 percent of Democrats and 64 percent of Republicans, with an eyebrow-raising 57 percent of conservative Republicans in agreement.[8]

The polling profile of a progressive majority on attitudes supporting social security, health care, education, job security, higher minimum wages, higher taxes on the rich, getting big money out of politics, and protecting the environment are consistently documented in public polling. Attitudes toward US wars and foreign policy show both right- and leftwing disenchantment with what Trump called "silly wars," and a population that wants continued US engagement and shared leadership but not hegemonic control over the world, that costs trillions in military spending, outsources jobs and requires huge loss of American and other lives.

- 59 percent . . . think Wall Street has too much power and influence in Washington.
- 65 percent of Americans think our economic system "unfairly favors powerful interests."
- 66 percent of Americans think money and wealth should be distributed more evenly.
- 72 percent of Americans say it is "extremely" or "very" important . . . to reduce poverty . . .
- 80 percent of Americans think some corporations don't pay their fair share of taxes . . .
- 74 percent of registered voters . . . support requiring employers to offer paid parental and medical leave . . .
- 72 percent of voters think it is a "bad idea" to cut funding for scientific research on the environment and climate change . . .
- 68 percent of Americans . . . believe the country's openness to people from around the world "is essential to who we are as a nation."[9]

None of this ensures rejection of the glorious cause. A majority of Germans in Weimar Germany in the 1920s and early 1930s opposed Hitler. The left did not have a majority but neither did the Nazis. But German aristocratic and big business elites turned to Hitler to save themselves from the Left. Since the 1960s, US corporate elites have largely done the same thing by embracing and funding the Reagan revolution and Republicans for the last several decades. But the breadth of the progressive majority of Americans, while hardly a guarantee of a rejection of glory, suggests new possibilities. If revived popular movements and the "red-green" wave of the Democratic Party find traction in the progressive majority, as they did in 2018, the possibilities are real that urgent social needs – such as jobs, better wages and health care for all – will get increasing attention. And, as in the New Deal era, glory may be seen increasingly as a dangerous or unaffordable indulgence.

The Green New Deal, proposed in 2019 as a major Democratic Party agenda, is an important step toward rejecting glory and addressing real public needs. The Republican Senate will kill it as long as the GOP is in control, but it opens right away a new conversation in Congress about survival of humanity, the greatest real crisis ever facing the public. This has the makings of an existential anti-glory politics that can attract not only progressives but many populists who supported Trump in 2016.

The threat of extinction of all life dwarfs any other threat in history and should make spending money on glory appear insane. A Green New Deal at a scale capable of stopping extinction can only be funded by major new taxes on the rich and drastic cuts of the military budget. Again, the Democrats have taken some early steps, with Elizabeth Warren's proposed wealth taxes on those making $50 million or more getting a lot of Democratic and public support. Cortez and the younger wave of progressive Democratic Representatives have also proposed their own taxes on wealth, reflecting a general outrage about extreme wealth and income inequality shared by millennials, Generation Z and a majority of the public.

Inequality has become such a big issue that President Trump had to denounce the rising acceptance of "socialism" in America, saying socialism will make worker conditions far worse and that "the US will never be a socialist country." That he had to make such a proclamation was a sign of how anxious billionaires – and the capitalist class broadly – are alarmed about the super-majority of the public expressing anger at extreme inequality, growing poverty, a middle class living paycheck to paycheck, and the fact that the 1% now has more wealth than the bottom 90% of the population. Indeed, a majority of Democrats and of young people have more positive associations with socialism than capitalism. In a major report from the Gallup Poll, Gallup's director, Frank Newport, writes that:

> For the first time in Gallup's measurement over the past decade, Democrats have a more positive image of socialism than they do

of capitalism. Attitudes toward socialism among Democrats have not changed materially since 2010, with 57% today having a positive view. The major change among Democrats has been a less upbeat attitude toward capitalism, dropping to 47% positive this year – lower than in any of the three previous measures. Republicans remain much more positive about capitalism than about socialism, with little sustained change in their views of either since 2010.[10]

All of this is an indication that the Green New Deal could become, as the New Deal itself did, part of a powerful serious political challenge to the established order and a rejection of glorious causes that legitimate that order as unaffordable. As Cortez has accurately noted: "Every single policy proposal that we have adopted and presented to the American people has been overwhelmingly popular."[11]

The appeal of the wealth taxes and the Green New Deal, as well as the greater popularity of the term "socialism," doesn't mean what President Trump suggested when he demonized the term as Stalinist authoritarianism. Bernie Sanders, Alexandra Cortez and most "democratic socialists" today have, as noted earlier, a passion not for "big government" but for decentralized power and democratizing business, government and all big institutions. They have in mind, at least initially, something looking more like Sweden than the old Soviet Union. As Nobel economist Paul Krugman observes:

> What Americans who support "socialism" actually want is what the rest of the world calls social democracy: A market economy, but with extreme hardship limited by a strong social safety net and extreme inequality limited by progressive taxation. They want us to look like Denmark or Norway, not Venezuela.
>
> And in case you haven't been there, the Nordic countries are not, in fact, hellholes. They have somewhat lower G.D.P. per capita than we do, but that's largely because they take more vacations. Compared with America, they have higher life expectancy, much

less poverty and significantly higher overall life satisfaction. Oh, and they have high levels of entrepreneurship — because people are more willing to take the risk of starting a business when they know that they won't lose their health care or plunge into abject poverty if they fail.[12]

This means that many working people who are culturally conservative but feel their jobs and survival are in jeopardy can get behind the Green New Deal and another version of a New Deal that helped get Americans out of the Depression while delivering social security, unions and health care. This is not revolution but it is the beginning of a conversation about big change that could refocus people on meeting their real needs rather than chasing glory.

But the Democratic Party – including its progressive wing – has not made the same turn toward big cuts in the military. Even the most senior and progressive Democratic leaders such as Sanders and Warren, as well as the younger generation symbolized by Cortez, have focused on domestic policy. They have been way too quiet about US wars and the legitimacy of US military power in the world. But there can be no repudiation of the reigning American glorious cause without a focused attack on US militarism.

The failure of the Democratic Party in this area is very serious – and reflects both the deep flaws in the anti-Trumpist movement as well as weakness in US popular movements for peace. As noted repeatedly, both liberal and conservative anti-Trumpists have felt it necessary to legitimate their attack against Trump by accusing him of undermining American national security. The anti-Trump movement has bordered on being a pro-war and New Cold War movement, a sign of how powerful glory is in America and how even liberals and Leftists either support US global military dominance or feel they will lose public legitimacy if they challenge US militarism.

The Democrats and liberal media have attacked Trump in the safe company of CIA, FBI and military leaders. By kow-towing to traditional security interests, they believe they have space to critique Trump's domestic policies. It's a sign of the strength of the American glorious cause that liberals are so reluctant to challenge US wars and feel they must shield themselves behind anti-Trumpist leaders of the national security establishment.

This weakness in the Democratic Party is reflected as well in the Left popular movements. The Left has become focused on identity politics, and has only recently, since the Occupy Wall Street movement after the 2008 Wall Street crisis and bank bail-outs, begun to focus more on extreme inequality, economic policies which serve corporations, not people and, to some degree, climate change. But the peace movement, which played a central role in the Left of the 1960s when the Vietnam War was raging, has virtually disappeared. There are many local and even national anti-war and peace organizations, including ones led by or composed of veterans. These include Vets for Peace, Code Pink, Massachusetts Peace Action, ANSWER, and many other anti-war groups. But peace activism and the peace movement are struggling to survive and gain visibility in the public. To be a "true" American who can be taken seriously, one has to "honor" America's wars and the service of the soldiers, even if Trump himself is proposing pull-outs. Ironically, Trump's call for getting troops out of Syria, Iraq and Afghanistan, which should be turned into full withdrawal rather than modest and symbolic reforms, are not generally supported by the Democrats or the Left. Or, at best, they are viewed as acceptable if carried out "responsibly," which means maybe never pulling out all the troops or stopping the bombs and drones.

This is the most serious obstacle to ending glorious causes in the US. Peace movements are the most important popular force that can turn the nation away from glory. The Democratic Party will never champion an end to US global power and wars unless peace movements, helping channel a popular revulsion against US endless wars, force them to do so. The political establishment will resist this above all else, but the public's mood may be changing.

The parallels with Europe after two world wars are not perfect, since US wars have not yet created the collapse of the nation as experienced by European countries. But the US is seeing endless wars in Afghanistan, Iraq and other "terrorist" nations or groups. Nobel economist

Joseph Stiglitz called Iraq the $3 trillion war. That's a huge sum for the catastrophes in the Mideast created by that war alone. But it's not just the economic cost. The defeat after defeat in US endless wars have cost America respect and "exceptionalism" abroad, and increasingly at home.

As in Europe, such defeats weaken glory. They make it less seductive. Even President Trump played on the public resentment of giving up their tax-dollars and social wellbeing for a pursuit of increasingly tarnished glory after so many disastrous wars.

Moving beyond glory, nonetheless, is an overwhelmingly difficult challenge. Glory is embedded in Western civilization and the US is now its main champion. That will not change quickly. It will require a new universalizing politics to root out the deep economic, political and cultural forces driving war and glorious causes. Such a politics can build on progressive struggles for universal health care, better wages and a Green New Deal. But it won't become real until the Democratic Party and the Left both move beyond their current failures.

If history is any lesson, the Left – led by human rights advocacy tied to progressives in the Democratic Party – will have to champion this movement. But they will have to speak passionately to the real needs of working people and to the Trumpists who were attracted to Trump's rhetoric about "silly wars." This is not a struggle that can be won if it doesn't win over much of the populist Right as well as the progressives on the Left. It will take changes in the Right to bring an end to glory. They will have to repudiate their obsession with "national security," expose the entrenched construction of foreign enemies to fight, and focus on economic transformation, social welfare, and environmental survival.

But the Left, to realize its historic mission, will need to transform itself. It will have to abandon its shift since the 1960s to an identity politics that largely has abandoned class politics and the struggle against America's militarized capitalism. It won't reach either liberal or conservative working people, nor even minorities and other racially oppressed people, without challenging capitalist empires. The way forward here was taught by Martin Luther King, who recognized that civil rights and the struggle to end racism was impossible as long as Americans supported wars such as Vietnam. Here is his clear recognition, that world peace and human rights cannot be divided and there will not be any racial or any other form without non-violence and peace.

> At Oslo I suggested that the philosophy and strategy of non-violence become immediately a subject for study and serious experimentation in every field of human conflict, including relations between nations. This was not, I believe, an unrealistic suggestion. World peace through non-violent means is neither absurd nor unattainable. All other methods have failed. Thus we must begin anew. Non-violence is a good starting point. Those of us who believe in this method can be voices of reason, sanity and understanding amid the voices of violence, hatred and emotion. We can very well set a mood of peace out of which a system of peace can be built. Racial injustice around the world. Poverty. War. When man solves these three great problems he will have squared his moral progress with his scientific progress. And more importantly, he will have learned the practical art of living in harmony.[13]

Nothing is more powerful today – as a political vision for the Left and for the nation – than King's passion to tie the civil rights movement and all other freedom and equality struggles to a peace movement that lies at the foundation of any struggle for equality and survival, whether waged by the Left or Right.

> I want to say one other challenge that we face is simply that we must find an alternative to war and bloodshed. Anyone who feels, and there are still a lot of people who feel that way, that war can solve the social problems facing mankind is sleeping through a great revolution. . . . Our involvement in the war in Vietnam has torn up the Geneva Accord. It has strengthened the military-industrial complex; it has strengthened the forces of reaction in our nation. It has put us against the self-determination of a vast majority of the Vietnamese people, and put us in the position of protecting a corrupt regime that is stacked against the poor.

It has played havoc with our domestic destinies. This day we are spending five hundred thousand dollars to kill every Vietcong soldier. Every time we kill one we spend about five hundred thousand dollars while we spend only fifty-three dollars a year for every person characterized as poverty-stricken in the so-called poverty program, which is not even a good skirmish against poverty . . . And we force young black men and young white men to fight and kill in brutal solidarity. Yet when they come back home that [i.e. they] can't hardly live on the same block together . . .

It is no longer a choice, my friends, between violence and nonviolence. It is either nonviolence or nonexistence. And the alternative to disarmament, the alternative to a greater suspension of nuclear tests, the alternative to strengthening the United Nations and thereby disarming the whole world, may well be a civilization plunged into the abyss of annihilation, and our earthly habitat would be transformed into an inferno that even the mind of Dante could not imagine.[14]

King is speaking here not only to the true mission of the Left but to the real interests of conservative workers on the Right and everyone in the nation and world. Rejection of war and violence is the only way to ensure survival with justice, or indeed survival at all. King quoted John F. Kennedy, "Mankind must put an end to war or war will put an end to mankind."[15] Perhaps even Trumpists rejecting "silly wars" can find some common ground with this vision of politics.

For what King has prophesized, correctly, is that the pursuit of glory is now suicidal. Europe learned that lesson. Can the US –and the rest of the world – do the same? King offers hope, for if the most oppressed can reject violence and pursue peace, then surely the vast majority of working people can see the wisdom that King preached.

It is the wisdom that there is no more glory in glorious causes.

NOTES

Introduction
1. Robert Zemeckis and Bob Gale. *Back to the Future*; Hollywood, Ca: Universal Pictures; 1985
2. *Mad Magazine.* N.Y., N.Y.: Time Warner; 1988
3. Glenne Currie. "Jimmy Stewart's Son." United Press International; March 14, 1982
4. Uri Friedman. "Trump's New Term for Terrorists: 'Evil Losers'." *The Atlantic*; May 23, 2017
5. Jose Pagliery. "Donald Trump was a Nightmare Landlord in the 1980s." *CNNMoney*; March 28, 2016
6. Alan Greenspan. *New York Times*; 1958
7. Ayn Rand. *Capitalism: The Unknown Ideal*; N.Y., N.Y.: Penguin; 1967; pp. 61–62
8. Institute for Policy Studies. "The CEO-Worker Pay Gap." February 2019
9. Ryan Struyk and Sam Petulla. "How Good the Stock Market Under Trump Really Is, In One Chart." *CNN*; January 5, 2018
10. David Leonhardt. "For Wages, a Trump Slump." *New York Times*; August 5, 2018
11. Wofgang Streeck. "Trump and the Trumpists." Inference; April 2017
12. Other people have used a similar vocabulary; for example: Stephen Kinzer, "The Enlightenment Had a Good Run." *Boston Globe*; December 23, 2016 and Sean Trende; "Why Trump? Why Not." Chicago, Ill; *Real Clear Politics*; January 29, 2016
13. Eric Fromm. *Escape From Freedom*; Austin, Tx: Holt, Rinehart and Winston; 1969; p. 34
14. Ibid., p. 36
15. Robert Baden-Powell. *Scouting for Boys*; London, U.K.: C. Arthur Pearson Ltd; 1967; p. 211
16. King James Bible. Nashville, Tn: Thomas Nelson; 2017; Timothy: 6:10
17. Max Weber (translated by Anthony Giddens). *The Protestant Ethic and the Spirit of Capitalism*; N.Y., N.Y.: Routledge; 2015; p. 124
18. Max Weber (translated by Ephraim Fischoff). *Sociology of Religion*; Boston, MA: Beacon; 1963; p. 125
19. Max Weber (translated by Guenther Roth, Claus Wittich). *Economy and Society*; 1978; Oakland, Ca: University of California Press; p. 125

20. Kurt Gauger. "Psychotherapy and Political World View." In George Mosse; *Nazi Culture*; N.Y., N.Y.: Schocken; 1966; p. 219
21. Jerry Falwell. *Listen America*; N.Y., N.Y.: Bantam; 1980; p. 12
22. Richard Santorum. www.brainyquote.com/quotes/quotes/r/ricksantor425210.html
23. "10 Questions with Rick Santorum." *New York Times*; March 1, 2012
24. Cornor Friedorsdorf. "Rick Santorum's Case for Big Government." *The Atlantic*; June 9, 2011
25. Richard Santorum. First Redeemer Church. Forsyth County, GA; February 19, 2012
26. Darwin Porter and Danforth Prince. *Love Triangle*; N.Y, N.Y.: Blood Moon; 2015

Chapter 1

1. Hugh Hudson. *Chariots of Fire*; Hollywood, Ca: Twentieth Century Fox; 1981
2. This is Magrass' and Derber's paraphrasing
3. Revised Standard Bible. Nashville, Tn: Abingdon; 2010; Matthew Chapter 5
4. Chuck Collins. *Born on Third Base*; White River Junction, Vt.: Chelsea Green; 2016
5. Ayn Rand. "What is Capitalism?" In *Capitalism*; N.Y., N.Y.: Penguin; 1967; p. 12
6. For a more detailed discussion, see Charles Derber, William Schwartz and Yale Magrass, *Power in the Highest Degree*; N.Y., N.Y.: Oxford; 1990
7. James A. Herrick. *The Making of the New Spirituality*; ISBN 0-8308-3279-3: InterVarsity Press; 2004; pp. 75–76
8. I, Vardi. "The French Revolutionary Calendar." §3.5.4. In *Computational Recreations in Mathematica*; Reading, Ma: Addison-Wesley, pp. 45–46, 1991
9. Jeremy Bentham. *An Introduction to the Principles of Morals and Legislation;* Oxford, U.K.: Clarendon; 1907; Preface
10. Bentham; ibid., Chapter 1.1
11. Charles Dickens. *Oliver Twist.*, U.K.: Penquin; 2003; p. 53
12. See Charles Derber, William Schwartz and Yale Magrass, *Power in the Highest Degree*; N.Y., N.Y.: Oxford; 1990
13. Tim Hindle. "Scientific Management." *The Economist*; February 9, 2009
14. Ibid.
15. Ibid.
16. Ibid.
17. See Charles Derber and Yale Magrass, *The Surplus American*. Boulder, Co.: Routledge; 2012
18. See Charles Derber, *Greed to Green*. Boulder, Co.: Routledge; 2010
19. Richard Polenberg. *In the Matter of J. Robert Oppenheimer*; Ithaca, N.Y.: Cornell; 2002; p. 97
20. Tom Demerly. "'Red Flag Confirmed F-35 Dominance with a 20:1 Kill Ratio' U.S. Air Force says." *The Aviator*; February 28, 2017
21. Hollie McKay. "More Than 180,000 Iraqi Civilians Killed Since 2003." *Fox News*. June 18, 2017
22. Paul Wood and Richard Hall. "U.S. Killing More Civilians in Iraq, Syria Than it Acknowledges." *USA Today*. February 4, 2016
23. Micho Kaku and Daniel Alexrod. *To Win a Nuclear War*. Montreal, Canada: Black Rose; 1987; p. 23
24. Joseph de Maistre. *Considerations on France* (translated by Richard Lebrun); Montreal, Canada: McGill-Queen's University Press; 1974; p. 23
25. *Muskogee Herald* (Muskogee Alabama) quoted in *New York Herald* September 16, 1856 (156)

26. Robert Baden-Powell. *Scouting for Boys*. London, U.K.: C. Arthur Pearson; 1967; p. 262
27. Colin Jones. "Did Emotions Cause the Terror." *New York Review of Books*; June 22, 2017; p. 38
28. Martin Daunton. "London's 'Great Stink' and Victorian Urban Planning." BBC History Trail, London; 2004
29. Karl Marx and Frederick Engels. "Manifesto of the Communist Party." Moscow, Russia: Progress Publishers; 2010; p. 15
30. De Maistre; op. cit.; p. 95
31. Stephen Kinzer. "The Enlightment Had a Good Run." *Boston Globe*; December 23, 2016
32. See "Conservative Thought" and "The Democratizaton of Culture." In Kurt Wolff; *From Karl Mannhein*; New Brunswick, N.J.: Transaction; 2011
33. De Maistre. Essay on the Generative Principle of Political Constitutions and other Human Institutions; 1809; Section XII (can be found on http://maistre.uni.cx/generative_principle.html)
34. De Maistre; ibid., Section XX
35. Oscar Hammerstein. *The King and I*; Hollywood, Ca: Twentieth Century Fox; 1956
36. De Maistre; op. cit.; Section XV
37. Horatio Alger. *Ragged Dick*; N.Y., N.Y: Signet; 2014
38. David Selznick. *Gone With the Wind*; Hollywood, Ca: Selznick International Pictures; 1939
39. Baden-Powell; op. cit.; p. 10
40. Baden-Powell; op. cit.; p. 39
41. Kristen Majewsk. "Marie Antoinette Built A Fake Peasant Village; Real Peasants Not Pleased." *Modern Notion*; Reno, Nv: Waldo Media; 2014
42. Eden Maxwell. Paul Gauguin – The Art Story. The Art Story Foundation; 2017 (see also www.theartstory.org/artist-gauguin-paul.htm)
43. Paul Gauguin; quoted in the Seattle Art Museum: Seattle, Wa; 2014
44. Wolfgang Streeck. "Trump and the Trumpists." *Inference: International Review of Science* April 7, 2017; p. 7
45. Nancy Isenberg. *White Trash. The 400 Year History of Class in America*; N.Y., N.Y: Penguin; 2016; p. 313
46. Streeck; op. cit.
47. Marc Lawrence. *Did You Hear About the Morgans*; Hollywood, Ca: Columbia Pictures; 2009
48. Marx; op. cit.
49. Fran Lebowitz. *Metropolitan Life*; N.Y., N.Y.: Dutton; 1978; p. 16
50. Woody Allen. *Love and Death*; Hollywood Ca; MGM; 1975
51. Tony Perkins. "FRC Gets to the Bottom of Spanking." *Washington Watch Daily*; December 26, 2007
52. Richard Santorum. First Redeemer Church. Forsyth County, Ga. February 19, 2012
53. Victor Volsky. "Gay Marriage: The Hidden Agenda." *American Thinker*, May 27, 2012
54. Isenberg; op. cit.; p. 285
55. Constance Grady. "Almost 30 Million People Watched the Royal Wedding on US Broadcast Alone." *Vox*; May 21, 2018
56. Thorstein Veblen. *Theory of the Leisure Class*; Oxford, U.K.: Oxford University Press; 2009
57. "The Industrial Age in America: Robber Barons and Captains of Industry." *National Endowment for the Humanities*; https://edsitement.neh.gov/lesson-plan/industrial-age-america-robber-barons-and-captains-industry
58. Amy Vanderbilt. *Complete Book of Etiquette: A Guide to Gracious Living*; N.Y., N.Y.: Doubleday; 1954

59. Isenberg; op. cit.; p. 302
60. Oliver Stone. *JFK*; Hollywood, Ca: Warner Bros.; 1991
61. Donald Trump. Acceptance Speech; Republican National Convention; Cleaveland, Ohio; July 21, 2016
62. Richard Nixon. Interview by David Frost; San Clemente, Ca.; May 1977
63. John F. Kennedy. Inaugural Address. Washington, D.C.; January 21, 1961
64. Michael Harrington. *The Other America*; N.Y., N.Y.: Scribner; 1997
65. Lisa Gordon. "Donald Trump's Home vs. the White House: Which Is More Posh?" November 15, 2016; www.realtor.com/news/trends/donald-trumps-home-vs-white-house
66. Kinzer; op. cit.
67. Ropper Center for Public Opinion Research. Cornell University; https://ropercenter.cornell.edu/polls/us-elections/how-groups-voted/how-groups-voted-2012/
68. Tanzina Vega. "The Wage Gap Between Blacks and Whites is the Worst It's Been in Nearly Four Decades." *CNN Money*; September 20, 2016; http://money.cnn.com/2016/09/20/news/economy/black-white-wage-gap/index.html
69. Cornell West. "Good-bye American Neoliberalism. A New Era is Here." *The Guardian*; November 17, 2016
70. Barack Obama. ABC News; Chicago, Ill. November 4, 2008
71. William Astore. "Make Sports, Not War." *Tom Dispatch*; August 19, 2018
72. James Stavridis. "We Have a Military to Defend Our Values, Not Tear Them Down as Trump is Doing." *Boston Globe*; August 24, 2017
73. Barack Obama. Acceptance Speech for the Democratic Nomination; Denver, Colorado. *New York Times*; August 28, 2008
74. Leonard Bernstein & Stephen Sondheim. *West Side Story*. N.Y., N.Y.: 1957
75. Bible, English Standard Version. 1 Peter 2: 16–17; Wheaton, Ill: Good News Publishers; 2016
76. Stavridis; op. cit.
77. General William Boykin. Speech in an Oregon Church; October 2003
78. Lauren Markoe. "Did God Choose Trump? What it Means to Believe in Divine Intervention." *Religious News Service*; January 17, 2017
79. Joseph De Maistre; *Considerations on France*; Cambridge, U.K.: Cambridge University Press; 2003; p. 51
80. Rudolf Friml. *The Vagabond King* (an operetta in four acts); N.Y., N.Y.; 1925
81. Brian Skoloff. "Jodi Arias: 'Death Is The Ultimate Freedom'." *Huffington Post*; May 8, 2013
82. Lynyrd Skynyrd. "God and Guns." Nashville, Tn: Blackbird Studios. 2009
83. Graeme Wood. "Why We Fear and Admire the Military Sniper." *Boston Globe*; January 16, 2015
84. William Boykin, quoted in Greg Corombos. "U.S. General: America Craves More 'heroes' Like Chris Kyle." WND Radio; February 3, 2015
85. Stanley Kramer. *High Noon*; Hollywood, Ca: United Artists; 1952
86. Cyryl Mockridge and Alfred Newman. *The Man Who Shot Liberty Valance*; Hollywood, Ca: Paramount; 1962
87. Alfred Lord Tennyson. "The Charge of the Light Brigade." 1854
88. David Williamson, *Gallipoli*; Hollywood, Ca: Paramount; 1981
89. Frederick Wiseman. *High School*; Cambridge, Ma: Zipporah Films; 1968
90. Russell W. Glennt. "Man Against Fire." *Vietnam Magazine*; April 2002
91. Army News Service. "Understanding Why Soldiers Decide to Fight"; 2018
92. Jean Renoir. *The Grand Illusion*. Paris, France: Réalisations d'Art Cinématographique; 1937

93. Malcolm Brown and Shirley Seaton. *The Christmas Truce*; London, U.K.: Pan; 1999
94. Eugene Debs Canton, Ohio; June 16, 1918
95. Sgt Barry Sadler. "The Ballad of the Green Berets." RCA Victory; 1966
96. Arlo Guthrie. "Alice's Restaurant." Warner Bros.; 1967
97. "'March Against Death' Commences in Washington D.C." *This Day in History*. History Channel. November 13, 1969
98. Alfred Bryan. "I Didn't Raise My Boy to Be a Soldier." 1915
99. Lieutenant Colonel John McCreae. "In Flanders Fields." 1915
100. Stephen Magagnini, Ellen Garrison and Sam Stanton. "At Least 10 Hurt at Chaotic, Bloody Neo-Nazi Rally at Capitol." The Sacramento Bee; Sacramento, Ca.
101. www.marineband.marines.mil/About/Library-and-Archives/The-Marines-Hymn/
102. Hillel quote by Yaakov Astor. *Me, Myself and I: Ethics of the Fathers* 1:14; June 5, 2004 (see www.aish.com/sp/pg/48893292.html)

Chapter 2

1. George Gershwin and Michael Feinstein. "Swanee." 1919
2. Stephen Foster. "Old Black Joe." The Minnesota Heritage Songbook; 1860
3. Paul Robeson. "Born to Be Free." Black 47
4. Paul Robeson. *Paul Robeson Speaks*; N.Y., N.Y.: Kensington; 2002; p. 230
5. Tony Perucci. *Paul Robeson and the Cold War Performance Complex*; Ann Arbor, Michigan: University of Michigan Press; 2012; p. 169
6. Benjamin T. Arrington. "Industry and Economy During the Civil War." National Park Service; www.nps.gov/articles/industry-and-economy-during-the-civil-war.htm
7. Jim Kirwan. Slavery Transformed America; November 25, 2009
8. Waters McIntosh. In George P. Rawick, ed., *The American Slave: A Composite Autobiography*; Westport, Ct: Greenwood; 1972–79; Vol. 2 (AR), Part 5, 20
9. Hammond, quoted in George M. Weston, *The Poor Whites of the South* Washington, D.C.: Buell & Blanchard; 1856; p. 3
10. James Hammond. *Selections from the Letters and Speeches of Hon. James H. Hammond*; N.Y., N.Y.: J. F. Trow; 1966; p. 124
11. Al Carroll (Professor Northern Virginia Community College and Fulbright Scholar). "What Percentage of Southern Population Owned Slaves at the Beginning of the American Civil War." April 20, 2015 (see also www.quora.com/What-percentage-of-the-Southern-population-owned-slaves-at-the-beginning-of-the-American-Civil-War)
12. www.civilwar.org/learn/articles/civil-war-facts
13. William M. Brewer. "Poor Whites and Negroes in the South Since the Civil War." *The Journal of Negro History*; Vol. 15, No. 1; January 1930; p. 26
14. Gerald Horne. *The Counter-Revolution of 1776*; N.Y., N.Y.: NYU Press; 2016; Introduction
15. Ibid.
16. "The Middle Passage." *The Terrible Transformation*. PBS.org.; 2000
17. Olaudah Equiano. *The Interesting Narrative of the Life of Olaudah Equiano or Gustavus Vassa the African*. First published in 1789 in London, U.K.
18. Horne; op. cit.
19. Horne; op. cit.
20. Howard Zinn. *A People's History of the United States*; N.Y., N.Y.: Harper; p. 85
21. Donald Trump, quoted in John M. Crisp. "Are George Washington and Thomas Jefferson next?" *Tribune News* Service; August 22, 2017

22. Jacey Fortin. "What Robert E. Lee Wrote to *The Times* About Slavery in 1858." *New York Times*; August 18, 2017
23. David Selznick. *Gone With the Wind*; Hollywood, Ca: Selznick International Pictures; 1939
24. Eugene Genovese. *The Political Economy of Slavery*; Middletown, Ct: Wesleyan; 1988
25. Elizabeth Fox-Genovese and Eugene Genovese. *The Mind of the Master Class*; Cambridge, U.K.: Cambridge University Press; 2005
26. George Fitzhugh, quoted in Ta-Nehisi Coates. "If White Slavery Be Wrong, the Bible Cannot Be True." *The Atlantic*; May 27, 2011
27. George Fitzhugh. *Cannibals All*; Richmond, Va: A. Morris; 1857
28. Ibid.
29. Karl Marx. Letter to Abraham Lincoln. *The Bee-Hive Newspaper*; No. 169; November 7, 1865
30. Frederick Engels. *The Principles of Communism*; Moscow, Russia; Progress Press; 1969; pp. 81–97
31. Catherine Lavender. "Liberty Rhetoric and Nineteenth-Century American Women." Department of History, College of Staten Island; 1998
32. Richie Havens. "Follow the Drinking Gourd." 1991
33. Quoted in Ta-Nehisi Coates. "Slaves Who Like Slavery." *Atlantic Monthly*; June 24, 2010
34. Solomon Northrup. *Twelve Years a Slave*; Auburn, N.Y.: Derby & Miller; 1853
35. Breen Patrick H. *The Land Shall Be Deluged in Blood: A New History of the Nat Turner Revolt*; Oxford, U.K.: Oxford University Press; 2015, pp. 98, 231
36. Thom Hartman. "The Second Amendment was Ratified to Preserve Slavery." *Truth-Out*; January 15, 2013
37. Alexander H. Stephen. "Corner Stone" Speech: Savannah, Georgia; March 21, 1861; http://teachingamericanhistory.org/library/document/cornerstone-speech/
38. Jim Burgess, Museum Specialist at the Manassas National Battlefield Museum. "Blood in Bull Run: The Battlefield Today." *Hallowed Ground Magazine*; Spring 2011
39. *Guinness World Records, 60 (2015 edn.); 2014; pp. 160–161*
40. *The Daily Mail; April 4, 2008*
41. Gavin Lambert. "The Making of Gone With the Wind, Part II." *Atlantic Monthly*; March 1973
42. Selznick; op. cit.
43. Margaret Mitchell. *Gone With the Wind*; N.Y., N.Y.: Pocket Books; 2008; p. 320
44. Mitchell; ibid., p. 319
45. Abraham Lincoln (Peoria, Ill; 1854); *Collected Works of Abraham Lincoln. Volume 2*. Rockville, Md: Wildside Press; 2008; p. 250.
46. https://store.ushistory.org/products/men-of-virginia-civil-war-recruiting-poster-1861
47. https://images.search.yahoo.com/images/view;_ylt=A2KJkP2T99ZPzWIAokm-JzbkF;_ylu=X3oDMTB1MTQ4cGxyBHNlYwNzcgRzbGsDaW1n?back=http://images.search.yahoo.com/search/image
48. www.theatlantic.com/national/archive/2011/10/civil-war-recruitment-posters/247420/
49. Abraham Lincoln. "Open Letter to Horace Greeley." Washington D.C.; April 22, 1862
50. Abraham Lincoln. "The Lincoln-Douglas Debates 4th Debate Part I." Charleston, Ill.; September 18, 1858
51. Henry Mayer. *All on Fire: William Lloyd Garrison and the Abolition of Slavery*; N.Y., N.Y.: St. Martin's Press; 1998; pp. 201–204
52. William T. Sherman. Message to William J. Hardee, December 17, 1864, recorded in Memoirs of General William T. Sherman; Boston, Ma: Library of America; 1990

53. Henry Clay Work. "Marching Through Georgia." Chicago, Ill: Root & Cady; 1865
54. Lincoln biography. Americanpresident.org; October 13, 2006.
55. "Subject To Death: The Confederate Response To Black Union Troops." On the Battlefield; www.thiscruelwar.com; April 5, 2016
56. Larry Holzwarth. "10 of the Most Heinous Forgotten War Crimes of the American Civil War." https://historycollection.co
57. Stefan G. Chrissanthos. *Warfare in the Ancient World*; Westport, CT; Praeger; 2008. p. 80
58. M. Wheelis. "Biological Warfare at the 1346 Siege of Caffa." Emerg Infect Dis (Center for Disease Control); 2002
59. Guy Gugliotta. "New Estimate Raises Civil War Death Toll." *New York Times*; April 2, 2012
60. Eric Foner. *Freedom's Lawmakers: A Directory of Black Officeholders During Reconstruction*; Baton Rouge, La: LSU Press; 1996
61. James W. Loewen. "Five Myths About Reconstruction." *Washington Post*; January 21, 2016
62. Tracey Baptiste. "The Civil War and Reconstruction Era." *Britannica Educational Publishing*; 2015; p. 48
63. Noah Weiland. "Howard University Stares Down Challenges and Hard Questions on Black Colleges." *New York Times*; April 26, 2018
64. "Carpetbaggers and Scalawags." The History Channel; www.history.com/topics/american-civil-war/carpetbaggers-and-scalawags
65. David Pilgrim. *What Was Jim Crow*; Museum of Racist Memorabilia. Ferris State University: Big Rapids, Mich; September 2000
66. Andrew Johnson, quoted in Keith E. Whittington. *American Political Thought*; Chapter 6: "Secession, Civil War, and Reconstruction – Equality and Status"; Oxford, U.K.: Oxford University Press; 2016
67. Eric Foner. *Reconstruction: America's Unfinished Revolution, 1863–1877*; N.Y.,N.Y.: Harper; 2014; pp. 555–556
68. Loewen; op. cit.
69. Emily Glaser. "The Scourge of the South: Carpetbaggers and Scalawags." *The Voice of the South*; Potterbrigs.com
70. W. P. Trent. "A New South View of Reconstruction." *The Sewanee Review*; Vol. 9, No. 1; January, 1901; p. 6
71. Eric Foner. *Reconstruction: America's Unfinished Revolution 1863–1877*; N.Y., N.Y.: Harpers; 2014; p. 296
72. Maury Klein. "Southern Railroad Leaders, 1865–1893: Identities and Ideologies." *Business History Review*; 1968; p. 42
73. Ibid.
74. Foner; op. cit.
75. Glaser; op. cit.
76. "Carpetbaggers and Scalawags." History Channel; op. cit.
77. "Carpetbaggers and Scalawags." History Channel; op. cit.
78. D. W. Griffith. *Birth of a Nation*; Hollywood, Ca: D.W. Griffith Corp; 1915
79. Woodrow Wilson; quoted in *Birth of a Nation*; op. cit.
80. Ibid.
81. Mitchell; op. cit.
82. Cited by Suzanne Ashmore. *AP US Chapter 22;* January 7, 2016; /prezi.com/ny02mbgnn79r/ap-us-chapter-22/
83. Kkk.com/ttps://americanheritagecommittee.com/main/product/american-by-birth-southern-by-choice-dixie-outfitters/

84. www.justsomelyrics.com/1553627/the-klansmen-stand-up-&-be-counted-lyrics.html
85. www.brainyquote.com/quotes/billy_graham_626325
86. Thornwell, quoted in Eugene Genovese. "James Henley Thornwell and Southern Religion." Abbeville, Va: Abbeville Institute; May 5, 2015
87. George Wallace. Inaugural Address as Governor; Montgomery, Al; January 14, 1963
88. Howell Raines. "George Wallace, Segregation Symbol, Dies at 79." *New York Times*; September 14, 1998
89. Glenn Eskew. "George C. Wallace." *Encyclopedia of Alabama*; Auburn, Al.; 2008
90. US Census Bureau. "American Factfinder." July 2017
91. Lyndon, Johnson quoted in Bill Moyers. "What a Real President was Like." *Washington Post*; November 13, 1988
92. Katherine Steward. "Eighty-one Percent of White Evangelicals Voted for Donald Trump. Why?" *The Nation*; November 17, 2016
93. Arlie Hochschild. *Strangers in Their Own Land*; N.Y., N.Y.: New Press; 2016; p. 47
94. Ibid., p. 92
95. Sean Braswell. "Why the U.S. Military Is So Southern." *Daily Dose*; November 20, 2016
96. Deborah White. "What Is Gun Ownership Like State by State." *ThoughtCO*; May 10, 2018.
97. Paul Thurman. *Deep South*; Boston, Ma: Houghton Mifflin; 2015; p. 106
98. https://civilwartalk.com/threads/world-war-2-recruiting-poster-back-then-they-admired-robert-e-lee.89310/
99. Karen Cox. *Dixie's Daughters: The United Daughters of the Confederacy and the Preservation of Southern Culture*; Gainesville, Fl: University Press of Florida; 2003
100. Leonard Rabon Poe. *Self-Description of Southern Pride: An Alternative Civil War History for the Southern Mind*; Independently published; ISBN-10: 1521995842; 2017
101. Carol Stocker: "Student's Response to Confederate Flag Touches off Free Speech Dispute at Harvard." *Boston Globe*; April 21, 1991
102. Karl Marx. "The Eighteenth Brumaire of Louis Bonaparte." Marx/Engels Internet Archives; 2006
103. Kristin Toussant. "Black Advocates Make Final Plea to Avoid 'Racial Showdown' Over Faneuil Hall Name." Boston, Ma: *METROUS*; August 1, 2018
104. The Papers of Jefferson Davis; Houston, Tx: Rice University; October 11, 1858
105. Nancy Isenberg. *White Trash. The 400 Year History of Class in America*; N.Y., N.Y.: Penguin; 2016; p. 159
106. Kathleen Banks Nutter. "'Militant Mothers': Boston, Busing, and the Bicentennial of 1976." (PDF) *Historical Journal of Massachusetts*; Vol. 38; No. 1 (Fall 2010): 52–75. Retrieved April 6, 2017
107. Kathleen Kilgore. "Militant Mothers: The Politicization of ROAR Women." *The Real Paper*; November 13, 1976; Section 4; p. 6
108. Louise Day Hicks, quoted in *Michigan Daily*; June 15, 1976; p. 9
109. Louise Day Hicks, quoted in Dominic Sandbroook. *Mad as Hell: The Crisis of the 1970s and the Rise of the Populist Right*; N.Y., N.Y.: Alfred A. Knopf; 2011; p. 53

Chapter 3

1. Brian Murdoch. *Fighting Songs and Warring Words: Popular Lyrics of Two World Wars*, pp. 121–122, Routledge 1990
2. Lyrics of "Deutschland erwache"
3. "Queen Victoria Died in the Crook of the Kaiser's Perfect Arm." *Look and Learn*; London, U.K.: Fleetway; March 31, 1973

4. Sir Edward Grey quoted in John Alfred Spender. *Life, Journalism and Politics*; Wahroonga, NSW Australia: Sagwan; 2018; pp. 14–15
5. Imperial War Museums. "Voices of the First World War: Outbreak." May 26, 2018
6. Ibid.
7. Reveille Press. A Division of Tommies Guides Military Book Specialists; Tommies Guides Ltd; 2014
8. Imperial War Museums. "Voices of the First World War" op. cit.
9. Walter Mühlhausen. "Social Democratic Party of Germany (SPD)." *International Encyclopedia of the First World War*; December 8, 2015
10. Rosa Luxemburg. "The Junius Pamphlet." 1915; Chapter 1
11. Molly Billings; "The Influenza Pandemic of 1918." February, 2005 (see https://virus.stanford.edu/uda/)
12. *"Twentieth Century Atlas – Death Tolls." necrometrics.com*; April 14, 2018
13. John Moody. *The Masters of Capital*; New Haven, CT: Yale University Press; 1919; pp. 164–165.
14. Harry Hopps (artist, 1918); Library of Congress, Washington D.C.; https://www.loc.gov/pictures/item/2010652057http://sites.utexas.edu/acc/files/2014/04/85_140_1215.jpg
15. David Mikics. "The Jews Who Stabbed Germany in the Back." *Tablet*; November 9, 2017
16. "The Silent Holocaust: The Belgian Genocide of the Congo." *Black Voices*; July 12, 2009
17. Collin M. Anderson. "The Industrial Workers of the World in the Seattle General Strike." Seattle General Strike Project; 1999
18. Michael Kazin. *War Against War*; N.Y., N.Y.: Simon & Schuster; 2017; p. 188
19. John Steinbeck. *East of Eden*; N.Y., N.Y.: Penquin; 1992; Chapter 46
20. George M. Cohen. "Over There." https://genius.com/George-m-cohan-over-there-lyrics
21. Walter Donaldson. "How Ya Gonna Keep 'Em Down on the Farm?" Transcribed from Lieut. Jim Europe's 369th U.S. Infantry ("Hell Fighters") Band; March 3–7, 1919
22. David Jarmul. "By 1920, America Had Become World's Top Economic Power." The Making of a Nation; Voice of America; July 12, 2006.
23. "X-Kaiser Dead at 82, Turned Anti-semitic After Germany's Defeat." Jewish Telegraphic Agency; June 5, 1941
24. Mikics; op. cit.
25. John Simkin. "Versailles Treaty." Sparatacus; 1997
26. Charles Derber. *Sociopathic Society*; Boulder, Co: Routledge; 2013
27. Volker Ullrich. *Hitler: Ascent, 1889–1939*; N.Y., N.Y.: Random House; 2016
28. Joseph Boskin. *Urban Racial Violence*; Beverly Hills, Ca: Prentice Hall; 1976, p. 37
29. Emma Goldman. *Emma Goldman, Vol. 2: A Documentary History of the American Years, Volume 2*; Urbana, Ill: University of Illinois Press; p. 377
30. Walter Donaldson; op. cit.
31. Josef von Sternberg. *The Blue Angel*; Berlin, Germany: UFA Tonfilm; 1930
32. Christopher Isherwood. *The Berlin Stories*; N.Y., N.Y.: New Direction; 2008
33. Bob Fosse. *Cabaret;* Hollywood, Ca: Allied Artists; 1972
34. Peter Gay. *Weimar Culture*; N.Y., N.Y.: Norton; 2001
35. Jack Eidt. "Dada as the Antidote to War and Capitalism." Los Angeles, Ca: WilderUtopia; April 25, 2015
36. Tristan Tzara. "Dada Manifesto." Paris, France; 1918
37. Jean Arp, in Dadaland; quoted in Cosana Maria Eram and Debabrata Dash. *The Autobiographical Pac*; Charleston, S.C.: BiblioBazaar; 2010; p. 20
38. Bertolt Brecht. *The Threepenny Opera*; N.Y., N.Y.: Grove Press; 1994

39. Rosa Luxemburg (1918) *The Russian Revolution*; Chapter 6; www.marxists.org/archive/luxemburg/1918/russian-revolution/ch06.htm
40. Erich Maria Remarque. *All Quiet on the West Front*; London, U.K.: Atlantic; 1995; p. 263
41. Patrick Sauer. "The Most Loved and Hated Novel About World War I." Washington D.C.: Smithsonian; 2015 (see also www.smithsonianmag.com/history/most-loved-and-hated-novel-about-world-war-I-180955540/)
42. Karl Marx and Frederick Engels. *The Communist Manifesto*; Moscow, Russia: Progress Press; 1848
43. Adolph Hitler, quoted in the *Daily Express*; September 28, 1930
44. George Mosse. *The Crisis of German Ideology*; N.Y., N.Y.: Howard Fertig; 1999
45. Adolph Hitler. Speech of February 20, 1938. Quoted *in My New Order*
46. Adolph Hitler. quoted in *Danziger Vorposten*; May 2, 1938
47. Ian Buruma. "Art in a Degenerate World." *New York Review of Books*; September 27, 2018; p. 84
48. Adolph Hitler. Speech of July 19, 1937; Quoted in *Domarus*
49. Joseph Dietrich, quoted in George Mosse; *Nazi Culture*; N.Y., N.Y: Schocken; 1966; p. 31
50. Hitler, quoted in Mosse; ibid., p. 39
51. Rudolf Hess, quoted in Mosse, ibid.; p. 31
52. Adolph Hitler. *Mein Kampf*; Alingsås, Sweden: Midgaard; 2015
53. Adolph Hitler. Speech of January 30, 1939. Quoted in Domarus
54. Quoted in Richard Koenigsberg. *Nations Have The Right to Kill; Hitler, The Holocaust and War*; N.Y., N.Y.: Library of Social Science; 2009; p. 5
55. Ibid., pp. 5 and 6
56. Adolph Hitler, February 24, 1940. Quoted in *Hitler's Words*; Washington, D.C.: American Council on Public Affairs; 1944
57. Adolph Hitler. Obersalzberg Speech; August 22, 1939
58. Richard J. Evans. *The Coming of the Third Reich;* N.Y., N.Y.: Penguin; 2004; p. 317
59. Adolph Hitler, quoted in "Hitler's Words", op. cit; April 20, 1923.
60. Adolph Hitler, quoted in *Domarus*; speech of January 30, 1941.
61. James Pool. *Who Financed Hitler*; N.Y., N.Y.: Simon & Schuster; 1997; p. 75
62. Karl Wiehe, quoted in Lasha Darkmoon. "The Sexual Decadence of Weimar Germany." *Veterans Today*; September 24, 2014
63. http://fyeah-history.tumblr.com/post/51190782519/a-leaflet-published-in-1920-by-the-reichsbund
64. Arthur Waskow. *God-Wrestling*; N.Y., N.Y.: Schocken, 1978; p. 129
65. Quoted in Miriam Weinstein. *Yiddish*; N.Y., N.Y.: Ballentine Books; 2001; p. 127
66. Paul Breines. *Tough Jews*; N.Y., N.Y.: Basic; 1992
67. Bruno Bettelheim. *The Informed Heart*; N.Y., N.Y.: Free Press, 1979; p. 149
68. Yehuda Bauer. *Rethinking the Holocaust*. New Haven, Ct.: Yale University Press; 2001; pp. 80–82
69. Hannah Arendt. *Eichmann in Jerusalem*; N.Y., N.Y.: Penguin; 2006; p. 104
70. Thomas Hobbes. *Leviathan*; N.Y., N.Y.: Penguin; 2017
71. Louise Ridley. "The Holocaust's Forgotten Victims." *Huffington Post*; January 27, 2015
72. Winston Churchill, quoted in Peter Millett. "The Worst Form of Government." U.K.: Foreign & Commonwealth Office; March 5, 2014
73. Office of the Historian. "The Allende Years and the Pinochet Coup, 1969–1973." U.S. Department of State; 2016
74. Milton Friedman. "Commanding Heights." PBS Interview; October 1, 2010
75. Fosse; op. cit.
76. Pool; op. cit.
77. Winston Churchill, quoted in Richard Langworth. *Churchill by Himself*; N.Y., N.Y: Public Affairs; 2008; p. 346

78. Evans; op. cit.
79. William L. Hosch. "*The Reichstag Fire and the Enabling Act of March 23, 1933.*" *Encyclopaedia Britannica*; March 23, 2007
80. See our other book: Charles Derber and Yale R. Magrass. *Capitalism: Should You Buy It?*; Boulder, Co; Routledge; Ch 4
81. John Simkin. "Unemployment in Nazi Germany." Taunton, U.K.: Spartacus Educational Newsletter; January 2016
82. Sheri Berman. "It Wasn't Just Hate. Fascism Offered Robust Social Welfare." *Aeon*; March 27, 2017
83. Richard J. Evans. "A Community of Defeat." *The Nation*; October 29, 2018; p. 33
84. *Joan Gearin*. "Movie vs. Reality: The Real Story of the Von Trapp Family." Washington, D.C.: *Prologue Magazine*; Winter 2005; Vol. 37; No. 4
85. Albert Einstein. Letter to President Roosevelt; www.atomicarchive.com/Docs/Begin/Einstein.shtml; August 2, 1939
86. Atomic Heritage Foundation; "Scientific Refugees and the Manhattan Project." June 20, 2018
87. Raffaele Laudani (editor). "Secret Reports on Nazi Germany. The Frankfurt School Contribution to the War Effort by Franz Neumann, Herbert Marcuse & Otto Kirchheimer." Princeton, N.J.: Princeton University Press; 2013; p. 2
88. Steven Bach. *Marlene Dietrich: Life and Legend*; Minneapolis, Mn: University of Minnesota Press: 2013
89. Stephen Parker. *Bertolt Brecht: A Literary Life*; N.Y., N.Y.: Methuen Drama; 2015
90. Dominic Selwood. "Dresden Was a Civilian Town With No Military Significance. Why Did We Burn Its People?" *The Telegraph*; February 13, 2015
91. John Maynard Keynes. *The Economic Consequences of Peace*; Chicago, ll: Rogers; 2013
92. Winston Churchill, quoted in Geoffrey Wheatcroft. "Imperial Son." *New York Times*; August 15, 2014
93. Emma Goldman, quoted in Alice Wexler. *Emma Goldman in Exile*; Boston, Ma: Beacon; 1989; p. 236
94. Hillel Italie. "David S. Wyman, Holocaust Scholar, Dead at 89." *The Times of Israel*; March 15, 2018
95. Arthur Ponsonby quoted in Nicholson Baker. "Why I'm A Pacifist." *N.Y.: Harpers*; May 2011
96. Vera Brittain; quoted in Baker; ibid.
97. Baker; op. cit.
98. "Second Source List and Detailed Death Tolls for the Twentieth Century Hemoclysm." erols.com; March 4, 2016.
99. Wirtschaft und Statistik November 1949 pp. 226–229, journal published by Statistisches Bundesamt Deutschland (German Federal Statistical Office)
100. Koenigsberg; op. cit.; p. 105
101. "A Black Day for Germany." *The Times*; November 11, 1938 (the 20th anniversary of Germany's surrender in World War I)

Chapter 4

1. Janet Greene. "Fascist Threat." www.musixmatch.com/lyrics/Janet-Greene/Fascist-Threat
2. Antoine Prost. "War Losses." *International Encyclopedia of the First World War*; Berlin, Germany; October 8, 2014; https://encyclopedia.1914-1918-online.net/home.html
3. "Research Starters: Worldwide Deaths in World War II"; National World War II Museum; New Orleans, LA: www.nationalww2museum.org/students-teachers/student-resources/research-starters/research-starters-worldwide-deaths-world-war

NOTES

4. Richard J. Evans. "A Community of Defeat." *The Nation*; October 29, 2018; p. 33
5. Ibid.
6. History Channel. "Federal Republic of Germany Is Established." A&E Television Networks; November 13, 2009
7. General George Patton. Speech to the Third Army; July 5, 1944
8. Commonwealth War Graves Commission Annual Report 2014–2015; p. 39
9. Commonwealth War Graves Commission Annual Report 2014–2015; p. 38
10. "1945: Churchill Loses General Election." On This Day; BBC; July 26, 2005
11. Arthur Allen. "The Problem with Trump's Admiration of Patton." Politico; December 26, 2016
12. George Patton. Letter to Beatrice (29 September 1945), published in *The Patton Papers*, edited by Martin Blumenson; Boston, Ma: Da Cappo Press; 1996; Vol. 2; p. 786
13. Diaries, General Patton, quoted in Stanley P. Hirshson. *General Patton: A Soldier's Life*; N.Y., N.Y.: Harper; 2002; p. 661
14. Richard Cohen. "What Bill O'Reilly ignored about George Patton." *Washington Post*; September 29, 2014
15. Phyllis Schlafly. *A Choice Not an Echo*. Alton, Il: Pere Marquette, 1964; p. 23
16. Wayne Biddle. *The Dark Side of the Moon*; N.Y., N.Y.: Norton; 2009
17. Fiedermann, Heß, and Jaeger. *Das KZ Mittelbau Dora. Ein historischer Abriss*; Berlin, Germany: Westkreuz Verlag; 1993; p. 100
18. Niall Ferguson. *Empire*; N.Y., N.Y.: Basic; 2004; pp. 126, 127
19. Gar Alperovitz. "Did America Have to Drop the Bomb to End the War?" *Washington Post*; August 4, 1985
20. Charles E. Wyzanski. "Nuremberg: A Fair Trial? A Dangerous Precedent." *The Atlantic*; April 1946
21. Ibid.
22. Hannah Arendt. *Eichmann in Jerusalem*; N.Y., N.Y.: Penguin; 2006; p. 91
23. Nelson Mandela. "Statement On Receiving Truth and Reconciliation Commission Report." October 29, 1998
24. Jason Beaubien. "The Country With The World's Inequality Is… " NPR; April 2, 2018
25. Sarah Wildman. "Why You See Swastikas In American But Not Germany." *Vox*; August 16, 2017
26. Herbert Marcuse. *Repressive Tolerance*. Boston, Ma: Beacon; 1965
27. Ibid.
28. Katrin Bennhold. "Can Europe's Liberal Order Survive As The Memory Of War Fades?" *Boston Globe*; November 10, 2018
29. Jordan Stancil. "Rioting in Germany Exposes the Growing Power of the Far Right." *The Nation*; September 7, 2018
30. Ibid.
31. "GDP (current US$)." World Development Indicators. World Bank. July 2018.
32. Monica Lungu. "University Tuition Fees and Living Costs in Germany." www.mastersportal.com/articles/358/university-tuition-fees-and-living-costs-in-germany-low-cost-german-degrees.html
33. Andres Roman-Urrestarazu. "Private Health Insurance in Germany and Chile." *International Journal for Equity in Health*; August 3, 2018
34. Audrey Goodson Kingo. "This is What Happened When Germany Paid Women $25K More During Maternity Leave." *Working Mom*; September 13, 2017
35. "Social Security in Germany." InterNations; www.internations.org/germany-expats/guide/29458-social-security-taxation/social-security-in-germany-15970

36. Bureau of Economic Analysis. "Chart of US Gross Domestic Product, 1929–2004." Economic-Chart.com, 2007
37. Victor Zarnowitz. *Business Cycles*; Chicago, Ill: University of Chicago Press; 1966; p. 229
38. Garry L. Thompson. *Army Downsizing*; Fort Leavenworth, KS: Army University; 2002; p. 4
39. David Horowitz. *The Free World Colossus*; N.Y., N.Y.: Hill and Wang; 1971; p. 74
40. Alice Slater. "The US Has Military Bases in 80 Countries." *The Nation*; January 24, 2018
41. Peter Peterson Foundation. "U.S. Defense Spending to Other Countries." May 7, 2018
42. www.goodreads.com/quotes/287464-every-man-i-meet-wants-to-protect-me-i-can-t
43. Winston Churchill. The Second World War, Vol. 2: Boston, Ma.: Houghton Mifflin; 1952; p. 832
44. Viktor Zemskov. "The Extent of Human Losses USSR in the Great Patriotic War ('Военно-исторический архив' in Russian)." Democcope.ru, 2012; pp. 59–71.
45. J. Edgar Hoover. "Communist 'New Look'." *The Elks Magazine*; August 1956
46. General Douglas MacArthur, speech to the Corps of Cadets. "Duty, Honor, Country." West Point, N.Y.; May 12, 1962
47. Raymond J. Mauer. *Duck and Cover*; Civil Defense Film; 1951
48. Glenn C. Altschuler. *The GI Bill*; N.Y., N.Y.: Oxford; 2006
49. Charles Siegel. *The Politics of Simple Living*; Berkeley, Ca: Preservation Institute; 2008
50. Jim Klein and Martha Olson. *Taken For a Ride*; PBS Film; 1996
51. Stephen Ambrose. *Eisenhower, Soldier and President*; N.Y., N.Y.: Simon & Schuster; 1990; p. 573
52. Vance Packard. *The Waste Makers*; N.Y., N.Y.: Simon and Schuster; 1978
53. "Reuther's Guaranteed Wage." *Life Magazine*; February 14, 1955; p. 49

Chapter 5

1. Hollis Archives. Harvard University Library; Cambridge, Mass.; 1968
2. Paul Blumberg. *Inequality in an Age of Decline*; N.Y., N.Y.: Oxford; 1980; p. 93
3. Jim Manzi. "The American Scene." Oakland, Ca; May 7, 2007
4. "Foreign Interventions by the United State." Wikipedia; 2012
5. "Dien Bien Phu: Did the US Offer France an A-bomb?" BBC News; May 5, 2014
6. Dwight D. Eisenhower. *Mandate for Change*; N.Y., N.Y.: Doubleday; 1994; p. 372
7. Seth Jacobs. *Cold War Mandarin: Ngo Dinh Diem and the Origins of America's War in Vietnam, 1950–1963*; Lanham, Maryland: Rowman & Littlefield; 2006; p. 20
8. Micheal Clodfelter. *Vietnam in Military Statistics*: A History of the Indochina Wars, 1792–1991. Jefferson, N.C.: McFarland & Company, Inc. Publishers; 1995; p. 225.
9. Ann Hornaday. "Most Dangerous Man in America Revisits War Dissenter Daniel Ellsberg's Critical Choice." *Washington Post*; February 12, 2010
10. Oliver Stone and Peter Kuznick. *The Untold History of the United States*; N.Y. N.Y.: Gallery Books; 2012; p. 384, citing Daniel Ellberg, *Secrets: A Memoir of Vietnam and the Pentagon Papers*; N.Y., N.Y.: Viking; 2002; pp. 258–260
11. "Destroying the Village in Order to Save It." Students for Liberty: Arlington, Va.; 2014
12. This and much of the description here relies on a report by a US soldier: Joe Allen, "Vietnam: The War the U.S. Lost." ISR, January–February 2004.
13. Norman Lear. *All in the Family*. Hollywood, Ca: CBS; 1971–1972
14. Pete Seeger; "Little Boxes." https://genius.com/Pete-seeger-little-boxes-lyrics
15. "Educational Attainment Over Time, 1940–2009." The College Board; U.S. Census Bureau, 2009b, Table A-1.
16. "*The Sit-in: 40 Years Later.*" *Chicago Maroon*; December 2, 2008

17. Newton N. Minow. "Unlikely Allies Against Vietnam War." *Chicago Tribune*; September 16, 1996
18. Penny Lewis. *Hardhats, Hippies, and Hawks: The Vietnam Antiwar Movement as Myth and Memory*; Ithaca, N.Y.: Industrial and Labor Press; 2013
19. David Dellinger. *From Yale to Jail*; Eugene, Or: Rose Hill; 1993; p. 5
20. David Dellinger. *Revolutionary Nonviolence*; Indianapolis, In; Bobs Merrill; 1970
21. Martin Luther King. "Beyond Vietnam." Riverside Church, N.Y., N.Y.; April 4, 1967
22. Martin Luther King. "March on Washington for Jobs and Freedom." Washington, D.C.; August 28, 1964
23. John Marciano. "Walter Cronkite Opposed the Vietnam War Because It Was Unwinnable." *LA Progressive*; June 26, 2016
24. Ibid.
25. Timothy Ferris. "David Brinkley vs. Woeful Ignorance." *Rolling Stone*; September 14, 1972
26. Alan Watts. "The Taoist View of the Universe." https://creativesystemsthinking.wordpress.com; July 31, 2015
27. Kurt Anderson. "How America Lost Its Mind." *The Atlantic*; September 2017
28. Dave Lifton. "When John Lennon and Yoko Oko Held a Bed-In For Peace." Ultimate Classic Rock; March 25, 2016
29. John Lennon and Paul McCartney. "You Say You Want a Revolution." Sony Music; 1968
30. Allen Ginsberg. Testimony in Chicago Eight Trial; Chicago, Ill; December 11 and 12, 1969
31. Country Joe McDonald. "Vietnam Song." Woodstock, N.Y.; 1969
32. Steve Chapman. "Political Violence is 'as American as Cherry Pie'." *Chicago Tribune*; June 16, 2017
33. The Beatles. "All You Need is Love;" London, U.K.; 1967; Rolling Stones, "Street Fighting Man;" London, U.K.; 1968
34. Martin Luther King. Nobel Price Acceptance Speech; Oslo, Norway; December 11, 1964
35. Martin Luther King. *The Trumpet of Conscience*; N.Y., N.Y.: Harper; 1967
36. Martin Luther King. "Letter From a Birmingham Jail." April 16, 1963
37. www.brainyquote.com/quotes/malcolm_x_532915
38. Malcolm X Introduces Fannie Lou Hamer. December 20, 1964
39. Malcom X, quoted in Michael Brown. *Revolution*: Bellingham, Wa: Kirkdale; 2013; Chapter 9
40. Malcom X, quoted in Amechi Okolo. *The State of the American Mind*: Bloomington, In: Xliberis; 2010; p. 1112
41. Malcolm X. Oxford Union Debate; Oxford, U.K.; December 3, 1964
42. Jeff Gray. "US Deserter's Canadian campaign." *BBC; July 6, 2004*
43. Gerald Gioglio. *Days of Decision*; Trenton, N.J.: Grgbookseller; 1989; p. 319
44. Fred Halstead. *Out Now!* N.Y., N.Y.: Pathfinder; 1991; pp. 174–184
45. John Kerry. Vietnam Veterans Against the War Statement to the Senate Committee of Foreign Relations; April 23, 1971
46. John Kerry. Acceptance Speech, Democratic National Convention; Boston, Ma; July 29, 2004
47. Arlo Guthrie. "Alice's Restaurant." Warner Bros.; 1967
48. Daniel S. Levy. *1968: The Year That Changed the World*; N.Y., N.Y.: Time-Life; 2018
49. Judith Orr. "Fort Hood: Iraq and Afghanistan – the Resurgence of Anti-War Cafes." *Socialist Review*; October 2009

50. Jerry Lembcke. *The Spitting Image: Myth, Memory and the Legacy of Vietnam*; N.Y., N.Y.; NYU Press; 1998; p. 6
51. Ibid., p. 29
52. Jon Wiener. "Was Nixon Worse?" *Truthdig*; December 12, 2006
53. Peter Baker. "Nixon Tried to Spoil Johnson's Vietnam Peace Talks in '68." *New York Times*; January 2, 2017
54. Richard Nixon. "Silent Majority Speech." Washington, D.C.; November 3, 1969
55. Ibid.
56. Terry Leonard. "Vietnam: The Loss of American Innocence." *Stars and Stripes*; November 11, 2014
57. Richard Nixon. Acceptance Speech; Republican National Convention; Miami Beach, Fl; August 8, 1968
58. "Spiro Agnew: The King's Taster." *Time*; November 14, 1969
59. Jefferson Cowie. *Stay' Alive*. N.Y., N.Y.: New Press; p. 135
60. George Wallace. Campaign brochure; 1968
61. George Wallace. Madison Square Garden; N.Y., N.Y.; October 24, 1968
62. Lasha Darkmoon. "The Sexual Decadence of Weimar Germany." *Veterans Today*; September 24, 2013
63. Samuel Huntington. Trilateral Commission Report; 1975
64. David Saradohn. "The Republican War on Public Universities." *New Republic*; August 10, 2016
65. Ronald Reagan, speaking about the Berkeley rioters; April 7, 1970
66. Ronald Reagan. Letter to Glenn Dumke, Chancellor of San Francisco State College; 1967
67. Ronald Reagan, quoted in Patrick Hagopian. *The Vietnam War in American Memory*; Amherst, Ma: University of Massachusetts Press; 2009; p. 38
68. Ronald Reagan. Acceptance Speech. Republican Convention; Detroit, Mi; July 17, 1980
69. www.goodreads.com/quotes/179719-in-this-present-crisis-government-is-not-the-solution-to
70. Max Rafferty. "Guidelines for Moral Instruction in California Schools." Sacramento, Ca: California State Department of Education; 1969
71. Jerry Falwell. *Listen America*; N.Y., N.Y.: Bantam; 1980
72. Tim LaHaye. *Battle for the Mind*; Grand Rapids, Mi: Fleming H. Revell; 1980
73. Lynne Cheney. *Telling the Truth*. N.Y., N.Y.: Touchstone; 1996
74. John Marciano. *The American War in Vietnam*; N.Y., N.Y.: Monthly Review Press; 2016; p. 140
75. James Cullen. "The History of Mass Incarceration." The Brennan Center for Justice; N.Y., N.Y.; July 20, 2018
76. Peter Wagner and Wendy Sawyer. "Mass Incarceration: The Whole Pie." Prison Policy Initiative; 2018
77. Douglas C. McDonald. "The Cost of Corrections." Research in Corrections; February 1989; p. 3
78. Sanford Schram. "Welfare Spending and Poverty." *American Journal of Economics and Sociology*; April 1991; p. 138
79. "Income Inequality." Institute for Policy Studies; Washington, D.C.; 2016

Chapter 6

1. Tom Lutey. "Trump: 'We're Going To Win So Much'." *Billings Gazette*; May 26, 2016
2. Jenny Cheng and Rebecca Harrington. "17 of the Most Legendary Quotes From James Mattis." *Business Insider*; December 20, 2018

3. Mark Z. Barabak. "In Stunning Attack, George W. Bush Rebukes Trump, Suggesting He Promotes Falsehoods and Prejudice." *Los Angeles Times*; October 19, 2017
4. Gregory Krieg. "10 Colorful Donald Trump Insults from Mitt Romney's Speech." *CNN*; March 3, 2016
5. Emily Schulteis and Julia Boccagno. "Quotes from Steve Bannon, Trump's New White House Chief Strategist." *CBS News*; November 16, 2016
6. Samuel Huntington. *Class of Civilizations*; N.Y., N.Y.: Simon and Schuster; 1997; Introduction, p. 20
7. https://myemail.constantcontact.com/-America-needs-God-more-than-God-needs-America—-Reagan-stated—-If-we-ever-forget-that-we-are-One-Nation-Under-God—then-we-wil.html?soid=1108762609255&aid=CdVnyN37msQ
8. Ronald Reagan. "Evil Empire Speech." Orlando Fl: National Association of Evangelicals; March 8, 1983
9. George Washington. Valley Forge Pa; 1778
10. Ayn Rand. *The Fountainhead*; N.Y., N.Y.: Signet; 1996
11. Ayn Rand. *Atlas Shrugged*; N.Y., N.Y.: Signet; 1996
12. Ayn Rand. *Capitalism: The Unknown Ideal*; N.Y., N.Y.: Signet; 1986; p. 22
13. Ibid., p. 47
14. Frank Capra. *Mr. Smith Goes to Washington*; Hollywood Ca: Columbia Pictures; 1939
15. www.change.org/p/donald-trump-put-donald-trump-s-face-on-mount-rushmore
16. Frank Sinatra and Paul Anka. "I Did It My Way." LA, Ca: Reprise; 1968
17. Donald Trump; Speech Announcing Presidential Candidacy; N.Y., N.Y.; June 16, 2015
18. Matt Ford. "Donald Trump's Racially Charged Advocacy of the Death Penalty." Washington, D.C.: *The Atlantic*; December 18, 2015
19. Samuel Huntington. *Who Are We?*; N.Y., N.Y.: Simon & Schuster; 2005
20. Z. Bryon Wolf. "Trump's Attacks on Judge Curiel are Still Jarring to Read." CNN: February 27, 2018
21. Scott Horton. "Lord Shiva's Dance." *N.Y. Harpers*; January 15, 2008
22. Ian Schwarz. "Sarah Huckabee Sanders: 'God Wanted Trump To Become President'." Real Clear Politics; January 30, 2019; www.realclearpolitics.com/video/2019/01/30/sarah_huckabee_sanders_god_wanted_donald_trump_to_become_president.html
23. Joe Heim. "Jerry Falwell Jr. interview: Evangelical Leader Praises Trump's Business Acumen, Says Poor Don't Give to Charity." *Washington Post*; January, 2019
24. Robert Jones. "White Evangelicals Can't Quit Donald Trump." *The Atlantic*; April 20, 2018
25. Nick Allen, David Lawler and Ruth Sherlock. "Donald Trump Asked Why US Couldn't Use Nuclear Weapons if He Becomes President." *The Telegraph*; August 3, 2016
26. Eileen Sullivan. "Trump Disputes 'Naive' Intelligence Chiefs, Suggests They 'Go Back to School'." *New York Times*; January 30, 2019
27. Ibid.
28. Ibid.
29. "Rachel Maddow interviews John Brennan." MSNBC; August 8, 2018
30. President Donald Trump's Davos Address. World Economic Forum; January 26, 2018
31. Jon Sharman. "John Bolton: What Does Donald Trump's New National Security Advisor Believe." *Independent*; March 23, 2017
32. Samuel Osborne. "Donald Trump Promises 'Historic' Increase in US Military Budget." *Independent*; February 27, 2017
33. Donald Trump. White House; Washington, D.C.; February 27, 2017
34. Jair Bolsonaro. "After Visiting Brazil's Lula in Prison, Noam Chomsky Warns Against 'Disaster'." *Democracy Now*, November 22, 2018

35. Matt Egan. "The Myth of Donald Trump, CEO President." *CNN Business*; November 6, 2018
36. Javier David. "Trump Applauds Riders Who Boycott Harley Davidson." *CNBC*; August 12, 2018
37. Tessa Berenson; "Donald Trump's Speech on Jobs and the Economy." *Time*; September 15, 2016
38. Diana Hembree. "CEO Pay Skyrockets to 361 Times That of the Average Worker." *Forbes*; May 22, 2018
39. Thomas Piketty. *Capital in the Twenty-First Century*; Cambridge, Ma: Harvard; 2014
40. Brandy X. Lee. *The Dangerous Case of Donald Trump*; N.Y., N.Y.: Thomas Dunne; 2017
41. Jeff Mason and Richard Cowan. "Trump Threatens to Use Emergency Power to Build Wall, End Shutdown." Boston, Ma: *Reuters*; January 10, 2019
42. Jake Coyles. "In Trump's Rise, Michael Moore Sees the Hallmarks of Hitler." Toronto; Associated Press; September 7, 2018; www.apnews.com/e62ce3a926fc450c97d614d8988b0a7d

Chapter 7

1. Noam Chomsky. "Talk on U.S. Foreign Policy in Central America." University of California; Berkeley, Ca; May 14, 1984
2. Erich Maria Remarque (translated by A. W. Wheen). *All Quiet on the Western Front*; N.Y., N.Y.: Ballantine; 1987
3. Donald Trump. State of the Union Address; Washington, D.C.; CNN; February 5, 2019
4. Michael Sontheimer. "Why Germans Can Never Escape Hitler's Shadow." *Spiegel*; March 10, 2005
5. Trump; op. cit.
6. Alexander C. Kaufman. "Alexandria Ocasio-Cortez Unveils Landmark Green New Deal Resolution." *Huffington Post*; February 7, 2019
7. Frank Newport. "Democrats More Positive About Socialism Than Capitalism.' *Gallop*; August 13, 2019
8. Alexander Kaufman. "Alexandria Ocasia Cortez Unveils Landmark Green New Deal Resolution." *Huffington Post*; February 6, 2019
9. Peter Dreier. "Most Americans Are Liberals, Even If They Don't Know It." *The American Prospect*; November 10, 2017
10. Newport; op. cit.
11. Alexandria Ocasio-Cortez. MSNBC; February 4, 2019
12. Paul Krugman. "Trump Versus the Socialist Menace." *New York Times;* February 8, 2019
13. Martin Luther King, Jr. "Dreams of Brighter Tomorrows." *Ebony Magazine*; March 1965
14. Martin Luther King, Jr. "Remaining Awake Through a Great Revolution." March 31, 1968
15. Ibid.

INDEX

Abrahams, Harold 1
absolutist feudalism 22
AFD (Alternative for Germany, *Alternative für Deutschland*) 143, 238
Afghanistan 34, 191, 213–218, 240–243
Agnew, Spiro 181
Air Force 9
al Qaeda 240
Alexandra Feodorovna, Empress of Russia 82
Alger, Horatio 14
All in the Family (ABC) 158
All Quiet on the Western Front (Remarque) 97, 235
Allen, Woody 17, 108
Allende, Salvador 114
America traditional white Christianity 230
American capitalism 220–221
American Civil War (1861–1865) 38–47, 59–62, 69, 76, 82–83, 88–89, 129–130, 177
American civilization 210
American Dream 62, 149, 153
American exceptionalism 145–152, 197
American Federation of Labor (AFL) 87
American Revolution (1775–1783) 41–43, 72
American Sniper (2015) 29
Americanism 79
AmeriKa 174
Andersen, Hans Christian 3
Anderson, Kurt 167,168

Anglo-Americans 128, 131, 135–137
Another Mother for Peace (AMP) x
ante-bellum 38–50
anti-capitalist values 200
anti-Reagan 207
Anti-Trumpism 195–231
anti-Trumpists 196, 204, 207, 213–215
apartheid system, USA 61, 62
Arendt, Hannah 112, 138
Arias, Jody 28
aristocracy 4, 13, 19
aristocrats xvi, xvii, 10
Arpt, Hans (or Jean) 95
Aryan term 67, 103
Aryanness 67
Aryans 89, 106, 117; non- 117
Ashkenazic Jewry 108–110
Asia 238
al-Assad, Bashar 197
Astore, William 24
Atlantic, The 167
Atlas Shrugged (Rand) xi, 202
Attlee, Clement 135
Auschwitz 26, 123
authoritarianism 229; Stalinist 246
autocracy 228

Back to the Future (1985) ix
Baden-Powell, Robert xv, 10–11, 14
Baez, Joan 127
Baker, Josephine 93
Ballin, Albert 89

INDEX

Bannon, Steven 197–198
Bauer, Yehuda 112
Bavaria 133
Beatles, The 169, 170
Begin, Menachem 109
Belgium 91
Bellichek, William (Bill) 226
bellum 50–60
Bentham, Jeremy 7
Berlin (Germany) 93, 99
Berlin Stories (Isherwood) 94
Berthe, Hans 119
Bezos, Jeff 222
Big Brother 229
Bin Laden, Osama 213
Birth of a Nation (1915) 64–66
Bismarck, Otto von 152
Black Panther Party (USA) 166, 171–172
Blue Angel, The (1930) 94
Bolsheviks 99
Bolsonaro, Jair 219
Bolton, John 217
Borscht belt 108
bourgeois term 99–100
bourgeoisie 7–11, 15, 19, 46, 84
Boykin, William 26, 27, 29, 30
Brady, Tom 225
Brandeis University 166
Braun, Wernher von 134
Brazil 219
Brecht, Bertolt 96, 120
Brennon, John 215, 216
Brewer, William 40
Brinkley, David 164
Brittain, Vera 123
Brooks, Mel 108
Brown Sr, Edmund 187
Bruce, Blache 60
Buchanan, Pat 211
Buddhism 167
Bundestag 143
bureaucracy xviii
Burr, Aaron 30, 171
Bush Jr, George W. 26–27, 176, 196, 211
Bush Sr, George H.W. 186, 191–192
Butler, Rhett 52–54

Cabaret (1972) 94, 115
Cambridge University (UK) 1
Canada 174

capitalism xiii, 2–13, 38, 52–53, 92, 246; American xiii–xiv, 220–221; global 223; industrial 47; national 105
capitalist consumerism 169
capitalist democracy 11
capitalist glory 202–205, 220
capitalist ideology 2, 44
capitalist irrational rational (CIR) 167
capitalist secular ideology xiv
capitalists xix, 4
Carpetbagger 63, 64
Carter, James (Jimmy) 19, 186, 205
CBS News 163
Central Europe 122
Central Intelligence Agency (CIA, USA) 120, 173, 196, 214–215
Chadwick, Edwin 7
Chariots of Fire (1981) 1
Chavez, Cesar 219
Cheney, Lynne 191
Cheney, Richard 191
Chicago Eight 170
Chile 114
China 156, 216, 224–225
Choice Not and Echo, A (Schafly) 133
Chomsky, Noam 219, 233
Christian America 208
Christian evangelicals 200
Christian Right 190
Christian Trinity 12
Christianity 76; America traditional white 230; feudal xiv
Churchill, Winston 114, 122, 132, 147
Civil Defense Agency, American 149
Civil Rights Era 157
civil rights movements (USA, 1960s) 198
civilization: American 210; European 208; Islamic 209
civilizational backwater 213
civilizational glory 199–201, 208–213
Clark, Ramsey 161
class: political 198; professional-managerial (PMC) xii, xxi
Clinton, Hilary 224
Clinton, William (Bill) xi, 70, 190, 196
CNN 196, 211, 215, 240
Coghill, Kendal 136
Cohan, George M. 87
Cohn, Michael 227
Cold War (1947–1991) 127

Collins, Chuck 3, 227
colonies 234
colonized peoples 237
Columbia University 159, 165
communism 68, 105, 114, 236
Communist Party USA 164
communists 113, 116
community, feudal 2
Confederacy (USA) 55, 59–60, 67, 73, 121
Confederate army (USA) 55–56, 59, 65
Congo 91, 137
Congress (USA) 228–230
conservatism, modern 12
conservatives 161, 210
constitutional democracy 228
consumerism, capitalist 169
Cortez, Alexandria Ocasio- 240–247
cosmopolitan leftists 158
cosmopolitan life 93
cosmopolitanism 23, 91–93, 108, 111; leftwing 200
cosmopolitans xiii, 1–36, 91, 161
Costner, Kevin 21
Coulter, Ann 196
Country Joe McDonald 170
counter-culture 169
Cox, Karen 74
Crimea 216
Crimean War (1853–1856) 30
Cronkite, Walter 163–164
Crow, Jim 74, 131
Curiel, Gonzalo 210
Czar Nicholas II 82

Dadaism 94, 95
Daily Mail 115
Daily Mirror 116
Daley Sr, Richard 160
Dangerous Case of Donald Trump, The (Ed. Lee) 226
Davis, Clara 49
Davis, Jefferson 59, 72, 76
Davis, Rennie 166–167
Day, Doris xx
Dead Lagoon (Oibdin) 200
Debs, Eugene 33, 84–85, 141
Defense Intelligence Agency (USA) 214
Dellinger, David 161, 162
democracy 101, 114, 196, 206, 228–230; capitalist 11; constitutional 228; social 128; Western capitalist xiii

Democratic Party 203, 205, 221, 244–249
Democrats xi, 196, 202, 210, 214, 239–240, 243–246; Reagan 221
Depression, Great (1929–1939) 113, 130, 146, 158, 239, 247
denazification 128–134
Denmark 110, 246
Deterding, Sir Henri 115
diaspora 108
Did You Hear About the Morgans? (2009) 17
Dien Bien Phu, Battle of (1954) 154, 178
Dietrich, Joseph "Sepp" 100
Dietrich, Marlene 94, 120
disenchantment xvii–xviii
Disney 3
Douglass, Frederick 76
Dow Jones Industrial Average xiii
Dulles, John Foster 154
Dresden 121, 136
Dylan, Bob 127

East (Asian religions) 167
East of Eden (Steinbeck) 87
East Germany 238
Eastern Europe 108, 123, 202, 218
Ebert, Friedrich 105
economy, global 223–225
Edward VIII, King of Britain 1–2, 116
egalitarianism 173
Einstein, Albert 13, 119, 122
Eisenhower, Dwight D. 154, 236
Ellsberg, Daniel 155
Engels, Frederick 48
enlightenment science 6
equality 232–251
Europe 86–88, 127–129, 143–144, 150–152, 217–218, 236–237, 249–251; Central 122; Eastern 108, 123, 202, 218
European civilization 208
European nations 234
European Union (EU) 237
euthanasia 124
evangelicals 212; Christian 200
evangelicism, Southern 208
evangelism 71
exceptionalism, American 145–152, 197
expressionism 95
Exxon Mobil 181

Falwell Jr, Jerry 212
Falwell Sr, Jerry xix, 189

Faneuil, Peter 76
Far Right 130, 229, 237
fascism xviii, 91, 124, 144
Federal Bureau of Investigation (FBI, USA) 171–173, 196, 215
Ferdinand, Franz 82
feudal Christianity xiv
feudal community 2
feudal ideology xiv–xv
feudal idyllic relations 9–11
feudalism xiii–xv, 2–3, 9–12, 19, 22, 25, 29, 38; absolutist 22; neo- 53; Western 2
Fitzgerald, F. Scott 93
Fitzhugh, George 45–48
Follow the Drinking Gourd 48
Ford, Henry 106–107, 116, 205
Forrest, Nathan 59
Foster, Stephen 38
Fountainhead, The (Rand) 202
Fox News 196
France 82, 85, 88, 91, 132, 146–147, 154, 235
Franck, James 119
Franco-Prussian War (1870–1871) 82
Frazier, Ken 222
free trade 224; arrangements 222
Frankfort School 119, 184
French Revolution (1789–1799) 6, 11, 99
Friedman, Milton 114
Fromm, Eric xiv
Fuchs, Klaus 119

Gallipoli (1981) 31
Gallup surveys 238, 242, 245
Gandhi, Mahatma 171
Gardner, Ava xx
Garrison, William Lloyd 58
Gauguin, Paul 15
Gavin, James 161
Gaza xvi
GDP (gross domestic product) 144–146, 154
Generation Z 242, 245
Genghis Khan 104
Genovese, Eugene 44–46
George V, King of Britain 82
German Left 95
Germany xv, 84–90, 95–97, 100–108, 119–126, 128–137, 140–147, 156–157, 235–237; AFD 238; Berlin 93, 99; East 238; Holocaust xv, 86, 109–110, 113, 124–125, 141, 148, 168; Nazi 174–175, 185; Reichstag 86; Weimar 4, 89–90, 90–98, 105, 116, 152, 158–159, 167, 185, 230, 244; West 131, 140
Gershwin, George 37
GI Bill 149, 150
Gilded Age 20
Ginsberg, Allen 169–170
global capitalism 223
global economy 223–225
global hegemony 213
global hostile powers 216
global war on terrorism 216
globalism 36, 222; national 35–36
globalization 222
Goebbels, Joseph 98
Goldman, Emma 92, 123, 164, 171
Goldwater, Barry 134
Gone With The Wind (1939) 14, 44, 51, 65
Grable, Betty xx
Graham, Billy 68
Grand Illusion, The (1937) 32
Grant, Hugh 17
Great Britain 85–88, 132, 146–147, 238; Cambridge University 1; London 83
Great Depression (1929–1939) 113, 130, 146, 158, 239, 247
great leader glory 205–207
great man glory 225–231
Great Society (President Johnson) 203
Green New Deal 239, 243–249
Greene, Janet 127
Greenspan, Allan xi, 43, 114, 188
Greun, Dieter 119
Grey, Edward 83
Grimm brothers 3
Guatemala 211
Guthrie, Arlo 34, 177
Guthrie, Woody 165

Haase, Hugo 105
Hallowed Ground Magazine 51
Hamilton, Alexander 30, 171
Hammond, James 39–40, 46
Hancock, John 42
Hanfstaengl, Ernst Putzi 115
Hardee, William 58
Harden, Maximillian 89
Harley Davidson 222–223
Harmsworth, Harold 115
Harrington, Michael 22

hegemony, global 213
Hemmingway, Ernest 93
Henry, Patrick 55
Herzl, Theodor 89
Hess, Rudolph 101
Hicks, Louise Day 78
High Noon (1952) 30
High School (1968) 31
Hillel 36
Hindenburg, Paul von 116
Hinduism 167
hippies 167–170, 186
Hirohito (Emperor of Japan) 137
Hispanics 209–210
Hitler, Adolf xviii, 2–4, 89–91, 98–106, 117–125, 134–136, 145–147, 236–237; *Mein Kampf* 115, 125, 140
Hitler Youth 118
Ho Chi Minh 154
Hobbes, Thomas 113
Hochschild, Arlie 71
Hollywood 19
Hollywood Ten ix, 120
Holocaust xv, 86, 109–110, 113, 124–125, 141, 148, 168
Hoover, Edgar J. 148
Horne, Gerald 41
hostile powers, global 216
House of Morgan 85
House of Representatives (USA) 239
human survival 232–251
humanistic socialism 2
Humiliation with Honour (Britain) 123
Humphrey, Hubert 161
Hun, The 86
Huntington, Samuel 185, 199, 208–210
Hussein, Saddam 213

ideology 103; capitalist 2, 44; capitalist secular xiv; feudal xiv–xv; Nazi 90, 103; of Rand-Reagan-Trumpism xii; volkish 106
I.G. Farben Chemical Trust 115
immigration 210; Middle East 237
Indochina 154–157
industrial capitalism 47
industrialism 13
industrialization 50, 106
inequality xiii, 234
Inflation, German (1920s) 113
intellectualism xvii

International Workers of the World (IWW or Wobblies) 86
Iran 193, 214, 217
Iraq 9, 32–34, 176, 191, 215–218, 243
Iraq invasion (2003) 213
irrational liberation 29–35
irrational rationality 5–9
irrational reality 13
Isenberg, Nancy 17, 21
ISIS 197, 216–217, 240
Islam 28
Islamic civilization 209
Israel 110, 123
It's a Wonderful Life (1946) ix–x

Jackson, Andrew 30
Japan 137, 147, 150–152, 154, 193, 236
Jewry, Ashkenazic 108–110
Jews xvi, 4, 86, 106–113, 118–120, 123–124, 133
JFK (1991) 21
Johnson, Andrew 62
Johnson, Lyndon B. 71, 177–178, 205; Great Society 203
Jolson, Al 37
Judenrate (Ghetto Jewish Police) 113
Junkers. 30, 84, 98, 114, 115, 119

3 Ks 100
Kaiser Wilhelm II 82, 86, 89, 100
Kaminer, Wladimir 238
Keith, James 59
Kennedy, John F. 22, 251
Kennedy, Robert 161
Kent State University 166
Kerry, John 176
Keynes, John Maynard 116–117, 122
Keynesianism 117, 205
King and I, The (1956) 13
King, Martin Luther 162, 171–174, 241, 249–251
Kinzer, Stephen 12, 23
Kirby, John 9
Kirchheimer, Otto 120
Koenigsberg, Richard 103
Korea 148
Kristol, William (Bill) 216
Krupp Steal 115
Ku Klux Klan (KKK) xviii, 59, 64–67, 92, 98
Kyle, Chris 29, 73
Kristallnacht 125

LaHaye, Tim 189
Landesberg, Otto 105
Latin America 209, 219–220
leader, great 205–207
League of German Girls 118
Lebowitz, Fran 17
Lee, Robert E. 43, 73
Left ix, xx–xxi, 15, 18, 98, 142, 153–194, 248–251; German 95; New 160–170, 174–175, 184–185, 191; Weimar 186, 193
Left Behind 189
Leftists 173, 186; cosmopolitan 158; New 177
leftwing cosmopolitanism 200
legitimacy 111, 118, 137
Lembcke, Jerry 178
Lennon, John 169
Leopold II (King of Belgium) 137
Leviathan (Hobbes) 113
LGBT (Lesbian, Gay, Bisexual and Transsexual) 93, 212
liberalism, neo- xxi
liberals 160–167, 196, 240, 248
liberation, irrational 29–35
Liberator, The 58
Limbaugh, Rush 196
Lincoln, Abraham 47, 57
London (Great Britain) 83
London Times 125
Los Angeles Transit System 150
Louis XIV (King of France) 22, 101, 199, 227
Löwenthal, Leo 120
Ludendoff, Erich 89, 98, 140
Lula da Silva, Luiz Inácio (Lula) 219
Luxemburg, Rosa 84–85, 96, 105, 164, 171
Lynyrd Skynyrd 29

MacArthur, Douglas 148
McCain, John xvi, 29, 136
McCarthy, Joseph 120, 164
McCreae, John 35
McGovern, George 160
McNamara, Robert 161
Mad Magazine ix
Maddow, Rachel 215
Madison, James 42
Maduro, Nicolas 219
Maistre, Joseph de 10, 12, 13

Make America Great Again (MAGA) 196, 202, 216, 223
Malcolm X 171–172
Man Who Shot Liberty Valance, The (1962) 30
Mandela, Nelson 139–140
Manhattan Project 119
Mao Tse Tung 181
Marciano, John 163
Marcuse, Herbert 119–120, 142, 165, 185
Marie Antoinette, Queen of France 15
Markey, Ed 241
Marshall, Samuel Lyman Atwood 32
Marx, Karl xvii–xviii, 2, 8, 11, 16–17, 47–48, 53, 75, 105
Marxism 95
Mattis, James 195, 215
Mein Kampf (Hitler) 115, 125, 140
Merkel, Angela 229
Mexico 193, 196, 209–211
Middle Ages xiv
Middle East 146, 202, 209, 213, 216, 219; immigration 237
millennials 245
modern conservatism 12
Mondale, Walter 186
Monroe, Marilyn x
Moore, Michael 229
Moral Majority xix–xx
morality 104
Moving Beyond Fear (Derber and Magrass) xxi
Mr Smith Goes to Washington (1939) 205
MSNBC 196, 215–216, 240
Mueller, Robert 227
multi-culturalism xiii
Muskie, Edmund 161
Muslims 209–211
Mussabini, Sam 1

NAFTA (North American Free Trade Agreement) 224
national capitalism 105
national globalism 35–36
National Liberation Front (NLF, Vietnam, Vietminh, Vietcong) 155, 174
National Socialism 100, 105
National and Space Administration (NASA) 134
nationalism 36, 143, 197, 223; patriotic 196

nationalist aims 223
nativism 197
NATO (North Atlantic Treaty Organization) 213–216
Nazi Germany 113–125, 130, 131s
Nazi ideology 98–107
Nazis xvi, 4, 36, 67, 81, 97–101, 105–121, 131–144, 174, 230; neo- 229
Nazism 104, 126, 131
Negroes 40
neo-classicism xii
neo-feudalism 53
neo-liberal Reaganism 205
neo-liberal trade system 222
neo-liberalism xxi
neo-Nazis 229
Neumann, Franz 120
New Deal America 204
New England Anti-Slavery Society 58
New Left 160–170, 174–175, 184–185, 191
New Leftists 177
New Orleans Times-Picayune 63
New Right xx, 200, 203, 227
New York Times xi, 155, 209
Newport, Frank 242, 245
Ngo Dinh Diem 154
nineteenth century 7, 13, 30
Nixon, Richard 22, 160, 166, 178–183, 187–189, 200, 204–205
nobility 227
non-Aryans 117
Norman, Montagu 115
North 39
North Vietnam 155
Northerners 55
Norway 246
November Criminals 89, 103, 105, 106
Nuremberg Trials xvi, 128, 135–138

Obama, Barack 9, 23, 26, 190, 202, 215
Ocasio-Cortez, Alexandria 240–247
Occupy Wall Street Movement 248
Office of War Information and the Office of Strategic Services (OSS, USA) 119–120
Oibdin, Michael 200
Oliver Twist (Dickens) 7
Olympics 1
Ono, Yoko 169

OPEC (Organization of Petroleum Exporting Countries) 181
Operation Paperclip 134, 135
Oppenheimer, J. Robert 9
Over There (George M. Cohan) 87

Palestinians xvi
Parker, Sarah Jessica 17
Patriotic Europeans against the Islamization of the West (PEGIDA) 144
patriotic nationalism 196
patriotism 56, 237–238
Patton, George 132–133, 137–138
Pelosi, Nancy 239
Pentagon Papers 155
Pentagon (USA) 9, 216, 242
Perkins, Tony 212
personalism 228–229
Philippines 193
Pietsch, Albert 115
Pinchback, Pickney 60
Pinochet, Augusto 114
Poe, Leonard Rabon 74
Poland 123, 134
political class 198
Pollack, Jackson 13
Ponsonby, Arthur 123
Porter, Cole 93
post-bellum 60–75
POW-MIA Flag 179
pre-capitalism 28
Prisoners of War (POW) 179
professional-managerial class (PMC) xii, xxi
Progressive Labor (PL) 165
Prohibition 91
Protestantism 190
Protocol of the Learned Elders of Zion 106
providential destiny 202
Prues, Hugo 105
Putin, Vladimir 213, 218

racism 209
radical Islamic terrorism 196, 213
Rafferty, Max 188
Ragged Dick (Alger) 14
Rand, Ayn xi–xii, xvi, 5, 43, 53, 114, 188, 202–204, 220
Rathenau, Walter 89

rationality, irrational 5–9
Reagan Democrats 221
Reagan, Nancy 19
Reagan, Ronald ix–xiii, xix–xx, 4, 16–19, 71–72, 153–194, 196–199, 204–206, 227–231; anti- 207; revolution 198–200, 203, 226, 244
Reaganism xi, 188–190, 199, 229; neo-liberal 203
realism 185; surrealism 95
reality, irrational 13
Reconstruction 63–65, 70, 131
Reed, Donna x
Reichstag (Germany) 86, 116
Reign of Terror 11
Remarque, Erich Maria 97, 120
Republican Party xix, 198, 204, 225–227
Republicans 239, 243–244
Reserve Officer Training Corp (ROTC) 165
Rhodes, Hiram 60
Ridgway, Mathew 161
Right xxi, 142, 153–194, 250–251; Christian 190; Far 130, 229, 237; New xx, 200, 203, 227
rightwing movements 18
Robertson, Pat 211–212
Robeson, Paul 37–38
Rockefeller, David 185
Rockefeller, Nelson 161
Rolling Stones 170
Romney, George 161
Romney, Mitt 197
Roosevelt, Franklin 70, 119, 133, 187, 238
Roxbury (Boston) 78
Russell, Bertrand 122
Russia 85, 106, 133–134, 156, 213–217, 235, 240; Revolution (1917) 92
Rust Belt (USA) 221

Sanders, Bernie 191, 241, 246–247
Sanders, Sarah Huckabee 212
Santorum, Rick xx
Saxe, Susan 172,173
Scalawags 64, 121
Schacht, Hjalmar 115
Schafly, Phyllis 134
Schlesinger, Arthur 161
Schroeder, Kurt von 115
scientific management 7

Screen Actors Guild ix
Seale, Bobby 166
secular ideology, capitalist xiv
secularism 211
Seeger, Pete 127, 159, 165
Sexual Revolution 169, 184, 185
Share croppers 62
Shell Oil 181
Sherman, William Tecumseh 58–59
Shite Muslim movements 213
Shoup, David 161
Silverman, Sarah 108–109
Simpson, Wallis 2
Singapore 193
Singer, Isaac Bashevis 109
slave trade 41, 44
slavery 40–46, 49, 54, 68, 141; wage 47
slaves 39–40, 45, 50
Smith, Ada (Bricktop) 93
social democracy 128
Social Democrats 84, 105, 116
social justice movements (1960s) 198
socialism 98–99, 242, 245–246; humanistic 2
socialist 98
Sociopathic society 90
Sontheimer, Michael 237
South Africa 139–140; Truth and Reconciliation Commissions (TRC) 139–140
South America 209
South Boston 77, 78
South China Sea 216
South Korea 224
South (USA) 30–75, 200
South Vietnam 155, 178
Southern evangelicism 208
Southern Quarterly Review 68
Southern Poverty Law Center 74
Southern traditionalism 71
Southerners 54–55
Southerness 52
Soviet Union 115, 131, 147–149, 164, 201–202, 213, 236
Spiegel 237
Stalin, Joseph 123, 164
Stalinist authoritarianism 246
Stavridis, James 25
Stein, Gertrude 93
Steinbeck, John 87

INDEX

Stephens, Alexander Hamilton 51
Stewart, James x, 30, 205–206
Stiglitz, Joseph 249
Stone, Oliver 21
Stone, Roger 227
Stouffer, Samuel 32
Streeck, Wolfgang xiii, 15–17, 90
Students for a Democratic Society (SDS) 165–166, 172
Sunday, Billy 92
super-power glory 201–202, 213–220
supremacy, white 61, 65, 131
surrealism 95
survival, human 232–251
Swanee (Gershwin) 37
Sweden 174
Switzerland 95
Syria 197, 215, 218, 240

Taliban 213
Taylor, Frederick 7–8
Taylorism 8
Tennyson, Baron Alfred 30
terrorism 216, 240; global war on 216; radical Islamic 196, 213
Theory of the Leisure Class (Veblen) 20
Third Reich 118, 127, 130–131, 141, 144
Third World 181
Thornwell, James Henley 68–69
Threepenny Opera (1928) 96
Thyssen, Fritz 115
trade: free 222, 224; neo-liberal system 222; slave 41, 44
traditionalism 36, 38, 79, 90–93, 105; Southern 71
traditionalists xix, 1–36, 91, 161
Trans-Pacific Partnership 224
Treaty of Versailles (1919) 116, 122
Trilateral Commission 185–186
Trudeau, Justin 229
Trump, Donald ix, xi, 16–18, 36, 43, 71–72, 90, 129, 187–188, 193–194, 195–231; Make America Great Again (MAGA) 196, 202, 216, 223
Trump era 210
Trumpism xi, 194, 197–199; AI 195–231
Truth and Reconciliation Commission (TRC, South Africa) 139–140
Tulsa Oklahoma riot (1921) 92
Turner, Lana xx

Turner, Nat 50
twentieth century 7, 90
twenty-first century 197, 205
tyranny 236
Tzara, Tristan 94

Ukraine 216
Underground Railroad 48
United Daughters of the Confederacy 74
United Nations (UN) 237
United States of America (USA) 38–41, 72–73, 85–88, 121–123, 127–135, 142–152, 155–158, 179–181, 201–203, 213–214; American Dream 62, 149, 153; Another Mother for Peace (AMP) x; apartheid system 62; Black Panther Party 171–172; CBS News 163; Central Intelligence Agency (CIA) 120, 173, 196, 214–215; Chicago Eight 170; civil rights movements (1960s) 198; Civil War (1861–1865) 38–47, 59–62, 69, 76, 82–83, 88–89, 129–130, 177; CNN 196, 211, 215, 240; Communist Party USA 164; Confederacy 55, 59–60, 67, 73, 121; Confederate army 55–56, 59, 65; Congress 228–230; Defense Intelligence Agency 214; Democratic Party 203, 205, 221, 244–249; Democrats xi, 196, 202, 210, 214, 239–240, 243–246; Federal Bureau of Investigation (FBI) 171–173, 196, 215; Federation of Labor 87; Fox News 196; Green New Deal 239, 243–249; hegemony 201; Hollywood 19; House of Representatives 239; Ku Klux Klan (KKK) xviii, 59, 64–67, 92, 98; MSNBC 196, 215–216, 240; National and Space Administration (NASA) 134; New England Anti-Slavery Society 58; North 39; Occupy Wall Street 248; Office of War Information and the Office of Strategic Services (OSS) 119–120; Pentagon 9, 216; President Johnson's Great Society 203; Progressive Labor (PL) 165; Republican Party xix, 198, 204, 225–227; Reserve Officer Training Corp (ROTC) 165; Revolution (1775–1783) 72; Rust Belt 221; Rust Belt workers 221; South 38, 200; Southerners 54–55; Southerness

52; Students for a Democratic Society (SDS) 165–166, 172; Vietnam Veterans Against the War 176; Wall Street 186, 220, 238; White House 34, 79, 178–179, 212, 226
urbanization 13, 106
utilitarianism 60

Vagabond King, The (1925) 28
values, anti-capitalist 200
Vanderbilt, Amy 21
Vanderbilt, Cornelius 21
Veblen, Thorstein 20
Venezuela 246
Versailles, Treaty of (1919) 116, 122
Veterans Today 107
Victoria (Queen of Great Britain) 82
Vietnam 153–194, 198, 202–204, 250; National Liberation Front (NLF) 155; North 155; South 155, 178
Vietnam Era 157–158, 197
Vietnam Veterans Against the War (USA) 176
Vietnam War (1954–1975) xxi, 34, 160–161, 174, 178, 248
Voice of the South website 63–64
volkish ideology 99, 100, 101, 102, 103.106
Volkswagen 117
Von Trapp family 119

wage slavery 47
Wall Street (USA) 186, 220, 238
Wallace, George 69–72, 184–186
Walsh, Martin J. 76
War Resisters International 124
Warren, Elizabeth 241, 245–247
Washington, George 43, 202
Washington, Martha Curtis 43
Waskow, Walter 108
Watts, Alan 167
Weathermen 172, 173
Weber, Max xvii–xviii, 53
Weimar Germany (Weimar Republic) 4, 89–90, 90–98, 105, 116, 152, 158–159, 167, 185, 230, 244

Weimar Left 186, 193
West (Euro-America) 13
West, Cornell 23
West Germany 131, 140
West Side Story (1957) 26
Western capitalist democracies xiii
Western civilization 208–211, 249
Western feudalism 2
white Christianity, America traditional 230
White House (USA) 34, 79, 178–179, 212, 226
white supremacy 61, 65, 131
white traditional American culture 210
White Trash 39–41, 54, 61–62
White Trash (Isenberg) 21
whiteness 40
Who Are We? (Huntington) 210
Wiehe, Karl 107
Wilder, Billy 120
Wilhelm II, Kaiser of Germany 82, 86, 89,100
Wilkie, Wendell 133
Wilson, Woodrow 65, 85, 235
Wise, Douglas H. 214
Wiseman, Frederick 31
Wong, Leonard 32
Woodstock 170
World Bank 114
World Trade Organization (WTO) 221, 224
World War I (1914–1918) 30–34, 86–87, 90–92, 105–107, 118–124, 129–132, 156, 180, 238; Treaty of Versailles (1919) 116, 122
World War II (1939–1945) 4, 86, 116–125, 128–129, 145–152, 154–161, 187, 236–239
Wyman, David 123
Wyzanski, Charles 137

Yad Vashem 109
Yemen 219
Yiddish 109

Zionism 108

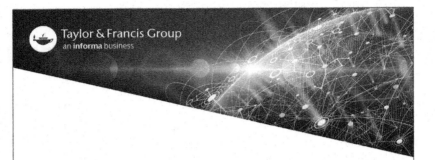